Mex[illegible]
Spanish

A ROUGH GUIDE
PHRASEBOOK

Compiled
by Lexus

Credits

Compiled by Lexus with Mike Gonzalez

Lexus Series Editor: Sally Davies
Rough Guides Phrasebook Editors: Jonathan Buckley, John Fisher
Rough Guides Series Editor: Mark Ellingham

This first edition published in 1996 by Rough Guides Ltd, 1 Mercer Street, London WC2H 9QJ.

Distributed by the Penguin Group.

Penguin Books Ltd, 27 Wrights Lane, London W8 5TZ
Penguin Books USA Inc., 375 Hudson Street, New York 10014, USA
Penguin Books Australia Ltd, 487 Maroondah Highway, PO Box 257, Ringwood, Victoria 3134, Australia
Penguin Books Canada Ltd, Alcorn Avenue, Toronto, Ontario, Canada M4V 1E4
Penguin Book (NZ) Ltd, 182–190 Wairau Road, Auckland 10, New Zealand

Typeset in Rough Serif and Rough Sans to an original design by Henry Iles.
Printed by Cox & Wyman Ltd, Reading.

272pp.

British Library Cataloguing in Publication Data
A catalogue for this book is available from the British Library.

ISBN 1-85828-176-8

CONTENTS

INTRODUCTION

The Rough Guide Mexican Spanish phrasebook is a highly practical introduction to the contemporary language. Laid out in clear A-Z style, it uses key-word referencing to lead you straight to the words and phrases you want – so if you need to book a room, just look up 'room'. The Rough Guide gets straight to the point in every situation, in bars and shops, on trains and buses, and in hotels and banks.

The main part of the Rough Guide is a double dictionary: English-Spanish then Spanish-English. Before that, there's a section called **The Basics**, which sets out the fundamental rules of the language, with plenty of practical examples. You'll also find here other essentials like numbers, dates, telling the time and basic phrases.

Forming the heart of the guide, the **English-Spanish** section gives easy-to-use transliterations of the Spanish words wherever pronunciation might be a problem, and to get you involved quickly in two-way communication, the Rough Guide includes dialogues featuring typical responses on key topics – such as renting a car and asking directions. Feature boxes fill you in on cultural pitfalls as well as the simple mechanics of how to make a phone call, what to do in an emergency, where to change money, and more. Throughout this section, cross-references enable you to pinpoint key facts and phrases, while asterisked words indicate where further information can be found in the Basics.

In the **Spanish-English** dictionary, we've given not just the phrases you're likely to hear (starting with a selection of slang and colloquialisms), but also all the signs, labels, instructions and other basic words you might come across in print or in public places.

Finally the Rough Guide rounds off with an extensive **Menu Reader**. Consisting of food and drink sections (each starting with a list of essential terms), it's indispensable whether you're eating out, stopping for a quick drink, or browsing through a local food market.

¡buen viaje!
have a good trip!

The Basics

PRONUNCIATION

In this phrasebook, the Spanish has been written in a system of imitated pronunciation so that it can be read as though it were English, bearing in mind the notes on pronunciation given below:

air	as in h**air**
ay	as in m**ay**
e, eh	as in g**e**t
g	always hard as in **g**oat
H	a harsh 'ch' as in the Scottish way of pronouncing lo**ch**
ī	as the 'i' sound in m**i**ght
o	as in n**o**t
ow	as in n**ow**
s	as in mi**ss**
y	as in **y**es

Letters given in bold type indicate the part of the word to be stressed.

As **i** and **u** are always pronounced 'ee' and 'oo' in Spanish, pronunciation has not been given for all words containing these letters unless they present other problems for the learner. Thus **María** is pronounced 'mar**ee**-a' and **fútbol** is 'f**oo**tbol'.

ABBREVIATIONS

adj	adjective	pl	plural
f	feminine	pol	polite
fam	familiar	sing	singular
m	masculine		

NOTE

In the Spanish-English section and Menu Reader, the letter **ñ** is treated as a separate letter, as is customary in Spanish. Alphabetically, it comes after **n**.

NOUNS

All nouns in Spanish have one of two genders: masculine or feminine. Generally speaking, those ending in **-o** are masculine:

el zapato
el sap**a**to
the shoe

Those ending in **-a**, **-d**, **-z** or **-ión** are usually feminine:

la cama
la k**a**ma
the bed

la pensión
la pens-y**o**n
the boarding house, the guesthouse

Nouns ending in **-or** are masculine. To form the feminine, add **-a**:

el señor	**la señora**
el sen-y**o**r	la sen-y**o**ra
the man	the woman
el profesor	**la profesora**
the (male) teacher	the (female) teacher

A small number of nouns ending in **-o** and **-a** (usually professions) can be either masculine or feminine:

el/la guía	**el/la violinista**
el/la g**ee**-a	el/la bee-oleen**ee**sta
the guide	the violinist

Plural Nouns

If the noun ends in a vowel, the plural is formed by adding **-s**:

el camino	**los caminos**
el kam**ee**no	los kam**ee**nos
the path	the paths
la mesera	**las meseras**
la mes**ai**ra	las mes**ai**ras
the waitress	the waitresses

If the noun ends in a consonant, the plural is formed by adding **-es**:

el chofer
el chof**air**
the driver

los choferes
los chof**air**-es
the drivers

la recepción
la reseps-y**o**n
the reception desk

las recepciones
las reseps-y**o**n-es
the reception desks

If the noun ends in a **-z**, change the **-z** to **-ces** to form the plural:

la luz	**las luces**
la l**oo**s	las l**oo**s-es
the light	the lights

ARTICLES

The different articles ('the' and 'a') in Spanish vary according to the number (singular or plural) and gender of the noun they refer to.

The Definite Article

The definite article 'the' is as follows:

	singular	plural
masculine	**el**	**los**
feminine	**la**	**las**

el cuchillo/los cuchillos
el kooch**ee**-yo/los kooch**ee**-yos
the knife/the knives

la mesa/las mesas
la m**e**sa/las m**e**sas
the table/the tables

When the article **el** is used in combination with **a** (to) or **de** (of) it changes as follows:

a + el = al
de + el = del

vamos al museo
v**a**mos al mooos**eh**-o
let's go to the museum

cerca del hotel
s**ai**rka del ot**e**l
near the hotel

The Indefinite Article

The indefinite article (a, an, some), also changes according to the gender and number of the accompanying noun:

	singular	plural
masculine	**un**	**unos**
	oon	**oo**nos
feminine	**una**	**unas**
	oona	**oo**nas

un sello — oon s**eh**-yo — a stamp
unos sellos — **oo**nos s**eh**-yos — some stamps

una chica — **oo**na ch**ee**ka — a girl
unas chicas — **oo**nas ch**ee**kas — some girls

ADJECTIVES AND ADVERBS

Adjectives must agree in gender and number with the noun they refer to. Unlike English, Spanish adjectives usually follow the noun. In the English-Spanish section of this book, all adjectives are given in the masculine singular. Adjectives ending in -o change as follows for the plural:

el precio alto
el pr**e**s-yo **a**lto
the high price

los precios altos
los pr**e**s-yos **a**ltos
the high prices

The feminine singular of the adjective is formed by changing the masculine endings as follows:

masculine	feminine
-o	-a
-or	-ora
-és	-esa

un cocinero estupendo
oon koseen**ai**ro estoop**e**ndo
a wonderful cook

una cocinera estupenda
oona koseen**ai**ra estoop**e**nda
a wonderful cook

un señor encantador
oon sen-y**o**r enkantad**o**r
a nice man

una señora encantadora
oona sen-y**o**ra enkantad**o**ra
a nice woman

un chico inglés
oon ch**ee**ko eeng-l**e**s
an English boy

una chica inglesa
oona ch**ee**ka eengl**e**sa
an English girl

For other types of adjective, the feminine forms are the same as the masculine:

un hombre agradable
oon h**o**mbreh agrad**a**bleh
a nice man

una mujer agradable
oona mooH**ai**r agrad**a**bleh
a nice woman

The plurals of adjectives are formed in the same way as the plurals of nouns, by adding an -s:

una silla roja
oona s**ee**-ya r**o**Ha
a red chair

dos sillas rojas
dos s**ee**-yas r**o**Has
two red chairs

Comparatives

The comparative is formed by placing **más** (more) or **menos** (less) before the adjective or adverb and **que** (than) after it:

lindo l**ee**ndo beautiful	**más lindo** mas l**ee**ndo more beautiful
tranquilo trank**ee**lo quiet	**menos tranquilo** m**e**nos trank**ee**lo less quiet

este hotel es más/menos caro que el otro
esteh ot**e**l es mas/m**e**nos k**a**ro keh el **o**tro
this hotel is more/less expensive than the other one

¿tiene un cuarto más soleado?
t-y**e**neh **oo**n kw**a**rto mas soleh-**a**do
do you have a sunnier room?

¿podría ir más de prisa, por favor?
podr**ee**-a **ee**r mas deh pr**ee**sa por fab**o**r
could you go faster please?

Superlatives

Superlatives are formed by placing one of the following before the adjective: **el más**, **la más**, **los más** or **las más** (depending on the noun's gender and number):

¿cuál es el más divertido?
kwal es el mas deebairt**ee**do
which is the most entertaining?

el carro más rápido
el k**a**rro mas r**a**peedo
the fastest car

la casa más linda
la k**a**sa mas l**ee**nda
the prettiest house

las mujeres más inteligentes
las mooH**ai**r-es mas eenteleeH**e**nt-es
the most intelligent women

The following adjectives have irregular comparatives and superlatives:

bueno	**mejor**	**el mejor**
bw**e**no	meH**o**r	el meH**o**r
good	better	the best
grande	**mayor**	**el mayor**
gr**a**ndeh	mī-y**o**r	el mī-y**o**r
big	bigger	the biggest
old	older	the oldest
malo	**peor**	**el peor**
m**a**lo	peh-**o**r	el peh-**o**r
bad	worse	the worst
pequeño	**menor**	**el menor**
pek**e**n-yo	men**o**r	el men**o**r
small	smaller	the smallest
	younger	the youngest

As ... as ... is translated as follows:

Oaxaca está tan linda como siempre!
waH**a**ka est**a** tan l**ee**nda komo s-y**e**mpreh
Oaxaca is as beautiful as ever!

The superlative form ending in **-ísimo** indicates that something is 'very/ extremely ...' without actually comparing it to something else:

guapo	**guapísimo**
gw**a**po	gwap**ee**seemo
attractive	very attractive

Adverbs

There are two ways to form an adverb. If the adjective ends in **-o**, take the feminine and add **-mente** to form the corresponding adverb:

exacto	**exactamente**
eks**a**kto	eks**a**ktam**e**nte
accurate	accurately, exactly

If the adjective ends in any other letter, add **-mente** to the basic form:

feliz	**felizmente**
fel**ee**s	feleesm**e**nteh
happy	happily

Possessive Adjectives

Possessive adjectives, like other Spanish adjectives, agree with the noun in gender and number:

	singular masculine	feminine	plural masculine	feminine
my	**mi**	**mi**	**mis**	**mis**
	mee	mee	mees	mees
your (sing, fam)	**tu**	**tu**	**tus**	**tus**
	too	too	toos	toos
his/her/its/your (sing, pol)				
	su	**su**	**sus**	**sus**
	soo	soo	soos	soos
our	**nuestro**	**nuestra**	**nuestros**	**nuestras**
	nw**e**stro	nw**e**stra	nw**e**stros	nw**e**stras
your (pl)/their	**su**	**su**	**sus**	**sus**
	soo	soo	soos	soos

tu bolsa	**sus pastillas**
too b**o**lsa	soos past**ee**-yas
your bag	his/her/your tablets
su maleta	**nuestros trajes de baño**
soo mal**e**ta	nw**e**stros tr**a**Hes deh b**a**n-yo
your suitcase	our swimming costumes

GRAMMAR

If when using **su/sus**, it is unclear whether you mean 'his', 'her', 'your' or 'their', you can use the following after the noun instead:

de él his
deh el
de ella her
deh **eh**-ya
de Usted your (sing, pol)
deh oost**eh**
de ellos their (m)
deh **eh**-yos
de ellas their (f)
deh **eh**-yas
de Ustedes your (pl)
deh oost**e**d-es

el dinero de Usted
el deen**ai**ro deh oost**eh**
your money

el dinero de ella
el deen**ai**ro deh **eh**-ya
her money

el dinero de él
el deen**ai**ro deh el
his money

POSSESSIVE PRONOUNS

To translate 'mine', 'yours' 'theirs' etc, use one of the following forms. Like possessive adjectives, possessive pronouns must agree in gender and number with the object or objects referred to:

	singular		plural	
	masculine	feminine	masculine	feminine
mine	**el mío**	**la mía**	**los míos**	**las mías**
	el m**ee**-o	la m**ee**-a	los m**ee**-os	las m**ee**-as
yours (sing, fam)	**el tuyo**	**la tuya**	**los tuyos**	**las tuyas**
	el t**oo**-yo	la t**oo**-ya	los t**oo**-yos	las t**oo**-yas
his/hers/yours (sing, pol)				
	el suyo	**la suya**	**los suyos**	**las suyas**
	el s**oo**-yo	la s**oo**-ya	los s**oo**-yos	las s**oo**-yas
ours	**el nuestro**	**la nuestra**	**los nuestros**	**las nuestras**
	el nw**e**stro	la nw**e**stra	los nw**e**stros	las nw**e**stras
yours (pl)/theirs	**el suyo**	**la suya**	**los suyos**	**las suyas**
	el s**oo**-yo	la s**oo**-ya	los s**oo**-yos	las s**oo**-yas

ésta es su llave y ésta es la mía
esta es soo y**a**beh ee **e**sta es la m**ee**-a
this is your key and this is mine

no es la suya, es de sus amigos
no es la s**oo**-ya es deh soos am**ee**gos
it's not his, it's his friends'

PERSONAL PRONOUNS

Subject Pronouns

yo yo	I
tú too	you (sing, fam)
él el	he/it
ella **eh**-ya	she/it
Usted oost**eh**	you (sing, pol)
nosotros nos**o**tros	we (m)
nosotras nos**o**tras	we (f)
ellos **eh**-yos	they (m)
ellas **eh**-yas	they (f)
Ustedes oost**e**d-es	you (pl)

Tú is used when speaking to one person and is the familiar form generally used when speaking to family, friends and children.
Usted is the polite form of address to be used when talking to someone you don't know or an older person.
Ustedes is the plural form used in Mexico whoever you are speaking to. The third person of verbs is used with Usted and Ustedes: Usted takes the same verb form as 'he/she/it'; Ustedes takes the same verb form as 'they'.

In Spanish the subject pronoun is usually omitted:

no saben no s**a**ben they don't know	está cansado est**a** kans**a**do he is tired

although it may be retained for emphasis or to avoid confusion:

¡soy yo! soy yo it's me!	¡somos nosotros! s**o**mos nos**o**tros it's us!

yo pago los tacos, tú pagas las cervezas
yo p**a**go los t**a**kos too p**a**gas las sairb**e**sas
I'll pay for the tacos, you pay for the beers

él es inglés y ella es americana
el es eeng-l**e**s ee **eh**-ya es amaireek**a**na
he's English and she's American

Subject pronouns are also used after prepositions:

para Usted
p**a**ra oost**eh**
for you

con él
kon el
with him

sin ella
seen **eh**-ya
without her

detrás de Usted
detr**a**s deh oost**eh**
behind you

después de nosotros
despw**e**s deh nos**o**tros
after us

The exceptions are **yo**, which is replaced by **mí**, and **tú** which is replaced by **tí**:

eso es para mí/tí
eso es p**a**ra mee/tee
that's for me/you

After **con** (with) **mí** and **tí** change as follows:

conmigo
konm**ee**go
with me

contigo
kont**ee**go
with you

Object pronouns

me	[meh]	me
te	[teh]	you (sing, fam)
lo	[lo]	him/it, you (sing, pol)
la	[la]	her/it, you (sing, pol)
nos	[nos]	us
los	[los]	them (m), you (mpl)
las	[las]	them (f), you (fpl)

Object pronouns usually precede the verb:

me la dio ayer
meh la d**ee**-o ī-y**air**
she gave it to me yesterday

las compré para ella
las kompr**eh** p**a**ra **eh**-ya
I bought them for her

cada viernes la compro flores
k**a**da b-y**ai**rn-es la k**o**mpro fl**o**r-es
every Friday I buy her flowers

los vi ayer
los bee a-y**air**
I saw them yesterday

When used with infinitives, pronouns are added to the end of the infinitive:

¿puede llevarme al aeropuerto?
pw**e**deh yeb**a**rmeh al airopw**air**to
can you take me to the airport?

intentaré recordarlo
eententar**eh** rekord**a**rlo
I'll try and remember it

When used with commands, pronouns are added to the end of the imperative form. See **Imperatives** page 23.
If you are using an indirect pronoun to mean 'to me', 'to you' etc (although 'to' might not always be necessarily said in English), you generally use the following:

me	[meh]	to me
te	[teh]	to you (sing, fam)
le/lo	[leh/lo]	to him, to you (sing, pol)
le/la	[leh/la]	to her, to you (sing, pol)
nos	[nos]	to us
les/los	[les/los]	to them (m), to you (mpl)
les/las	[les/las]	to them (f), to you (fpl)

me enseñó el camino
meh ensen-y**o** el kam**ee**no
he showed me the way

le pedí su dirección
leh ped**ee** soo deereks-y**o**n
I asked him/her for his/her address

Reflexive Pronouns

These are used with reflexive verbs like **lavarse** 'to wash (oneself)', that is where the subject and the object are one and the same person:

me	[meh]	myself (used with I)
te	[teh]	yourself (used with singular, familiar 'you')
se	[seh]	him/her/itself (used with singular, polite 'you')
nos	[nos]	ourselves (used with 'we')
se	[seh]	themselves (used with 'they' and plural 'you')

presentarse to introduce oneself
me presento: me llamo Richard
meh pres**e**nto: meh y**a**mo Richard
may I introduce myself? my name's Richard

divertirse to enjoy oneself
nos divertimos mucho en la fiesta
nos deebairt**ee**mos m**oo**cho en la f-y**e**sta
we enjoyed ourselves a lot at the party

DEMONSTRATIVES

The English demonstrative adjective 'this' is translated by the Spanish **este**. 'That' is translated by **ese** or **aquel**. **Ese** refers to something near to the person being spoken to. **Aquel** refers to something further away.

Like other adjectives, they agree with the noun they qualify in gender and number but they are placed in front of the noun. Their forms are:

masculine singular			feminine singular		
este	**ese**	**aquel**	**esta**	**esa**	**aquella**
esteh	**e**seh	ak**e**l	**e**sta	**e**sa	ak**eh**-ya
masculine plural			feminine plural		
estos	**esos**	**aquellos**	**estas**	**esas**	**aquellas**
estos	**e**sos	ak**eh**-yos	**e**stas	**e**sas	ak**eh**-yas

este restaurante
esteh restowr**a**nteh
this restaurant

ese mesero
eseh mes**ai**ro
that waiter

aquella playa
ak**eh**-ya plī-ya
that beach (in the distance)

'This one', 'that one', 'those', 'these' etc (as pronouns) are translated by the same words as above only they are spelt with an **é**:

éste	**ése**	**aquél**
esteh	**e**seh	ak**e**l
this one	that one	that one (over there)

quisiera éstos/ésos/aquéllos
kees-y**ai**ra **e**stos/**e**sos/ak**eh**-yos
I'd like these/those/those (over there)

The neuter forms **esto/eso/aquello** are used when no particular noun is being referred to:

esto	**eso**	**aquello**
esto	**e**so	ak**eh**-yo

eso no es justo
eso no es H**oo**sto
that's not fair

¿qué es esto?
keh es **e**sto
what is this?

VERBS

The basic form of the verb given in the **English-Spanish** and **Spanish-English** sections is the infinitive (e.g. to drive, to go etc). There are three verb types in Spanish which can be recognized by their infinitive endings: **-ar**, **-er** or **-ir**. For example:

hablar	[abl**a**r]	to talk
comer	[kom**ai**r]	to eat
abrir	[abr**ee**r]	to open

Present Tense

The present tense corresponds to 'I leave' and 'I am leaving' in English. To form the present tense for the three main types of verb in Spanish, remove the -ar, -er or -ir and add the following endings:

hablar to speak

habl-o	[**a**blo]	I speak
habl-as	[**a**blas]	you speak (sing, fam)
habl-a	[**a**bla]	he/she speaks, you speak (sing, pol)
habl-amos	[abl**a**mos]	we speak
habl-an	[**a**blan]	they speak, you speak (pl)

comer to eat

com-o	[k**o**mo]	I eat
com-es	[k**o**m-es]	you eat (sing, fam)
com-e	[k**o**meh]	he/she eats, you eat (sing, pol)
com-emos	[kom**e**mos]	we eat
com-en	[k**o**men]	they eat, you eat (pl)

abrir to open

abr-o	[**a**bro]	I open
abr-es	[**a**b-res]	you open (sing, fam)
abr-e	[**a**breh]	he/she opens, you open (sing, pol)
abr-imos	[abr**ee**mos]	we open
abr-en	[**a**bren]	they open, you open (pl)

Some common verbs are irregular:

dar to give

doy	[doy]	I give
das	[das]	you give (sing, fam)
da	[da]	he/she gives, you give (sing, pol)
damos	[d**a**mos]	we give
dan	[dan]	they give, you give (pl)

ir to go

voy	[boy]	I go
vas	[bas]	you go (sing, fam)
va	[ba]	he/she goes, you go (sing, pol)
vamos	[b**a**mos]	we go
van	[ban]	they go, you go (pl)

poder can, to be able

puedo	[pw**e**do]	I can
puedes	[pw**e**d-es]	you can (sing, fam)
puede	[pw**e**deh]	he/she can, you can (sing, pol)
podemos	[pod**e**mos]	we can
pueden	[pw**e**den]	they can, you can (pl)

querer to want

quiero	[k-y**ai**ro]	I want
quieres	[k-y**ai**r-es]	you want (sing, fam)
quiere	[k-y**ai**reh]	he/she wants, you want (sing, pol)
queremos	[kair**e**mos]	we want
quieren	[k-y**ai**ren]	they want, you want (pl)

tener to have

tengo	[t**e**ngo]	I have
tienes	[t-y**e**n-es]	you have (sing, fam)
tiene	[t-y**e**neh]	he/she has, you have (sing, pol)
tenemos	[ten**e**mos]	we have
tienen	[t-y**e**nen]	they have, you have (pl)

venir to come

vengo	[b**e**ngo]	I come
vienes	[b-y**e**n-es]	you come (sing, fam)
viene	[b-y**e**neh]	he/she comes, you come (sing, pol)
venimos	[ben**ee**mos]	we come
vienen	[b-y**e**nen]	they come, you come (pl)

The first person singular (the 'I' form) of the following verbs is irregular in some verbs:

decir to say	digo	[d**ee**go]
hacer to do, to make	hago	[**a**-go]
poner to put	pongo	[p**o**ngo]
saber to know	sé	[seh]
salir to go out	salgo	[s**a**lgo]

See page 21 for the present tense of the verbs ser and estar 'to be'.

Past Tense:

Preterite

The Preterite is the tense normally used to talk about the past:

habl-é	[ab**leh**]	I spoke
habl-aste	[abl**a**steh]	you spoke (sing, fam)
habl-ó	[abl**o**]	he/she spoke, you spoke (sing, pol)
habl-amos	[abl**a**mos]	we spoke
habl-aron	[abl**a**ron]	they spoke, you spoke (pl)
com-í	[kom**ee**]	I ate
com-iste	[kom**ee**steh]	you ate (sing, fam)
com-ió	[komee-**o**]	he/she ate, you ate (sing, pol)
com-imos	[kom**ee**mos]	we ate
com-ieron	[kom-y**ai**ron]	they ate, you ate (pl)
abr-í	[abr**ee**]	I opened
abr-iste	[abr**ee**steh]	you opened (sing, fam)
abr-ió	[abree-**o**]	he/she opened, you opened (sing, pol)
abr-imos	[abr**ee**mos]	we opened
abr-ieron	[abr-y**ai**ron]	they opened, you opened (pl)

¿quién te dijo eso?
k-yen teh d**ee**Ho **e**so
who told you that?

nos conocimos en Mérida
nos konos**ee**mos en m**e**reeda
we met each other in Mérida

lo compramos el año pasado
lo kompr**a**mos el **a**n-yo pas**a**do
we bought it last year

The verbs ser (to be) and ir (to go) are irregular and have the same form in the preterite:

fui	[fwee]	I was; I went
fuiste	[fw**ee**steh]	you were; you went (sing, fam)
fue	[fweh]	he/she/it was; you were (sing, pol); he/she/it went; you went (sing, pol)
fuimos	[fw**ee**mos]	we were; we went
fueron	[fw**ai**ron]	they were; you went (pl) they went; you went (pl)

Perfect Tense

The perfect tense corresponds to the English past tense using 'have' – i.e. 'I have seen', 'he has said' etc. It is formed by combining the appropriate person of the present tense of **haber** with the past participle of the verb. The present tense of haber is as follows:

he	[eh]	I have
has	[as]	you have (sing, fam)
ha	[a]	he/she/it has; you have (sing, pol)
hemos	[**e**mos]	we have
han	[an]	they have; you have (pl)

The past participle is formed by removing the infinitive ending (**-ar**, **-er** or **-ir**) and adding **-ado** or **-ido** as follows:

infinitive	past participle	
hablar	**hablado**	[abl**a**do]
comer	**comido**	[kom**ee**do]
vivir	**vivido**	[beeb**ee**do]

hemos dado una propina
emos d**a**do oona prop**ee**na
we have given a tip

hemos comido bien
emos kom**ee**do b-yen
we've eaten well, we've had a good meal

he encendido la luz
eh ensend**ee**do la loos
I (have) put the light on

Some verbs have irregular past participles:

hacer to do, to make	**hecho**	[**e**cho]
abrir to open	**abierto**	[ab-y**ai**rto]
decir to say	**dicho**	[d**ee**cho]
volver to return	**vuelto**	[bw**e**lto]
poner to put	**puesto**	[pw**e**sto]
ver to see	**visto**	[b**ee**sto]

Imperfect Tense

This tense is used to describe something or someone in the past, or to describe activities that were habitual in the past. It is also the tense you would use to talk about something that was going on over a period of time. It is formed as follows:

hablar to talk

habl-aba	[abl**a**ba]	I was speaking
habl-abas	[abl**a**bas]	you were speaking (sing, fam)
habl-aba	[abl**a**ba]	he/she was speaking, you were speaking (sing, pol)
habl-ábamos	[abl**a**bamos]	we were speaking
habl-aban	[abl**a**ban]	they were speaking, you were speaking (pl)

comer to eat

com-ía	[kom**ee**-a]	I was eating
com-ías	[kom**ee**-as]	you were eating (sing, fam)
com-ía	[kom**ee**-a]	he/she/it was eating, you were eating (sing, pol)
com-íamos	[kom**ee**-amos]	we were eating
com-ían	[kom**ee**-an]	they were eating, you were eating (pl)

abrir to open

abr-ía	[abr**ee**-a]	I was opening
abr-ías	[abr**ee**-as]	you were opening (sing, fam)
abr-ía	[abr**ee**-a]	he/she/it was opening, you were opening (sing, pol)
abr-íamos	[abr**ee**-amos]	we were opening
abr-ían	[abr**ee**-an]	they were opening, you were opening (pl)

Other useful regular verbs in the imperfect tense are:

estar to be

estaba	[est**a**ba]	I was
estabas	[est**a**bas]	you were (sing, fam)
estaba	[est**a**ba]	he/she/it was, you were (sing, pol)
estábamos	[est**a**bamos]	we were
estaban	[est**a**ban]	they were, you were (pl)

tener to have

tenía	[ten**ee**-a]	I had
tenías	[ten**ee**-as]	you had (sing, fam)
tenía	[ten**ee**-a]	he/she/it had, you had (sing, pol)
teníamos	[ten**ee**-amos]	we had
tenían	[ten**ee**-an]	they had, you had (pl)

The following are irregular in the imperfect tense:

ir to go

iba	[**ee**ba]	I was going
ibas	[**ee**bas]	you were going (sing, fam)
iba	[**ee**ba]	he/she/it was going, you were going (sing, pol)
íbamos	[**ee**bamos]	we were going
iban	[**ee**ban]	they were going, you were going (pl)

ser to be (see page 21 for more on this)

era	[**ai**ra]	I was
eras	[**ai**ras]	you were (sing, fam)
era	[**ai**ra]	he/she/it was, you were (sing, pol)
éramos	[**ai**ramos]	we were
eran	[**ai**ran]	they were, you were (pl)

todos los viernes salíamos a dar un paseo
t**o**dos los b-y**ai**rn-es sal**ee**-amos a dar oon pas**eh**-o
every Friday we used to go for a walk, every Friday we went for a walk

era alto y delgado
aira **a**lto ee delg**a**do
he was tall and slim

viajaban de México a Veracruz
bee-aH**a**ban deh m**e**Heeko a bairakr**oo**s
they were travelling from Mexico to Veracruz

Future Tense

To form the future tense in Spanish (I will do, you will do etc) add the following endings to the infinitive. The same endings are used whether verbs end in -ar, -er or -ir:

hablar-é	[abla**reh**]	I will speak
hablar-ás	[abla**ra**s]	you will speak (sing, fam)
hablar-á	[abla**ra**]	he/she/you will speak (sing, pol)
hablar-emos	[abla**re**mos]	we will speak
hablar-án	[abla**ra**n]	they/you will speak (pl)

llamaré más tarde
yama**reh** mas t**a**rdeh
I'll call later

The immediate future can also be translated by ir + a + infinitive:

vamos a comprar una botella de vino tinto
b**a**mos a kompr**a**r **oo**na bot**eh**-ya deh v**ee**no t**ee**nto
we're going to buy a bottle of red wine

iré a recogerlo
eer**eh** a rekoH**ai**rlo
I'll fetch him, I'll go and fetch him

In Spanish, as in English, the future can sometimes be expressed by the present tense:

tu avión sale a la una
too ab-y**o**n s**a**leh a la **oo**na
your plane takes off at one o'clock

However, Spanish often uses the present tense where the future would be used in English:

le doy ochocientos pesos
leh doy ochos-y**e**ntos p**e**sos
I'll give you 800 pesos

The following verbs are irregular in the future tense:

decir	to say	diré	I will say
hacer	to do	haré	I will do
poder	to be able	podré	I will be able
poner	to put	pondré	I will put
querer	to want	querré	I will want
saber	to know	sabré	I will know
salir	to leave	saldré	I will leave
tener	to have	tendré	I will have
venir	to come	vendré	I will come

The Verb 'To Be'

There are two verbs 'to be' in Spanish: ser and estar. The present tense is as follows:

ser

soy	[soy]	I am
eres	[**air**-es]	you are (sing, fam)
es	[es]	he/she/it is, you are (sing, pol)
somos	[s**o**mos]	we are
son	[son]	they are, you are (pl)

estar

estoy	[est**oy**]	I am
estás	[est**a**s]	you are (sing, fam)
está	[est**a**]	he/she/it is, you are (sing, pol)
estamos	[est**a**mos]	we are
están	[est**a**n]	they are, you are (pl)

Ser

Ser is generally used to describe a permanent state, for example, what something or someone looks like or what their nature is:

la nieve es blanca
la n-y**e**beh es bl**a**nka
snow is white

Ser is also used with occupations, nationalities, the time and to indicate possession:

somos escoceses
s**o**mos eskos**e**s-es
we are Scottish

mi madre es profesora
mi m**a**dreh es profes**o**ra
my mother is a teacher

éste es nuestro carro
esteh es nw**e**stro k**a**rro
this is our car

son las cinco de la tarde
son las s**ee**nko deh la t**a**rdeh
it's five o'clock in the afternoon

Estar

Estar, on the other hand, is used above all to answer the question 'where?':

el libro está en la mesa
el l**ee**bro est**a** en la m**e**sa
the book is on the table

Nuevo Laredo está en el norte del país
nw**e**vo lar**e**do est**a** en el n**o**rteh del pa-**ee**s
Nuevo Laredo is in the north of the country

It also describes the temporary or passing qualities of something or someone:

estoy enojado
est**oy** enoHado
I'm angry

estoy cansado
est**oy** kans**a**do
I'm tired

este filete está frío
esteh feel**e**teh est**a** fr**ee**-o
this steak is cold

Note the difference between the following two phrases:

Isabel es muy guapa
Isabel es mwee gw**a**pa
Isabel is very pretty

Isabel está muy guapa (esta noche)
Isabel est**a** mwee gw**a**pa **e**sta n**o**cheh
Isabel looks pretty (tonight)

soy inglés
soy eeng-l**e**s
I am English

estoy en México
est**oy** en m**e**Heeko
I am in Mexico

Negatives

To express a negative in Spanish, to say 'I don't want', 'it's not here' etc, place the word no in front of the verb:

entiendo
ent-y**e**ndo
I understand

no entiendo
no ent-y**e**ndo
I don't understand

me gusta este helado
meh g**oo**sta **e**steh el**a**do
I like this ice cream

no me gusta este helado
no meh g**oo**sta **e**steh el**a**do
I don't like this ice cream

lo alquilé aquí
lo alkeel**eh** ak**ee**
I rented it here

no lo alquilé aquí
no lo alkeel**eh** ak**ee**
I didn't rent it here

van a cantar
ban a kant**a**r
they're going to sing

no van a cantar
no ban a kant**a**r
they're not going to sing

To use negative words like:

nadie	nada	nunca
n**a**d-yeh	n**a**da	n**oo**nka
no-one, nobody	nothing	never

you can either place them before the verb, or put them after the verb with no in front, thus:

no llegó nadie/nadie llegó
no yeg**o** n**a**d-yeh/n**a**d-yeh yeg**o**
nobody came

no hay nadie ahí
no ī n**a**d-yeh a-**ee**
there's no-one there

no compramos nada
no kompr**a**mos n**a**da
we didn't buy anything

no sabemos nada de ella
no sab**e**mos n**a**da deh **eh**-ya
we don't know anything about her

To say 'there's no ...', 'I've no ...' etc, make the accompanying verb negative:

no hay vino
no ī b**ee**no
there's no wine

no tengo cerillas
no t**e**ngo sair**ee**-yas
I've no matches

To say 'not him', 'not her' etc just use the personal pronoun followed by no:

nosotros, no	ella, no	yo, no
nos**o**tros no	**eh**-ya no	yo no
not us	not her	not me

Imperatives

When giving a command to people you would normally address with Usted or Ustedes, you form the imperative by taking the first person singular of the present tense and changing the endings as follows:

	first person singular	singular	plural
hablar to speak	hablo	habl-e **a**bleh	habl-en **a**blen
comer to eat	como	com-a k**o**ma	com-an k**o**man
abrir to open	abro	abr-a **a**bra	abr-an **a**bran
venir to come	vengo	ven-ga b**e**nga	ven-gan b**e**ngan

coma despacio
k**o**ma desp**a**s-yo
eat slowly

When you are telling someone not to do something, use the forms above and place **no** in front of the verb:

no me moleste, por favor
no meh mol**e**steh por fab**o**r
please don't disturb me

¡no beba alcohol!
no b**e**ba alk**o**l
don't drink alcohol!

¡no venga esta noche!
no b**e**nga **e**sta n**o**cheh
don't come tonight!

To give a command to people you would normally address as **tú**, remove the endings **-ar**, **-er**, and **-ir** from the verb and add these endings:

hablar to speak
habl-a [**a**bla]
comer to eat
com-e [k**o**meh]
abrir to open
abr-e [**a**breh]

To form a negative imperative to people addressed as **tú**, **no** is placed in front of the verb and the endings change:

habla	**no habl-es**	[no **a**b-les]
come	**no com-as**	[no k**o**mas]
abre	**no abras**	[no **a**bras]

por favor, no hables tan rápido (to one person)
por fab**o**r no **a**b-les tan r**a**peedo
please don't speak so quickly

Pronouns are added to the end of the imperative form:

despiérteme a las ocho, por favor
desp-y**ai**rtemeh a las **o**cho por fab**o**r
wake me up at eight o'clock, please

bébelo	**ciérralas**
b**e**belo	s-y**ai**ralas
drink it	close them

ayúdeme, por favor
a-y**oo**demeh por fab**o**r
help me please

but when the imperative is negative, they are placed in front of it:

no lo bebas
no lo b**e**bas
don't drink it

no las cierres
no las s-y**air**-res
don't close them

The imperatives of the verb **ir** 'to go' are irregular:

forms	**Usted**	**Ustedes**	**tú**
	vaya	**vayan**	**ve**
	b**ī**-a	b**ī**-an	beh

QUESTIONS

Often the word order remains the same in a question, but the intonation changes, the voice rising at the end of the question:

¿quieres bailar?
k-y**air**-es bīl**ar**
do you want to dance?

¿quieres ir al cine?
k-y**air**-es eer al s**ee**neh
do you want to go to the cinema?

DATES

Use the numbers on page 26 to express the date:

el uno de septiembre [el **oo**no deh set-y**e**mbreh] the first of September
el dos de diciembre [dos deh dees-y**e**mbreh] the second of December
el treinta de mayo [tr**ay**nta deh m**ī**-yo] the thirtieth of May
el treinta y uno de mayo [tr**ay**ntī **oo**no deh m**ī**-yo] the thirty-first of May

DAYS

Sunday domingo
Monday lunes [l**oo**n-es]
Tuesday martes [m**a**rt-es]
Wednesday miércoles [m-y**air**kol-es]
Thursday jueves [Hw**e**b-es]
Friday viernes [b-y**ai**rn-es]
Saturday sábado

MONTHS

January enero [en**ai**ro]
February febrero [febr**ai**ro]
March marzo [m**a**rso]
April abril
May mayo [m**ī**-yo]
June junio [H**oo**n-yo]
July julio [H**oo**l-yo]
August agosto
September septiembre [set-y**e**mbreh]
October octubre [okt**oo**breh]
November noviembre [nob-y**e**mbreh]
December diciembre [dees-y**e**mbreh]

TIME

what time is it? ¿qué hora es? [keh **o**ra]
one o'clock la **u**na
two o'clock las dos
it's one o'clock es la **u**na
it's two o'clock son las dos
it's ten o'clock son las diez [d-yes]
five past one la **u**na y cinco [ee s**ee**nko]
ten past two las dos y diez [d-yes]
quarter past one la **u**na y cuarto [ee kw**a**rto]
quarter past two las dos y cuarto

half past ten las diez y media [d-yes ee m**e**d-ya]
twenty to ten veinte p**a**ra las diez [b**ay**nteh]
quarter to ten cuarto para las diez [kw**a**rto]
at eight o'clock a las ocho [**o**cho]
at half past four a las cuatro y media [kw**a**tro ee m**e**d-ya]
2 a.m. las dos de la mañana [deh la man-y**a**na]
2 p.m. las dos de la tarde [t**a**rdeh]
6 a.m. las seis de la mañana [seh-ees deh la man-y**a**na]
6 p.m. las seis de la tarde [t**a**rdeh]
noon mediodía [m**e**d-yo-d**ee**-a]
midnight medianoche [m**e**d-ya-n**o**cheh]
an hour **u**na hora [**o**ra]
a minute un min**u**to
two minutes dos min**u**tos
a second un seg**u**ndo
a quarter of an hour un cuarto de hora [kw**a**rto deh **o**ra]
half an hour media hora [m**e**d-ya]
three quarters of an hour tres cuartos de hora [kw**a**rtos deh **o**ra]

NUMBERS

0 cero [s**ai**ro]
1 **uno, una**
2 dos
3 tres
4 cuatro [kw**a**tro]
5 cinco [s**ee**nko]
6 seis [says]
7 siete [s-y**e**teh]
8 ocho [**o**cho]
9 nueve [nw**e**beh]
10 diez [d-yes]
11 once [**o**nseh]
12 doce [d**o**seh]
13 trece [tr**e**seh]
14 catorce [kat**o**rseh]
15 quince [k**ee**nseh]
16 dieciséis [d-yeseese-ees]
17 diecisiete [d-yesees-y**e**teh]
18 dieciocho [d-yesee-**o**cho]
19 diecinueve [d-yeseenw**e**beh]
20 veinte [b**ay**nteh]
21 veintiuno [bayntee-**oo**no]
22 veintidós [baynteed**o**s]
23 veintitrés [baynteetr**e**s]
30 treinta [tr**ay**nta]
31 treinta y uno [tr**ay**ntī **oo**no]
40 cuarenta [kwar**e**nta]
50 cincuenta [seenkw**e**nta]
60 sesenta
70 setenta
80 ochenta [och**e**nta]
90 noventa [nob**e**nta]
100 cien [s-yen]
120 ciento veinte [s-y**e**nto b**ay**nteh]
200 doscientos, doscientas [dos-y**e**ntos]
300 trescientos, trescientas [tres-y**e**ntos]
400 cuatrocientos, cuatrocientas [kwatros-y**e**ntos]

500 quinientos, quinientas [keen-yentos]
600 seiscientos, seiscientas [says-yentos]
700 setecientos, setecientas [setes-yentos]
800 ochocientos, ochocientas [ochos-yentos]
900 novecientos, novecientas [nobes-yentos]
1,000 mil
2,000 dos mil
5,000 cinco mil [seenko]
10,000 diez mil [d-yes]
1,000,000 un millón [meel-yon]

When **uno** is used with a masculine noun, the final **-o** is dropped:

un carro
oon karo
a/one car

una is used with feminine nouns:

una bicicleta
oona beeseekleta
a/one bike

With multiples of a hundred, the **-as** ending is used with feminine nouns:

trescientos hombres
tres-yentos omb-res
300 men

quinientas mujeres
keen-yentas mooHair-es
500 women

Ordinals

1st primero [preemairo]
2nd segundo
3rd tercero [tairsairo]
4th cuarto [kwarto]
5th quinto [keento]
6th sexto [sesto]
7th séptimo
8th octavo [oktabo]
9th noveno [nobeno]
10th décimo [deseemo]

BASIC PHRASES

yes
sí

no
no

OK
bueno
b**we**no

hello!/hi!
¡hola!
ola

good morning
buenos días
bw**e**nos

good evening
buenas t**a**rdes
bw**e**nas

good night
buenas noches
n**o**ches

goodbye/see you
hasta luego
asta lw**e**go

please
por favor
fab**o**r

yes please
sí, por favor

thanks, thank you
gracias
gr**a**s-yas

no thanks, no thank you
no gracias

thank you very much
muchas gracias
m**oo**chas

don't mention it
no hay de qué
ī deh keh

how do you do?
¡mucho g**u**sto!
m**oo**cho

how are you?
¿c**ó**mo le va?
leh

fine, thanks
bien gracias
b-yen gr**a**s-yas

nice to meet you
encant**a**do de conocerle
deh konos**ai**rleh

excuse me
(to get past) con perm**i**so
(to get attention) ¡por favor!
fab**o**r

(I'm) sorry
disculpe
deesk**oo**lpeh

sorry?/pardon (me)?
(didn't understand) ¿mande?
m**a**ndeh

what did you say?
¿qué dijo?
keh d**ee**Ho

I see/I understand
entiendo
ent-y**e**ndo

I don't understand
no entiendo

do you speak English?
¿habla inglés?
abla

I don't speak Spanish
no hablo español
ablo espan-y**o**l

could you speak more slowly?
¿podría hablar mas lento?
abl**a**r

could you repeat that?
¿puede repetir eso?
pw**e**deh

could you write it down?
¿puede escribírmelo?

I'd like a ...
quisiera un/una ...
kees-y**ai**ra

I'd like to ...
me gustaría ...
meh

can I have ...?
¿me da ...?

how much is it?
¿cuánto vale?
kw**a**nto b**a**leh

cheers!
(toast) ¡salud!
sal**oo**

it is ...
es ...; está ...

where is it?
¿dónde está?
d**o**ndeh

where are the ...?
¿dónde están los/las ...?

how far is it to ...?
¿cuánto hay de aquí a ...?
kw**a**nto ī deh ak**ee**

is it far?
¿queda lejos?
k**e**da l**e**Hos

how long does it take?
¿cuánto d**u**ra?
kw**a**nto

at what time ...?
¿a qué hora ...?
keh **o**ra

when is ...?
cuándo es ...?
kw**a**ndo

CONVERSION TABLES

1 centimetre = 0.39 inches

1 metre = 39.37 inches = 1.09 yards

1 kilometre = 0.62 miles = 5/8 mile

1 inch = 2.54 cm

1 foot = 30.48 cm

1 yard = 0.91 m

1 mile = 1.61 km

km	1	2	3	4	5	10	20	30	40	50	100
miles	0.6	1.2	1.9	2.5	3.1	6.2	12.4	18.6	24.8	31.0	62.1

miles	1	2	3	4	5	10	20	30	40	50	100
km	1.6	3.2	4.8	6.4	8.0	16.1	32.2	48.3	64.4	80.5	161

1 gram = 0.035 ounces

g	100	250	500
oz	3.5	8.75	17.5

1 kilo = 1000 g = 2.2 pounds
1 oz = 28.35 g
1 lb = 0.45 kg

kg	0.5	1	2	3	4	5	6	7	8	9	10
lb	1.1	2.2	4.4	6.6	8.8	11.0	13.2	15.4	17.6	19.8	22.0

kg	20	30	40	50	60	70	80	90	100
lb	44	66	88	110	132	154	176	198	220

lb	0.5	1	2	3	4	5	6	7	8	9	10	20
kg	0.2	0.5	0.9	1.4	1.8	2.3	2.7	3.2	3.6	4.1	4.5	9.0

1 litre = 1.75 UK pints / 2.13 US pints

1 UK pint = 0.57 l
1 US pint = 0.47 l

1 UK gallon = 4.55 l
1 US gallon = 3.79 l

centigrade / Celsius

C = (F - 32) × 5/9

C	-5	0	5	10	15	18	20	25	30	36.8	38
F	23	32	41	50	59	65	68	77	86	98.4	100.4

Fahrenheit

F = (C × 9/5) + 32

F	23	32	40	50	60	65	70	80	85	98.4	101
C	-5	0	4	10	16	18	21	27	29	36.8	38.3

English-Spanish

A

a, an* un [oon], una [**oo**na]
about: about 20 **u**nos v**ei**nte
it's about 5 o'clock son aproximadamente las c**i**nco [aprokseem**a**damenteh]
a film about Mexico **u**na película sobre México [s**o**breh]
above ... arr**i**ba de ... [arr**ee**ba deh]
abroad en el extranjero [estranH**ai**ro]
absolutely! (I agree) ¡cl**a**ro!
accelerator el acelerador [aselairad**o**r]
accept aceptar [asept**a**r]
accident el accidente [akseed**e**nteh]
there's been an accident hubo un accidente [**oo**bo]
accommodation alojamiento [aloHam-y**e**nto]
see **room** and **hotel**
accurate exacto
ache el dolor
my back aches me duele la esp**a**lda [meh dw**e**leh]
across: across the road al **o**tro l**a**do de la calle [k**a**-yeh]
adapter el adaptador
address la dirección [deereks-y**o**n]
what's your address? ¿cuál es su dirección? [kwal]

> Addresses are frequently written using just the street name and number, for example **Doctores 83**; sometimes the names of the streets themselves are numbers, which can be confusing – although if this is the case the word **calle**, which means street, will usually be included. **Avenida**, **Calzada** and **Paseo** are common names for streets, and you may sometimes see the words **callejón** (lane, alley) and **cerrada** (cul-de-sac). An address may be written like this: **Hidalgo, 39, 8° 2a** meaning number 39, Hidalgo Street, 8th floor, apartment 2. You might also see **planta baja** (**PB**), meaning ground floor, **sótano** (basement) or even **azotea** (roof). In some towns, streets may be laid out on a grid and have **Ote.** (**Oriente** east), **Pte.** (**Poniente** west), **Nte.** (**Norte** north) or **Sur** (south) added to the street name to show which side of two central dividing streets it is on. A typical address is as follows:
>
> Sr. José Gómez Ruiz
> Tacubaya, 38, 4° 2a
> Mexico D.F.
> 2P 00020

address book la libr**e**ta de direcciones [deh deereks-y**o**n-es]

admission charge la entr**a**da
adult el/la adulto [ad**oo**lto], el/ la pers**o**na mayor [mī-y**o**r]
advance: in advance por adelant**a**do
aeroplane el avión [ab-y**o**n]
after después (de) [despw**e**s (deh)]
after you pase Usted [p**a**seh oost**eh**]
after lunch después de com**e**r
afternoon la tarde [t**a**rdeh]
in the afternoon por la tarde
this afternoon esta tarde
aftershave el aftershave
aftersun cream la cr**e**ma p**a**ra después del sol [despw**e**s]
afterwards luego [lw**e**go]
again **o**tra vez [bes]
against c**o**ntra
age la edad [ed**a**]
ago: a week ago hace **u**na sem**a**na [**a**seh]
an hour ago hace una h**o**ra
agree: I agree de acuerdo [deh akw**ai**rdo]
AIDS el SIDA [s**ee**da]
air el aire [**ī**reh]
by air en avión [ab-y**o**n]
air-conditioned con cl**i**ma artificial [arteefees-y**a**l]
air-conditioning el aire acondicionado [**ī**reh akondees-yon**a**do]
airmail: by airmail por avión [ab-y**o**n]
airmail envelope el sobre aéreo [s**o**breh a-**ai**reh-o]
airplane el avión [ab-y**o**n]
airport el aeropuerto [īropw**ai**rto]
to the airport, please al aeropuerto, por favor [fab**o**r]
airport bus el camión del aeropuerto [kam-y**o**n]
aisle seat el asiento de pasillo [as-y**e**nto deh pas**ee**-yo]
alarm clock el despertad**o**r
alcohol el alcohol [alk**o**l]
alcoholic alcoh**ó**lico
all: all the boys t**o**dos los ch**i**cos
all the girls t**o**das las ch**i**cas
all of it t**o**do
all of them t**o**dos
that's all, thanks **e**so es todo, gracias [gr**a**s-yas]
allergic: I'm allergic to ... t**e**ngo alergia a ... [al**ai**rHee-a]
alligator el caimán [kīm**a**n]
allowed: is it allowed? ¿se permite? [seh pairm**ee**teh]
all right! ¡bueno! [bw**e**no]
I'm all right est**oy** bien [b-yen]
are you all right? (fam) ¿est**á**s bien?
(pol) ¿se encuentra bien? [seh enkw**e**ntra]
almond la alm**e**ndra
almost c**a**si
alone s**o**lo
alphabet el alfab**e**to

a a	n **e**neh
b beh l**a**rga	ñ **e**n-yeh
c seh	o o
ch cheh	p peh
d deh	q koo

e eh
f **e**feh
g Heh
h **a**cheh
i ee
j H**o**ta
k ka
l **e**leh
m **e**meh
r **ai**rreh
s **e**seh
t teh
u oo
v beh ch**ee**ka
w **oo**beh
x **e**kees
y ee gr-y**e**ga
z s**e**ta

already ya
also también [tamb-y**e**n]
although aunque [a-**oo**nkeh]
altogether del t**o**do
always siempre [s-y**e**mpreh]
am*: **I am** soy; est**o**y
a.m.: at seven a.m. a las si**e**te de la mañana [deh la man-y**a**na]
amazing (surprising) increíble [eenkreh-**ee**bleh]
(very good) extraordinario [estra-ordeen**a**r-yo]
ambulance la ambulancia [amboolans-ya]
call an ambulance! ¡llame a **u**na ambulancia! [y**a**meh]

> Most phone booths give the number for the local Red Cross (**Cruz Roja**).

America Est**a**dos Un**i**dos
American (adj) norteamericano [norteh-amaireek**a**no]
I'm American (man/woman) soy norteamericano/ norteameric**a**na
among entre [**e**ntreh]
amount la cantidad [kanteed**a**]
(money) la s**u**ma
amp: a 13-amp fuse el fusible de tr**e**ce amperios [foos**ee**bleh deh – amp**ai**ree-os]
and y [ee]
angry enojado [enoH**a**do]
animal el anim**a**l
ankle el tobillo [tob**ee**-yo]
anniversary (wedding) el aniversario de b**o**da [aneebairs**a**r-yo deh]
annoy: this man's annoying me este hombre me est**á** molest**a**ndo [**e**steh **o**mbreh meh]
annoying mol**e**sto
another **o**tro
can we have another room? ¿puede d**a**rnos **o**tro cuarto? [pw**e**deh – kw**a**rto]
another beer, please **o**tra cerv**e**za, por favor [fab**o**r]
antibiotics los antibióticos [anteeb-y**o**teekos]
antifreeze el anticongelante [anteekonHel**a**nteh]
antihistamines los antihistamínicos [antee-eestam**ee**neekos]
antique: is it an antique? ¿es antiguo? [ant**ee**gwo]
antique shop la tienda de antigüedades [t-y**e**nda deh anteegwed**a**d-es]
antiseptic el antiséptico
any: have you got any bread/ tomatoes? ¿tiene pan/ jitom**a**tes? [t-y**e**neh]

do you have any? ¿tiene?
sorry, I don't have any lo siento, no tengo [s-y**e**nto]

anybody cualquiera [kwalk-y**ai**ra]
does anybody speak English? ¿habla alguien inglés? [**a**bla **a**lg-yen eeng-l**e**s]
there wasn't anybody there (allí) no había nadie [(a-y**ee**) no ab**ee**-a n**a**d-yeh]

anything algo
(negative) nada

••••••• DIALOGUES •••••••

anything else? ¿algo más?
nothing else, thanks nada más, gracias [gr**a**s-yas]

would you like anything to drink? ¿quiere algo de beber? [k-y**ai**reh – deh beb**air**]
I don't want anything, thanks no quiero nada, gracias [k-y**ai**ro]

apart from aparte de [ap**a**rteh deh]
apartment el departamento, el piso
appendicitis la apendicitis [apendees**ee**tees]
appetizer la botana
aperitif el aperitivo [apereet**ee**bo]
apologize: I apologize disculpe [deesk**oo**lpeh]
apology la disculpa
apple la manzana [mans**a**na]
appointment la cita [s**ee**ta]

••••••• DIALOGUE •••••••

good afternoon, sir, how can I help you? buenas tardes, señor, ¿en qué puedo servirle? [bw**e**nas t**a**rd-es sen-y**o**r, en keh pw**e**do sairb**ee**rleh]
I'd like to make an appointment quisiera hacer cita [kees-y**ai**ra as**air** s**ee**ta]
what time would you like? ¿a qué hora le conviene? [keh **o**ra leh konb-y**e**neh]
three o'clock a las tres
I'm afraid that's not possible, is four o'clock all right? lamento que no será posible, ¿está bien a las cuatro? [keh no sair**a** pos**ee**bleh – b-y**e**n]
yes, that will be fine sí, está bien
the name was ...? ¿su nombre ...? [nombr**eh**]

apricot el chabacano, el damasco
April abril
are*: we are somos; estamos
you are (fam) eres [**air**-es]; estás
(pol) es; está
they are son; están
area la zona [s**o**na]
area code el prefijo [pref**ee**Ho]
arm el brazo [br**a**so]
arrange: will you arrange it for us? ¿nos lo organiza Usted? [organ**ee**sa oost**eh**]
arrival la llegada [yeg**a**da]
arrive llegar [yeg**a**r]
when do we arrive? ¿cuándo

llegamos? [kwando yegamos]
has my fax arrived yet? ¿llegó ya mi fax? [yego]
we arrived today llegamos hoy [yegamos oy]
art el arte [arteh]
art gallery la galería de arte [galeree-a deh]
artist (man/woman) el pintor, la pintora
as: as big as tan grande como
as soon as possible lo más pronto posible [poseebleh]
ashtray el cenicero [seneesairo]
ask preguntar
to ask for pedir
I didn't ask for this no pedí esto
could you ask him to ...? ¿puede decirle que ...? [pwedeh deseerleh keh]
asleep: she's asleep está dormida
aspirin la aspirina
asthma el asma
astonishing increíble [eenkreh-eebleh]
at: at the hotel en el hotel
at the station en la estación
at six o'clock a las seis
at Pedro's en casa de Pedro [deh]
athletics el atletismo
Atlantic Ocean el Océano Atlántico [oseh-ano]
attractive atractivo [atrakteebo]
aubergine la berenjena [berenHena]
August agosto
aunt la tía
Australia Australia [owstral-ya]
Australian (adj) australiano
I'm Australian (man/woman) soy australiano/australiana
automatic automático [owtomateeko]
automatic teller el cajero automático [kaHairo]
autumn el otoño [oton-yo]
in the autumn en otoño
avenue la avenida [abeneeda]
average (ordinary) mediano [med-yano]
(not good) regular [regoolar]
on average por término medio [tairmeeno med-yo]
avocado el aguacate [agwakateh]
awake: is he awake? ¿está despierto? [desp-yairto]
away: go away! ¡lárguese! [largeseh]
he's gone away se ha ido fuera [seh a eedo fwaira]
is it far away? ¿está lejos? [leHos]
awful horrible [oreebleh]
axle el eje [eHeh]
Aztec (adj) azteca [asteka]

B

baby el bebé [beh-beh]
baby food la comida de bebé [deh]
baby's bottle el biberón [beebairon]

baby-sitter la niñera [neen-y**ai**ra]
back (of body) la esp**a**lda
(back part) la parte de atr**á**s [p**a**rteh deh]
at the back en la parte de atrás
can I have my money back? ¿me devuelve el dinero? [meh debw**e**lbeh el deen**ai**ro]
to come/go back regres**a**r
backache el dol**o**r de esp**a**lda [deh]
bacon el jamón [Ham**o**n], el tocino [tos**ee**no]
bad m**a**lo
a bad headache un fuerte dol**o**r de cabeza [fw**ai**rteh – deh kab**e**sa]
badly mal
(injured) gravemente [grabem**e**nteh]
bag la b**o**lsa
(handbag) el b**o**lso
(suitcase) la mal**e**ta, la pet**a**ca
baggage el equipaje [ekeep**a**Heh]
baggage check la consigna [kons**ee**gna], la paquetería [paketair**ee**-a]
baggage claim la recogida de equipajes [rekoH**ee**da deh ekeep**a**H-es]
bakery la panadería [panadair**ee**-a]
balcony el balc**ó**n
a room with a balcony un cuarto con balcón [kw**a**rto]
bald calvo [k**a**lbo]
ball (large) la pel**o**ta, el bal**ó**n
(small) la b**o**la
ballet el ball**e**t
banana el pl**á**tano
band (musical) la orquesta [ork**e**sta]
bandage la venda [b**e**nda]
Bandaid® la tir**i**ta
bandit el band**i**do

> You should be aware of the danger of bandits when driving in Mexico, especially in a foreign vehicle. Sometimes robbers pose as police or hitchhikers so be wary of offering a lift or a helping hand. On the other hand, there are plenty of legitimate police checkpoints along the main roads, where you must stop. The US embassy in Mexico advises never driving after dark.

bank (money) el b**a**nco

> The easiest kind of foreign currency to change in Mexico is US dollars; US dollar travellers' cheques are the second easiest to exchange. Canadian dollars and other major international currencies such as sterling and Deutschmarks are harder to exchange and sometimes refused. In general it is usually only the larger branches of the main banks (and some other banks in main tourist resorts) that are willing to change anything other than dollars. →

Banks are generally open Monday to Friday from 9. 30 a.m. until 1. 30 p.m., though sometimes with shorter hours for exchange. The commission varies from bank to bank but the exchange rate is the same, fixed daily by the government. Cashpoints/ATMs are becoming more and more common. In some border towns, they pay out in US dollars. **Casas de cambio** (bureaux de change) are open longer hours and at weekends and have varying exchange rates and commission charges. Many hotels, shops and restaurants in tourist areas are prepared to change dollars or accept them as payment but the rate will be very low.

bank account la cuenta bancaria [kwenta]

bar el bar

a bar of chocolate una barra de chocolate [deh chokolateh]

The least heavy atmosphere is in hotel bars, tourist areas, or anything that describes itself as a 'ladies' bar'. Traditional **cantinas** are for serious and excessive drinking, have a thoroughly threatening, macho atmosphere, and there's almost inevitably a sign above the door prohibiting entry to 'women, members of the armed forces and anyone in uniform' (**se prohibe la entrada a mujeres, uniformados e integrantes de las fuerzas armadas**). Special bars called **pulquerías** [poolkairee-as] sell **pulque** [poolkeh], a mildly alcoholic milky beer made from cactus, but these too will be male preserves monopolized by serious drinkers.

barber's la peluquería [pelookairee-a]

bargain regatear [regateh-ar]

•••••• DIALOGUE ••••••

how much is this? ¿a cómo está?

100 pesos a cien pesos

that's too expensive, how about 50? es muy caro, ¿me lo deja en cincuenta? [mwee – deHa]

I'll let you have it for 80 se lo dejo en ochenta [seh lo deHo]

can't you reduce it a bit more, to 70 ? ¿me lo rebaja un poco más, en setenta? [rebaHa]

that's the lowest I'll go es lo último

OK de acuerdo [deh akwairdo]

If you're buying handicrafts in markets you're expected to bargain fiercely. But don't try bargaining in supermarkets. Most shops have fixed prices and don't take kindly to being →

offered half (though you might get a small discount), while even in markets produce and household goods usually have their prices clearly marked. Bargaining and haggling are very much a matter of personal style, highly dependent on your command of Spanish but to some extent on experience. Even if you intend to buy, never show the least enthusiasm or interest: walking away will often cut the price dramatically. Decide what you want in advance, find out what a reasonable price would be and decide how much you are prepared to pay. If you start to haggle then it is assumed that you genuinely want to buy.

baseball el béisbol [b**ay**sbol]
basement el s**ó**tano
basket la can**a**sta
(in shop) la cesta [s**e**sta]
bath el baño [b**a**n-yo], la t**i**na
can I have a bath? ¿puedo bañarme? [pw**e**do ban-y**a**rmeh]
bathroom el cuarto de baño [kw**a**rto]
with a private bathroom con baño privado [preeb**a**do]
bath towel la toalla de baño [to-**a**-ya deh]
battery la p**i**la
(car) la batería [batair**ee**-a]
bay la bahía [ba-**ee**-a]
be* ser [sair]; est**a**r
beach la playa [plī-ya]
on the beach en la playa

Mexico has thousands of miles of wonderful beaches, on many of which you can camp if you want to. For your own safety, however, you should check with locals before camping anywhere, and avoid very isolated situations. Some of the bigger resorts like **Acapulco, Puerto Vallarta** or **Cancún** will have stretches of beach to which access is restricted, but by and large the beaches are open and accessible.
see **campsite**

beach umbrella la sombrilla [sombr**ee**-ya]
beans los frijoles [freeH**o**l-es]
runner beans los ejotes [eH**o**t-es]
broad beans las habas [**a**bas]
beard la b**a**rba
beautiful l**i**ndo
because porque [p**o**rkeh]
because of ... deb**i**do a ...
bed la c**a**ma
I'm going to bed now me voy a acost**a**r ahora [meh boy – a-**o**ra]
bed and breakfast cuarto y desayuno [kw**a**rto ee desī-y**oo**no]
bedroom la rec**á**mara
beef la carne de res [k**a**rneh deh]

beer la cerveza [sair**be**sa]
two beers, please dos cervezas, por favor [fab**o**r]

> Mexican beer is excellent. Most is light, lager-style beer, fine examples being **Bohémia**, **Superior**, **Dos Equis** and **Tecate** (the last normally served with lime and salt); but you can also get dark beers of which the best are **Negra Modelo** and **Tres Equis**, or the fine **Nochebuena** (literally: Christmas Eve) which is normally only produced around the year's end. Locally-bottled beers, such as **Sol** on the east coast or **Pacífico** on the west, are often even better than the national labels. Beer is also sold in most shops, supermarkets and, cheapest of all, **agencias** (agents for just one brand). When buying from these places, it is normal to pay a deposit and bring your empties back to the same store.
>
> Some useful terms:
>
> **cerveza clara** light lager-style beer
> **cerveza oscura** dark beer
> **cerveza de barril** draught beer
> **una mediana** a bottle of beer

before **a**ntes
begin empezar [empes**a**r]
when does it begin? ¿cuándo empieza? [kw**a**ndo emp-y**e**sa]

beginner el/la principiante [preenseep-y**a**nteh]
beginning: at the beginning al principio [preens**ee**p-yo]

> **behaviour**
> At heart Mexico is still a conservative, Catholic place and there are obvious ways to avoid hurting local sensibilities, for example: dressing 'decently' in public and covering up in church. It is especially important to be careful in rural areas, where it's unwise even to enter a church without permission, or to take photographs without asking first.

behind atr**á**s
behind me detr**á**s de mí [deh]
beige beige [baysh]
believe creer [kreh-**air**]
Belize Belice [bel**ee**seh]
below abajo [ab**a**Ho]
belt el cinturón [seentooro**n**]
bend (in road) la curva [k**oo**rba]
berth (on ship) el camarote [kamar**o**teh]
beside: beside the ... al l**a**do de la ... [deh]
best el mejor [meH**o**r]
better mejor
are you feeling better? ¿se siente mejor? [seh s-y**e**nteh]
between entre [**e**ntreh]
beyond más allá [a-y**a**]
bicycle la bicicleta [beeseekl**e**ta]

big grande [gr**a**ndeh]
too big demasiado grande [demas-y**a**do]
it's not big enough no es lo suficientemente grande [soofees-yentem**e**nteh]
big game fishing la pesca mayor [mī-y**o**r]
bike la bicicleta [beeseekl**e**ta]
(motorbike) la moto
bikini el bikini
bill la cuenta [kw**e**nta]
(US: banknote) el billete [bee-y**e**teh]
could I have the bill, please? me pasa la cuenta, por favor [meh – fab**o**r]
bin el bote de la basura [b**o**teh deh]
bin liners las bolsas de basura
binding (ski) la atadura
bird el pájaro [p**a**Haro]
biro® el bolígrafo
birthday el cumpleaños [koompleh-**a**n-yos]
happy birthday! ¡feliz cumpleaños! [fel**ee**s]
biscuit la galleta [ga-y**e**ta]
bit: a little bit un poquito [pok**ee**to]
a big bit un pedazo grande [ped**a**so gr**a**ndeh]
a bit of ... un pedazo de ... [deh]
a bit expensive un poco caro
bite (by insect) la picadura
(by dog) la mordedura
bitter (taste etc) amargo
black negro [n**eh**-gro]
black coffee el café americano [kaf**eh**]
(strong) el café solo
blanket la cobija [kob**ee**Ha], la frazada [fras**a**da]
bleach (for toilet) la lejía [leH**ee**-a]
bless you! ¡Jesús! [Hes**oo**s]
blind ciego [s-y**e**go]
blinds las persianas [pers-y**a**nas]
blister la ampolla [amp**o**-ya]
blocked (road, pipe) bloqueado [blokeh-**a**do]
(sink) atascado
block (city) la cuadra [kw**a**dra]
block of flats el edificio de departamentos [edeef**ee**s-yo deh]
blond guero [gw**ai**ro]
blood la sangre [s**a**ngreh]
high blood pressure la tensión alta [tens-y**o**n]
blouse la blusa
blow-dry (verb) secar a mano
I'd like a cut and blow-dry quisiera un corte y un marcado [kees-y**ai**ra oon k**o**rteh ee]
blue azul [as**oo**l]
blusher el colorete [kolor**e**teh]
boarding house la pensión [pens-y**o**n], la hostería [ostair**ee**-a]
boarding pass la tarjeta de embarque [tarH**e**ta deh emb**a**rkeh]
boat el barco
body el cuerpo [kw**ai**rpo]

boiled egg el h**ue**vo pas**a**do (por agua) [w**e**bo pas**a**do por **a**gwa]
boiler la cald**e**ra [kald**ai**ra]
bone el h**ue**so [w**e**so]
bonnet (of car) el cap**ó**, el c**o**fre [k**o**freh]
book el l**i**bro
(verb) reserv**a**r [resairb**a**r]
can I book a seat? ¿p**ue**do reserv**a**r un asi**e**nto? [pw**e**do – as-y**e**nto]

•••••• DIALOGUE ••••••

I'd like to book a table for two quis**ie**ra reserv**a**r **u**na m**e**sa p**a**ra dos pers**o**nas [kees-y**ai**ra]
what time would you like it booked for? ¿p**a**ra qué h**o**ra la qui**e**re? [keh **o**ra la k-y**ai**reh]
half past seven las si**e**te y m**e**dia
that's fine de acu**e**rdo [deh akw**ai**rdo]
and your name? ¿y su n**o**mbre ...? [ee soo n**o**mbreh]

bookshop, bookstore la librer**í**a [leebrair**ee**-a]
boot (footwear) la b**o**ta
(of car) la mal**e**ta, la caju**e**la [kaHw**e**la]
border (of country) la front**e**ra [front**ai**ra]
bored: I'm bored (said by man/woman) est**oy** aburr**i**do/aburr**i**da
boring aburr**i**do, pes**a**do
born: I was born in Manchester nac**í** en M**a**nchester [nas**ee**]
I was born in 1960 nac**í** en mil nov**e**ci**e**ntos ses**e**nta
borrow ped**i**r prest**a**do
may I borrow ...? ¿p**ue**de prest**a**rme ...? [pw**e**deh prest**a**rmeh]
both los dos
both... and... t**a**nto ... c**o**mo ...
bother: sorry to bother you si**e**nto molest**a**rlo [s-y**e**nto]
bottle la bot**e**lla [bot**eh**-ya], el fr**a**sco
a bottle of house red **u**na bot**e**lla de t**i**nto de la c**a**sa [deh]
bottle-opener el abrebot**e**llas [abrebot**eh**-yas]
bottom (of person) el tras**e**ro [tras**ai**ro], el c**u**lo
at the bottom of the ... (hill/road) al pie del/de la ... [p-yeh del/deh]
(sea) al f**o**ndo de ...
box la c**a**ja [k**a**Ha]
box office la taqu**i**lla [tak**ee**-ya], la bolet**e**r**í**a [boletair**ee**-a]
boy el ch**i**co, el j**o**ven [H**o**ven], el ch**a**vo [ch**a**bo]
boyfriend el n**o**vio [n**o**b-yo]
bra el brassi**e**re [bras-y**ai**r]
bracelet la puls**e**ra [pools**ai**ra]
brake el fr**e**no
brandy el co**ñ**ac [kon-y**a**k]
bread el pan
white bread el pan bl**a**nco
brown bread el pan de cent**e**no [deh sent**e**no]
wholemeal bread el pan integr**a**l [eentegr**a**l]
break (verb) romp**e**r [romp**ai**r]

I've broken the ... rompí el ...
I think I've broken my ... creo que me he roto el ... [kreh-o keh meh eh]

break down descomponerse [deskomponairseh]
I've broken down se me ha descompuesto el carro [seh meh a deskompwesto]

breakdown (mechanical) la descompostura

> If you have a breakdown, there is a free highway mechanics service known as the **Angeles Verdes** (Green Angels). As well as patrolling all major routes looking for stranded motorists, they can be reached by phone (AT 02-684-9715/9761) and speak English. They don't operate inside the capital; there you should call the AAM (AA or AAA equivalent). Should you have a minor accident, try to come to some arrangement with the other party – involving the police will only make matters worse and Mexican drivers will be anxious to do the same. Also, if you witness an accident, don't get involved – witnesses can get locked up along with those responsible to prevent them leaving before the case comes up.

breakdown service el servicio de grúa [serbees-yo deh groo-a]

breakfast el desayuno [desī-yoono]

break-in: I've had a break-in entraron en mi casa a robar

breast el pecho

breathe respirar

breeze la brisa

bribe la mordida

bridge (over river) el puente [pwenteh]

brief breve [brebeh]

briefcase la cartera [kartaira]

bright (light etc) brillante [bree-yanteh]
bright red rojo vivo [roHo beebo]

brilliant (idea, person) brillante [bree-yanteh]

bring traer [tra-air]
I'll bring it back later lo devolveré luego [debolbaireh lwego]

Britain Gran Bretaña [bretan-ya]

British británico
I'm British (man/woman) soy británico/británica

brochure el folleto [fo-yeto]

broken roto

bronchitis la bronquitis [bronkeetees]

brooch el broche [brocheh]

broom la escoba

brother el hermano [airmano]

brother-in-law el cuñado [koon-yado]

brown color café [kafeh]
brown hair el pelo castaño [kastan-yo]

brown eyes los ojos castaños [oHos]
bruise el moretón
brush (for hair, cleaning) el cepillo [sepee-yo]
(artist's) el pincel [peensel]
bucket el cubo [koobo], el balde [baldeh]
buffet car el vagón-restaurante [bagon-restowranteh]
buggy (for child) el carrito de niño [deh neen-yo]
building el edificio [edeefees-yo]
bulb (light bulb) el foco
bull el toro
bullfight la corrida
bullring la plaza de toros [plasa deh]
bumper la defensa
bunk la litera [leetaira]
bureau de change el cambio [kamb-yo], la casa de cambio [deh]
see **bank**
burglary el robo con allanamiento de morada [a-yanam-yento]
burn la quemadura [kemadoora]
(verb) quemar [kemar]
burnt: this is burnt está quemado [kemado]
burst: a burst pipe la cañería rota [kan-yairee-a]
bus el camión [kam-yon]
(long-distance) el autobús [owtoboos]
what number bus is it to ...? ¿qué número tomo para ...? [keh noomairo]
when is the next bus to ...? ¿cuándo sale el próximo camión/autobús para ...? [kwando saleh]
what time is the last bus? ¿a qué hora sale el último camión? [keh ora – oolteemo]
could you let me know when we get there? ¿puede avisarme cuando llegamos [pwedeh abeesarmeh kwando yegamos]

Within Mexico, long-distance buses (called **camiones** or **autobuses**) are by far the most common and efficient form of transport. There are basically two classes of bus, first (**primera**) and second (**segunda**), though on major long-distance routes, there's often little to differentiate the two. The main differences are that second-class buses make more stops and first-class buses are more expensive. In addition there are luxury buses with comfortable seats and air-conditioning – particularly on the long-distance routes from the US border. These are called **pullman**. Most large towns have a 'central' bus station (**central camionera** or **central de autobuses**), which is often a long way from the town centre. →

Often the main terminals in towns are for local bus lines only. Wherever possible, you should reserve your seat in advance at the terminal or the bus company office. If you cannot book, you may be able to stand on second-class buses, but most first-class buses will not take standing passengers. It's worth remembering, too, that while trains are quite leisurely about times, buses almost always depart exactly on time.
Public transport within towns and cities is always plentiful and inexpensive, though also very crowded and not very comfortable. You may need to shout loudly to the driver if you want him to stop (the cry is **¡bajan!** [b**a**Han] – 'people getting off'). Usually, you'll be relying on buses, although Mexico City has a vast and excellent **metro** system and there are smaller metros in Guadalajara and Monterrey.
see **taxi**

•••••• DIALOGUE ••••••

does this bus go to ...? ¿este camión va a ...? [esteh kam-y**o**n ba]
no, you need a number ... no, tiene que tomar el ... [t-y**e**neh keh]

business el negocio [neg**o**s-yo]

bus station la central camionera [sentr**a**l kam-yon**ai**ra], la estación de autobuses [estas-y**o**n deh owtob**oo**s-es]
bus stop la parada de camión [kam-y**o**n]
bust el pecho
busy (restaurant etc) concurrido
I'm busy tomorrow (said by man/woman) estoy ocupado/ocupada mañana [man-y**a**na]
but pero [p**ai**ro]
butcher's la carnicería [karneesair**ee**-a]
butter la mantequilla [mantek**ee**-ya]
button el botón
buy (verb) comprar
where can I buy ...? ¿dónde puedo comprar ...? [d**o**ndeh pw**e**do]
buzzard el buitre [bw**ee**treh]
by: by bus/car en camión/carro
written by ... escrito por ...
by the window junto a la ventana [H**oo**nto]
by the sea a orillas del mar [or**ee**-yas]
by Thursday para el jueves
bye! ¡hasta luego! [**a**sta lw**e**go]

C

cabbage el repollo [rep**o**-yo]
cabin (on ship) el camarote [kamar**o**teh]
cable car el teleférico [telef**ai**reeko], el funicular

[fooneekoolar]
cactus el cacto
café la cafetería [kafetairee-a]
see restaurant
cagoule el chubasquero [choobaskairo]
cake el pastel
cake shop la pastelería [pastelairee-a]
call (verb) llamar [yamar]
(to phone) llamar (por teléfono)
what's it called? ¿cómo se llama ? [seh yama]
he/she is called ... se llama ...
please call the doctor llame al médico, por favor [yameh – fabor]
please give me a call at 7.30 a.m. tomorrow por favor, llámeme mañana a las siete y media de la mañana [yamameh man-yana]
please ask him to call me por favor, dígale que me llame [deegaleh keh meh yameh]
call back: I'll call back later regresaré más tarde [regresareh mas tardeh]
(phone back) volveré a llamar [bolbaireh a yamar]
call round: I'll call round tomorrow mañana paso
camcorder la videocámara [beedeh-o-kamara]
camera la cámara
camera shop la tienda fotográfica [t-yenda]
camp (verb) acampar
can we camp here? ¿se puede acampar aquí? [seh pwedeh – akee]
camping gas canister la bomba de butano [deh bootano]

> Kerosene or paraffin oil for camping stoves is called **petróleo para lámparas** and can normally be bought from an **expendio** or **despacho de petróleo** or from the **tlapaleria** (hardware store); it cannot be bought at petrol stations. Camping gas is widely available.

campsite el camping

> There is not usually much alternative to staying in hotels. Camping is easy enough if you are hiking in the back country or happy to crash on the beach. However, robberies are common, especially in places with a lot of tourists. There are few organized campsites and those that do exist are first and foremost trailer parks. In a lot of less official campsites, you can rent a hammock and a place to sling it. Beach huts (**cabañas** [kaban-yas]) are found at the more rustic, backpacker-oriented beach resorts, and sometimes inland. Usually just a wooden or palm-frond shack with a hammock or hooks to →

hang your own, they often do not have electricity. In less touristy areas that don't have cabañas, you should still be able to sling a hammock somewhere (probably the local bar or restaurant).

can la l**a**ta
  a can of beer **u**na lata de cerveza [deh sairb**e**sa]
can*: **can you ...?** ¿puede ...? [pw**e**deh]
  can I have ...? ¿me da ...? [meh]
  I can't ... no puedo ... [pw**e**do]
Canada el Canad**á**
Canadian (adj) canadiense [kanad-y**e**nseh]
  I'm Canadian soy canadiense
canal el can**a**l
cancel cancelar [kansel**a**r]
candies los dulces [d**oo**l-ses]
candle la vela [b**e**la]
canoe la can**o**a
canoeing el piragüismo [peeragw**ee**smo]
can-opener el abrel**a**tas
canyon el cañón [kan-y**o**n], la cañada [kan-y**a**da]
cap (hat) la g**o**rra
  (of bottle) el tap**ó**n
car el c**a**rro, el auto [**ow**to], el autom**ó**vil
  by car en carro
caravan la caravana [karab**a**na]
caravan site el c**a**mping
carburettor el carburad**o**r
card (birthday etc) la tarjeta [tarH**e**ta]
  here's my (business) card aquí tiene mi tarjeta (de visita) [ak**ee** t-y**e**neh – deh bees**ee**ta]
cardigan la cham**a**rra
cardphone el tel**é**fono de tarjeta [deh tarH**e**ta]
careful cauteloso [kowtel**o**so]
  be careful! ¡cuidado! [kweed**a**do]
caretaker el portero [port**ai**ro]
car ferry el f**e**rry, el transbordad**o**r de c**a**rros [deh]
car hire el alquiler de carros [alkeel**air** deh]
  see **car rental**
car park el estacionamiento [estas-y**o**nam-y**e**nto]
carpet la alf**o**mbra, el tapete [tap**e**teh]
car rental el alquiler de c**a**rros [alkeel**air** deh]

Renting a car avoids many of the problems associated with driving in Mexico. Local operators normally charge less than the well-known chains. Check the rates carefully and make sure that insurance, tax and mileage are included. Weekly rates are usually better value and unlimited mileage is almost always a bargain. For shorter distances, mopeds and motorbikes are also available in most resorts.
see **driving** and **rent**

carriage (of train) el vagón [bag**o**n]
carrier bag la bolsa de plástico [deh]
carrot la zanahoria [sana-**o**r-ya]
carry llevar [yeb**a**r]
carry-cot el capazo [kap**a**so]
carton la caja [k**a**Ha]
carwash el lavado de carros [lab**a**do deh]
case (suitcase) la maleta
cash el dinero [deen**ai**ro], la plata
to pay (in) cash pagar en efectivo [efekt**ee**bo], pagar al contado
will you cash this for me? ¿podría hacerme efectivo un cheque? [as**ai**rmeh – ch**e**keh]
see **bank** and **cheque**
cash desk la caja [k**a**Ha]
cash dispenser el cajero automático [kaH**ai**ro owtom**a**teeko]
cassette la cassette [kas**e**t]
cassette recorder el cassette
castle el castillo [kast**ee**-yo]
casualty department emergencias [emairH**e**ns-yas]
cat el gato
catch (verb) agarrar
where do we catch the bus to ...? ¿dónde se toma el camión para ...? [d**o**ndeh seh]
cathedral la catedral
Catholic (adj) católico
cauliflower el coliflor
cave la cueva [kw**e**ba]
ceiling el techo
celery el apio [**a**p-yo]
cellar (for wine) la bodega
cellular phone el teléfono celular [selool**a**r]
cemetery el cementerio [sement**ai**r-yo], el panteón [panteh-**o**n]
centigrade* centígrado [sent**ee**grado]
centimetre* el centímetro [sent**ee**metro]
central central [sentr**a**l]
Central America Centroamérica [sentro-am**ai**reeka]
Central American (adj) centroamericano
central heating la calefacción central [kalefaks-y**o**n sentr**a**l]
centre el centro [s**e**ntro]
how do we get to the city centre? ¿cómo se llega al centro? [seh y**e**ga]
cereals los cereales [sereh-**a**l-es]
certainly por supuesto [soopw**e**sto]
certainly not de ninguna manera [deh neeng**oo**na man**ai**ra]
chair la silla [s**ee**-ya]
champagne el champán
change (loose) el suelto [sw**e**lto]
(after payment) el vuelto [bw**e**lto]
(verb) cambiar [kamb-y**a**r]
can I change this for ...? ¿puedo cambiar esto por ...? [pw**e**do]
I don't have any change no tengo suelto

can you give me change for a 1,000 peso note? ¿puede cambiarme un billete de mil? [pwedeh kamb-yarmeh oon bee-yeteh deh meel]

•••••• DIALOGUE ••••••

do we have to change (trains)? ¿tenemos que hacer correspondencia? [keh aser korrespondens-ya]
yes, change at Xalapa/no it's a direct train sí, haga trasbordo en Xalapa/no, es directo [aga – Halapa]

changed: to get changed cambiarse [kamb-yarseh]
chapel la capilla [kapee-ya]
charge (verb) cobrar
charge card see **credit card**
cheap barato
do you have anything cheaper? ¿tiene algo más barato? [t-yeneh]
check (US) el cheque [chekeh]
(US: bill) la cuenta [kwenta]
see **bank** and **cheque**
check (verb) revisar [rebeesar]
could you check the ..., please? ¿puede revisar el ..., por favor? [pwedeh – fabor]
check book el libro de cheques [deh chek-es]
check-in la facturación [faktooras-yon]
check in facturar
where do we have to check in? ¿dónde se factura? [dondeh seh]
cheek la mejilla [meHee-ya]
cheerio! hasta ¡luego! [asta lwego]
cheers! (toast) ¡salud! [saloo]
cheese el queso [keso]
cheesecake el pay de queso [pī deh keso]
chemist's la farmacia [farmas-ya]
see **pharmacy**
cheque el cheque [chekeh]
do you take cheques? ¿aceptan cheques? [aseptan chek-es]

Although travellers' cheques are obviously safer in case of theft or loss, it is best to bring some cash in dollars with you as sometimes you won't be able to change anything else. It's a good idea to have a mixture of denominations, including some one-dollar bills, and to change a small amount into pesos before you leave home. When buying travellers' cheques you should also get a mixture of denominations and stick to the established names.
see **bank**

cheque book la chequera [chekaira]
cheque card la tarjeta de banco [tarHeta deh]
cherry la cereza [sairesa]
(black) la guinda [geenda]

chess el ajedrez [aHed-**res**]
chest el **pe**cho
chewing gum el chicle [ch**ee**kleh]
chicken el pollo [p**o**-yo], la gallina [ga-y**ee**na]
chickenpox la varicela [barees**e**la]
child (male/female) el niño [n**ee**n-yo], la n**i**ña
children los n**i**ños

> Children under 18 require the permission of both parents to enter Mexico. If you are travelling with your child or children on your own, you will need a notarized letter from the other parent giving permission for you to take the child abroad. When travelling with children bear in mind that climate and diet might create some problems at first but that children adapt quickly. Mexicans are generally well disposed towards kids and there are not many restrictions on where you take them other than bars and other obviously adult places.

child minder la niñera [neen-y**ai**ra]
children's pool la alberca infantil [alb**ai**rka eenfant**ee**l]
children's portion la ración pequeña (p**a**ra niños) [ras-y**o**n pek**e**n-ya – n**ee**n-yos]
chilli el chile [ch**ee**leh]

> Chillies are in most kinds of Mexican food. **Chiles jalapeños** or **rajas** (strips of pickled green chillies) are often on restaurant tables as a garnish. They are hot, but in the wide spectrum of Mexican chillies they are mild compared with, for example, the small green **chile de Pekin** or the innocent looking white **chile rubio**, whose effects are brutal. If you want to know if it is hot ask **¿pica mucho?** [p**ee**ka m**oo**cho] or **¿es muy picante?** [es mwee peek**a**nteh]. It may still be hot for tourist tastes but it is worth persevering to enjoy Mexico's wonderful cooking. If you do burn, water doesn't really help; try salt on the lips or bread.

chin la b**a**rba
china la porcelana [porsel**a**na]
Chinese (adj) chino [ch**ee**no]
chips las p**a**pas fr**i**tas
chocolate el chocolate [chokol**a**teh]
milk chocolate el chocolate con leche [l**e**cheh]
plain chocolate el chocolate negro [n**eh**-gro]
a hot chocolate **u**na taza de chocolate [t**a**sa deh]
choose elegir [eleH**ee**r], escoger [eskoH**air**]
Christian name el nombre de p**i**la [n**o**mbreh deh]

Christmas Navidad [nabeed**a**]
Christmas Eve Nochebuena [nocheh-bw**e**na]
merry Christmas! ¡Felices Pascuas! [fel**ee**s-es p**a**skwas]
see **holiday**
church la iglesia [eegl**e**s-ya]
cider la sidra
cigar el puro [p**oo**ro]
cigarette el cigarro [seeg**a**rro]

> Mexican brand cigarettes are cheap but generally dark and strong. Most American brands are readily available – there are hundreds of sellers in the street in addition to tobacconists' – but are much more expensive than local brands.

cigarette lighter el mechero [mech**ai**ro]
cinema el cine [s**ee**neh]

> Cinema is enormously popular in Mexico, particularly in the capital. Cinemas show all the latest Hollywood releases as well as Mexican films, and 'art films' are shown in most towns and cities. Last showings tend to begin at around 9.30 or 10 p.m.

circle el círculo [s**ee**rkoolo]
(in theatre) el anfiteatro [anfeeteh-**a**tro]
city la ciudad [s-yood**a**]
city centre el centro de la ciudad [s**e**ntro deh]
clean (adj) limpio [l**ee**mp-yo]
can you clean these for me? ¿puede limpiarme estos? [pw**e**deh leemp-y**a**rmeh]
cleaning solution (for contact lenses) el líquido limpiador para las lentillas [l**ee**keedo leemp-y**a**dor – lent**ee**-yas]
cleansing lotion la crema limpiadora
clear claro
clever listo
cliff el acantilado
cliff-diving el clavado de acantilado [deh]
climbing el montañismo [montan-y**ee**smo]
cling film el plástico de envolver [deh embolb**air**]
clinic la clínica
cloakroom el guardarropa [gwardarr**o**pa]
clock el reloj [rel**o**H]
close (verb) cerrar [serr**a**r]

•••••• DIALOGUE ••••••

what time do you close? ¿a qué hora cierran? [keh **o**ra s-y**ai**rran]
we close at 8 p.m. on weekdays and 1.30 p.m. on Saturdays cerramos a las ocho de la tarde entre semana y a la una y media los sábados [serr**a**mos – deh la t**a**rdeh **e**ntreh]
do you close for lunch? ¿cierra a mediodía? [s-y**ai**rra]
yes, between 1 and 3.30 p.m. sí, de la una hasta las tres y media de la tarde [deh – **a**sta]

ENGLISH ◆ SPANISH | Ch

closed cerrado [sairr**a**do]
cloth (fabric) la t**e**la
(for cleaning etc) el tr**a**po
clothes la r**o**pa
clothes line la cuerda para tender [kw**ai**rda p**a**ra tend**air**]
clothes peg la pinza de la r**o**pa [p**ee**nsa deh]
cloud la nube [n**oo**beh]
cloudy nubl**a**do
clutch el embrague [embr**a**geh]
coach (bus) el autobús [owtob**oo**s]
(on train) el vagón [bag**o**n]
coach station la estación de camiones [estas-y**o**n deh kam-y**o**n-es]
coach trip la excursión (en autobús) [eskoors-y**o**n]
coast la c**o**sta
on the coast en la c**o**sta
coat (long coat) el abr**i**go
(jacket) el s**a**co
coathanger la percha [p**ai**rcha]
cockroach la cucaracha [kookar**a**cha]
cocoa el cacao [kak**a**-o]
coconut el c**o**co
code (for phoning) el prefijo [pref**ee**Ho], el código
what's the (dialling) code for Veracruz? ¿cuál es el prefijo de Veracruz? [kwal – deh bairakr**oo**s]
coffee el café [kaf**eh**]
two coffees, please dos cafés, por favor [fab**o**r]

> A great deal of coffee is grown in Mexico, and in the growing areas and the coffee houses in the capital, you will be served excellent coffee. If you ask for just **café** you will be given black coffee. Some useful terms:
>
> **café americano** weaker, black coffee or instant coffee
> **café con leche** [l**e**cheh] coffee made with milk and no water
> **café cortado** or **café con un poquito de leche** [pok**ee**to deh] white coffee
> **café de olla** [**oh**-ya] coffee stewed in the pot with cinnamon and sugar
> **café solo** or **negro** black coffee, usually strong and often sweet
> **Nescafe** instant coffee
> **sin azúcar** [as**oo**kar] without sugar

coin la mon**e**da
Coke® la Coca-C**o**la
cold frío
I'm cold t**e**ngo frío
I have a cold t**e**ngo resfri**a**do [resfr-y**a**do]
collapse: he's collapsed se desmayó [seh desmī-y**o**]
collar el cuello [kw**eh**-yo]
collect recoger [rekoH**air**]
I've come to collect ... vine a recoger ... [b**ee**neh]
collect call la llamada por cobr**a**r [yam**a**da]

college la Universidad [ooneebairseed**a**]
colour el col**o**r
do you have this in other colours? ¿tiene **o**tros colores? [t-y**e**neh – kol**o**r-es]
colour film la pel**í**cula en color
comb el peine [p**ay**neh]
come venir [ben**ee**r]

•••••• DIALOGUE ••••••

where do you come from? ¿de dónde es? [deh d**o**ndeh]
I come from Edinburgh soy de Edimb**u**rgo

come back regres**a**r
I'll come back tomorrow regr**e**so mañ**a**na
come in entr**a**r
come in! ¡pase! [p**a**seh]
comfortable c**ó**modo
compact disc el compact disc
company (business) la compañía [kompan-y**ee**-a]
compartment (on train) el compartim**e**nto
compass la brújula [br**oo**Hoola]
complain quejarse [keh-H**a**rseh]
complaint la queja [k**e**Ha]
I have a complaint tengo queja
completely completamente [kompl**e**tamenteh]
computer la computad**o**ra
concert el concierto [kons-y**ai**rto]
concussion la conmoción cerebral [konmos-y**o**n sairebr**a**l]
conditioner (for hair) el acondicionador de pelo [akondees-yonad**o**r deh]
condom el cond**ó**n
condor el c**ó**ndor
conference el congr**e**so
confirm confirm**a**r
congratulations! ¡felicidades! [feleeseed**a**d-es]
connecting flight el vuelo de conexión [bw**e**lo deh koneks-y**o**n]
connection el enlace [enl**a**seh]
conscious consciente [kons-y**e**nteh]
constipation el estreñimiento [estren-yeem-y**e**nto]
consulate el consul**a**do
contact (verb) ponerse en cont**a**cto con [pon**ai**rseh]
contact lenses las lentes de cont**a**cto [l**e**nt-es deh], las lentillas [lent**ee**-yas]
contraceptive el anticonceptivo [anteekonsept**ee**bo]
convenient a m**a**no
that's not convenient no conviene [konb-y**e**neh]
cook (verb) cocinar [koseen**a**r]
not cooked p**o**co hecho [**e**cho]
cooker el horno [**o**rno]
cookie la galleta [ga-y**e**ta]
cooking utensils los utensilios de cocina [ootens**ee**l-yos deh kos**ee**na]
cool fr**e**sco
cork el c**o**rcho
corkscrew el sacac**o**rchos

corner: on the corner en la esquina [eskeena]
in the corner en el rincón
cornflakes los cornflakes
correct (right) correcto
corridor el pasillo [pasee-yo]
cosmetics los cosméticos
cost (verb) costar, valer [balair]
how much does it cost? ¿cuánto vale? [kwanto baleh]
cot la cuna
cotton el algodón
cotton wool el algodón
couch (sofa) el sofá
couchette la litera [leetaira]
cough la tos
cough medicine la medicina para la tos [medeeseena]
could: could you ...? ¿podría ...?
could I have ...? ¿quisiera ...? [kees-yaira]
I couldn't ... no podría ...
country (nation) el país [pa-ees]
(countryside) el campo
countryside el campo
couple (two people) la pareja [pareHa]
a couple of ... un par de ... [deh]
courgette la calabacita [kalabaseeta], el calabacín [kalabaseen]
courier el/la guía turístico [gee-a]
course (main course etc) el plato
of course por supuesto [soopwesto]
of course not! ¡claro que no! [keh]
cousin (male/female) el primo, la prima
cow la vaca [baka]
crab la jaiba [Hība]
cracker (biscuit) la galleta salada [ga-yeta]
craft shop la tienda de artesanías [t-yenda deh]
crash el accidente [akseedenteh]
(verb) chocar
I've had a crash tuve un accidente [toobeh]
crazy loco
cream la crema
(colour) color crema
creche la guardería infantil [gwardairee-a]
credit card la tarjeta de crédito [tarHeta deh kredeeto]

Major credit cards are widely accepted. Visa and Mastercard are the best; American Express and other charge cards are usually only accepted by expensive places. Credit cards are not accepted in the cheapest hotels and restaurants, or for most bus tickets, but you can use them to get cash advances from banks. You can also use credit cards from home to get cash 24 hours a day from cashpoint/ATM machines in larger towns. Machines are erratic, however, and sometimes debit your account without giving you any cash so keep all receipts for →

checking. Many cashpoints/ ATMs also accept debit cards from the Cirrus and PLUS systems, which enable customers to withdraw money from their accounts back home. You may get preferential exchange rates this way.

•••••• DIALOGUE ••••••

can I pay by credit card? ¿puedo pagar con tarjeta? [pwedo – kon tarHeta]
which card do you want to use? ¿qué tarjeta quiere usar? [keh – k-yaireh oosar]
yes, sir sí, señor [sen-yor]
what's the number? ¿qué número tiene? [noomairo t-yeneh]
and the expiry date? ¿y la fecha de caducidad? [deh kadooseeda]

crisps las patatas fritas (de bolsa)
crockery la loza [losa]
crocodile el caimán [kīman]
crossing (by sea) la travesía [trabesee-a]
crossroads el cruce [krooseh]
crowd la muchedumbre [moocheh-doombreh]
crowded atestado
crown (on tooth) la funda [foonda]
cruise el crucero [kroosairo]
crutches las muletas
cry (verb) llorar [yorar]
Cuban (adj) cubano
cucumber el pepino
cup la taza [tasa]
a cup of ..., please una taza de ..., por favor [deh – fabor]
cupboard el armario [armar-yo]
cure la cura [koora]
curly rizado [reesado]

currency
Since 1993 and the revaluation of the peso, the national currency has been the **nuevo peso** sometimes expressed as **N$**; you may also see **M.N.** for **moneda nacional** (national currency).

current la corriente [korr-yenteh]
curtains las cortinas
cushion el cojín [koHeen]
custom la costumbre [kostoombreh]
Customs la aduana [adwana]

Crossing the border, especially on foot, it's easy to go straight past the immigration and Customs checks. Make sure that you get your tourist card (**FMT – Folleto de Migración Turística**) stamped and your bags checked though, otherwise you'll be stopped after some 20km and sent back to complete the formalities. It is equally important to have a properly stamped tourist card on leaving the country, since you can be refused exit from the country without it. It's →

also wise to have receipts for any major items you are carrying into the country – radios, TVs, jewellery, cameras etc – to make sure that you are not charged duty on exit. It is illegal to take antiquities out of the country. The penalties for contravention are severe.
see **passport**

cut el corte [k**o**rteh]
(verb) cort**ar**
I've cut myself me corté [meh korteh]
cutlery los cubiertos [koob-y**ai**rtos]
cycling el ciclismo [seekl**ee**smo]
cyclist el/la ciclista [seekl**ee**sta]

D

dad el papá
daily cada día [d**ee**-a], todos los días
(adj) diario [d-y**ar**-yo], de cada día [deh]
damage: damaged dañado [dan-y**a**do]
damn! ¡caramba!
damp (adj) húmedo [**oo**medo]
dance el baile [bīleh]
(verb) bailar [bīl**ar**]
would you like to dance? ¿quiere bailar? [k-y**ai**reh]
dangerous peligroso
Danish danés [dan-**e**s]
dark (adj: colour) oscuro [osk**oo**ro]
(hair) moreno
it's getting dark está oscureciendo [oskoores-y**e**ndo]
date* la fecha
what's the date today? ¿qué fecha es hoy? [keh – oy]
let's make a date for next Monday quedamos para el próximo lunes [ked**a**mos – pr**o**kseemo]
dates (fruit) los dátiles
daughter la hija [**ee**Ha]
daughter-in-law la nuera [nw**ai**ra]
dawn el amanecer [amanes**air**]
at dawn al amanecer
day el día
the day after el día siguiente [seeg-y**e**nteh]
the day after tomorrow pasado mañana [man-y**a**na]
the day before el día anterior [antair-y**o**r]
the day before yesterday anteayer [anteh-ī-y**air**]
every day todos los días
all day todo el día
in two days' time dentro de dos días [deh]
have a nice day! ¡que pase buen día! [keh p**a**seh bwen]
day trip la excursión [ekskoors-y**o**n]
dead muerto [mw**ai**rto]
deaf sordo
deal (business) el negocio [neg**o**s-yo]

it's a deal trato hecho [**e**cho]
death la muerte [mw**ai**rteh]
decaffeinated coffee el café descafeinado [kaf**eh** deskafay-eena**do**]
December diciembre [dees-y**e**mbreh]
decide decidir [deseed**ee**r]
we haven't decided yet todavía no hemos decidido [todab**ee**-a no **e**mos deseed**ee**do]
decision la decisión [desees-y**o**n]
deck (on ship) la cubierta [koob-y**ai**rta]
deckchair la tumb**o**na
deduct descont**a**r
deep prof**u**ndo
definitely (certainly) sin d**u**da
definitely not ni hablar [abl**a**r]
degree (qualification) el t**í**tulo
delay la dem**o**ra
the train was delayed se demor**ó** el tren [seh]
deliberately a prop**ó**sito
delicatessen la charcutería [charkootair**ee**-a]
delicious delicioso [delees-y**o**so]
deliver entreg**a**r
delivery (of mail) el rep**a**rto
Denmark Dinam**a**rca
dental floss el hilo dent**a**l [**ee**lo]
dentist el/la dent**i**sta

•••••• DIALOGUE ••••••

it's this one here es ésta de aquí [deh ak**ee**]
this one? ¿ésta?
no, that one no, aquélla [ak**eh**-ya]
here? ¿aquí?
yes sí

see doctor

dentures la dentad**u**ra postiza [post**ee**sa]
deodorant el desodorante [desodor**a**nteh]
department el departam**e**nto
department store la tienda de departamentos [t-y**e**nda deh]
departure la sal**i**da
departure lounge la s**a**la de embarque [deh emb**a**rkeh]
depend: it depends depende [dep**e**ndeh]
it depends when según cuándo [kw**a**ndo]
it depends on ... depende de ... [deh]
deposit (as security) la fianza [fee-**a**nsa]
(as part payment) el enganche [eng**a**ncheh]
description la descripción [deskreeps-y**o**n]
desert el desierto [des-y**ai**rto]
dessert el postre [p**o**streh]
destination el dest**i**no
develop (photos) revelar [rebel**a**r]

•••••• DIALOGUE ••••••

could you develop these films? ¿puede revelar **e**stos carr**e**tes? [pw**e**deh – karr**e**t-es]

when will they be ready? ¿cuándo estar**á**n l**i**stos? [kw**a**ndo]

tomorrow afternoon mañana por la tarde [man-y**a**na – t**a**rdeh]

how much is the four-hour service? ¿cuánto es el servicio de cuatro horas? [kw**a**nto – sairb**ee**s-yo deh kw**a**tro **o**ras]

diabetic (man/woman) el diab**é**tico [dee-ab**e**teeko], la diab**é**tica
  diabetic foods la com**i**da p**a**ra diab**é**ticos
dial (verb) marc**a**r
dialling code el pref**i**jo [pref**ee**Ho], el c**ó**digo

> Calling from long-distance (**Ladatel**) phones dial the codes below, followed by the area code and number:
>
> Mexico inter-state: 91
> US and Canada: 95
>
> Omit the initial zero of the area code when dialling the following:
>
> UK: 98 44
> Ireland: 98 353
> Australia: 98 61
> New Zealand: 98 64
>
> To call collect or person-to-person outside Mexico, dial 09.

diamond el diam**a**nte [d-yam**a**nteh]
diaper el pañ**a**l [pan-y**a**l]
diarrhoea la diarr**e**a [d-yarr**eh**-a]
diary (business etc) la ag**e**nda [aH**e**nda]
  (for personal experiences) el di**a**rio [d-y**a**r-yo]
dictionary el diccion**a**rio [deeks-yon**a**r-yo]
didn't see not
die mor**i**r
diesel el gas**o**il, el d**i**esel [d**ee**sel]
diet la di**e**ta [d-y**e**ta]
  I'm on a diet est**oy** a r**é**gimen [r**e**Heemen]
  I have to follow a special diet t**e**ngo que segu**i**r **u**na di**e**ta especi**a**l [keh seg**ee**r – espes-y**a**l]
difference la difer**e**ncia [deefair**e**ns-ya]
  what's the difference? ¿cu**á**l es la difer**e**ncia? [kwal]
different dist**i**nto
  this one is different **é**ste es dist**i**nto [**e**steh]
  a different table **o**tra m**e**sa
difficult dif**í**cil [deef**ee**seel]
difficulty la dificult**a**d [deefeekoolt**a**]
dinghy el b**o**te [b**o**teh]
dining room el comed**o**r
dinner (evening meal) la c**e**na [s**e**na]
  to have dinner cen**a**r [sen**a**r]
direct (adj) dir**e**cto
  is there a direct train? ¿hay un

tren directo? [ī]
direction la dirección [deereks-y**o**n], el sentido
which direction is it? ¿en qué dirección est**á**? [keh]
is it in this direction? ¿es por aquí? [ak**ee**]
directory enquiries información [eenformas-y**o**n]

For directory enquiries ring 01 for Mexico, 04 for the Federal District, 07 for other information.

dirt la suciedad [soos-yed**a**], la mugre [m**oo**greh]
dirty sucio [s**oo**s-yo]
disabled minusválido [meenoosb**a**leedo]
is there access for the disabled? ¿hay acceso p**a**ra minusv**á**lidos? [ī aks**e**so]
disappear desaparecer [desaparesa**ir**]
it's disappeared desapareció [desapares-y**o**]
disappointed decepcionado [deseps-yon**a**do]
disappointing decepcionante [deseps-yon**a**nteh]
disaster el desastre [des**a**streh]
disco la discot**e**ca
discount el descuento [deskw**e**nto]
is there a discount? ¿hay descuento? [ī]
disease la enfermedad [enfairmed**a**]
disgusting repugnante [repoogn**a**nteh]
dish (meal) el pl**a**to
dishcloth el tr**a**po de cocina [deh kos**ee**na]
disinfectant el desinfectante [deseenfekt**a**nteh]
disk (for computer) la disqueta [deesk**e**ta]
disposable diapers/nappies los pañales desechables [pan-y**a**l-es desech**a**b-les]
distance la distancia [deest**a**ns-ya]
in the distance a lo lejos [l**e**Hos]
distilled water el agua destil**a**da [**a**gwa]
district el b**a**rrio
disturb molest**a**r, estorb**a**r
diversion (detour) el desvío [desb**ee**-o]
diving board el trampol**í**n
divorced divorciado [deebors-y**a**do]
dizzy: I feel dizzy (said by man/woman) est**o**y mareado/mare**a**da [mareh-**a**do]
do hacer [as**air**]
what shall we do? ¿qué hacemos? [keh as**e**mos]
how do you do it? ¿c**ó**mo se hace? [seh **a**seh]
will you do it for me? ¿me lo puede hacer Usted? [meh lo pw**e**deh as**air** oost**eh**]

•••••• DIALOGUES ••••••

how do you do? ¿cómo está? [**ko**mo]
nice to meet you encant**a**do de conocerle [deh konos**ai**rleh]
what do you do? (work) ¿a qué se ded**i**ca? [keh seh]
I'm a teacher, and you? soy profes**o**r, ¿y Usted? [ee oost**eh**]
I'm a student soy estudiante [estood-y**a**nteh]
what are you doing this evening? ¿qué hace **e**sta t**a**rde? [as**eh**]
we're going out for a drink; do you want to join us? sal**i**mos a tom**a**r **u**na c**o**pa, ¿nos acompaña? [akomp**a**n-ya]

do you want cream? ¿quiere cr**e**ma? [k-y**ai**reh]
I do, but she doesn't yo sí, pero ella no [p**ai**ro **eh**-ya]

doctor el/la médico
we need a doctor necesitamos un médico [neseseet**a**mos]
please call a doctor por favor, llame a un médico [fab**o**r y**a**meh]

There are no reciprocal health arrangements between Mexico and any other country, so travel and health insurance is essential. You can get a list of English-speaking doctors from your government's nearest consulate. Big hotels and tourist offices may also be able to recommend someone. Every border town has hundreds of doctors and dentists experienced in treating English-speaking tourists. In every reasonably-sized town, you should be able to find a state- or Red Cross-run health centre (**centro de salud**), where emergency treatment is free but very elementary. The State Social Security System (IMSS) also has emergency facilities which may be of a slightly higher standard, but you will need to pay for anything beyond the most basic attention.
If you suffer from any chronic condition it is important to carry with you clear and legible documentation from your own doctor and if possible some of your normal medication, since the brand name may not be familiar to a Mexican pharmacist.

•••••• DIALOGUE ••••••

where does it hurt? ¿dónde le duele? [d**o**ndeh leh dw**e**leh]
right here justo aquí [H**oo**sto ak**ee**]
does that hurt now? ¿le duele ahora? [leh dw**e**leh a-**o**ra]
yes sí
take this to the chemist's lleve esto a la farmacia [y**e**beh – farm**a**s-ya]

document el documento [dokoom**e**nto]
dog el perro [p**ai**rro]
doll la muñeca [moon-y**e**ka]
domestic flight el vuelo nacional [bw**e**lo nas-y**o**nal]
donkey el burro [b**oo**rro]
don't! ¡no lo haga! [**a**ga]
don't do that! ¡no haga eso!
see **not**
door la puerta [pw**ai**rta]
doorman el portero [port**ai**ro]
double doble [d**o**bleh]
double bed la cama matrimonial [matreem**o**n-yal]
double room el cuarto doble [kw**a**rto d**o**bleh]
doughnut la dona
down: down here aquí abajo [ak**ee** ab**a**Ho]
downwards hacia abajo [**a**s-ya]
put it down over there déjelo ahí [d**eh**-Helo a-**ee**]
it's down there on the right está ahí a la derecha [dair**e**cha]
it's further down the road está bajando la calle [baH**a**ndo la k**a**-yeh]
downhill skiing el esquí alpino [esk**ee** alp**ee**no]
downmarket (restaurant etc) popular [popool**a**r]
downstairs abajo [ab**a**Ho]
dozen la docena [dos**e**na]
half a dozen media docena [m**e**d-ya]
drain (in sink, road) el desagüe [des**a**gweh]
draught beer la cerveza de barril [sairb**e**sa deh]
draughty: it's draughty hay corriente [ī korr-y**e**nteh]
drawer el cajón [kaH**o**n]
drawing el dibujo [deeb**oo**Ho]
dreadful horrible [orr**ee**bleh]
dream el sueño [sw**e**n-yo]
dress el vestido [best**ee**do]
dressed: to get dressed vestirse [best**ee**rseh]
dressing (for cut) el vendaje [bend**a**Heh]
salad dressing el aliño [al**ee**n-yo]
dressing gown la bata
drink (alcoholic) la copa
(non-alcoholic) la bebida
(verb) beber [beb**air**]
a cold drink una bebida fría
can I get you a drink? ¿quiere beber algo? [k-y**ai**reh]
what would you like (to drink)? ¿qué le apetece beber? [keh leh apet**e**seh]
no thanks, I don't drink no gracias, no bebo alcohol [gr**a**s-yas – alk**o**l]
I'll just have a drink of water sólo agua [**a**gwa]

> Apart from beer and wine, Mexico produces its own alcoholic specialities; the agave cactus (**maguey**) produces **tequila** and **mezcal** as well as **pulque** (a type of milky beer) which is less familiar and takes some →

getting used to. **Puro de caña** (also called **posh** in the south) is the local sugar cane liquor. There is a wide variety of non-alcoholic drinks from fizzy soft drinks (**refrescos**) to the wonderful fruit juices (**jugos**) or milkshakes (**licuados**) to be found in specialist shops or on pavement stalls. **Aguas de fruta** are delicious but are made with water, so tourists should beware.
see **water**

drinking water agua potable [**a**gwa pot**a**bleh]
is this drinking water? ¿esto es agua potable?
drive (verb) manejar [maneH**a**r]
we drove here vinimos en carro [been**ee**mos]
I'll drive you home te llevaré a casa en carro [teh yebar**eh**]
driver (man/woman) el/la chofer [chof**air**]

driving
To drive your own car in Mexico (apart from in Baja and the free zone), you must obtain a vehicle permit from the **Delegación de Servicios Migratorios** at the border. This will cover you for a period of 180 days, but remember to insist that you are given the maximum time. And make sure, too, that you are given (and always display) the windscreen sticker that comes with it. If you drive without renewal you can then become subject to large fines. The permit must be paid using a major credit card, otherwise you'll be asked for a minimum $500 refundable bond plus non-refundable tax and commission. To make sure you don't sell the car in Mexico, you'll also be required either to post a cash bond equal to the vehicle's book value or give the imprint of a major credit card. You must also have Mexican insurance, available from dozens of places on either side of the border.
Drivers from the US, Canada, Britain, Ireland, Australia and New Zealand will find their licences are valid in Mexico, though an international one is still advisable. You are required to have all your documents with you when driving.
Traffic circulates on the right, and the normal speed limit is 40km/h (25mph) in built-up areas, 70km/h (43mph) in open country, and 110km/h (68mph) on the motorway. Some of the new motorways are excellent and the toll motorways (**cuota**) are better still, though extremely expensive. Away from the major centres, roads are often narrow, →

winding and potholed, with livestock wandering across them. Keep out of the way of Mexican bus and truck drivers (and remember that if you signal left to them on a stretch of open road, it means it's clear to overtake). One convention to be aware of is that the first driver to flash their lights at a junction or where only one vehicle can pass has right of way, so someone who flashes you is not inviting you to go first. Most people recommend that you avoid driving at night for reasons of road safety and because of bandits.
see **rent** and **breakdown**

driving licence el carnet de chofer [karn**eh** deh chof**ai**r]
drop: just a drop, please (of drink) un poquito n**a**da más [pok**ee**to]
drug la medicina [medees**ee**na]
drugs (narcotics) la dr**o**ga
drunk (adj) borr**a**cho
drunken driving manejar en est**a**do de embriaguez [maneH**a**r – deh embr-yag-**e**s]
dry (adj) s**e**co
dry-cleaner la tintorería [teentorair**ee**-a]
duck el p**a**to
due: he was due to arrive yesterday tenía que llegar ayer [keh yeg**a**r ī-y**air**]
when is the train due? ¿a qué hora llega el tren? [**o**ra y**e**ga]
dull (pain) s**o**rdo
(weather) gris [grees]
dummy (baby's) el chupete [choop**e**teh]
during durante [door**a**nteh]
dust el polvo [p**o**lbo]
dustbin el bote de la bas**u**ra [b**o**teh deh]
dusty polvoriento [polbor-y**e**nto]
duty-free (goods) (los prod**u**ctos) sin impuestos [seen eempw**e**stos]
duty-free shop el duty free

Duty-free allowances in Mexico are three bottles of liquor (including wine), plus 400 cigarettes or two boxes of cigars or a 'reasonable quantity' of tobacco for your own use, plus twelve rolls of camera film or camcorder tape.

duvet el edred**ó**n

E

each c**a**da
how much are they each? ¿a c**ó**mo est**á** cada **u**no?
ear el oido [o-**ee**do]
earache: I have earache tengo dol**o**r de oídos [deh]
early pr**o**nto
early in the morning de madrug**a**da
I called by earlier pasé antes [pas**eh** **a**nt-es]

earring el arete [areteh]
earthquake el temblor
east oriente [or-yenteh]
 in the east en el oriente
Easter la Semana Santa
 see **holiday**
easy fácil [faseel]
eat comer [komair]
 we've already eaten, thanks ya comimos, gracias [gras-yas]

> **eating habits**
> Traditionally, Mexicans eat a light breakfast very early, a snack of **tacos** or eggs mid-morning, lunch (the main meal of the day) around two o'clock or later – in theory followed by a **siesta** – and a late, light supper. Eating a large set-menu meal (**comida corrida**) at lunchtime can be a great moneysaver.
> Breakfast (**desayuno**) might simply be coffee and **pan dulce** (sweet rolls and pastries that usually come in a basket); you pay for as many as you eat. Alternatively, breakfast can consist of eggs in any number of forms, or a **licuado** (fruit drink) fortified with raw egg (**blanquillo**). Freshly-squeezed orange juice (**jugo de naranja**) is always available from street stalls in the early morning. Snack meals mostly consist of some variation on the **taco**/**enchilada** theme (stalls selling them are called **taquerías**), but **tortas** – rolls heavily filled with meat or cheese or both, garnished with avocado or chilli and toasted on request – are also wonderful, and you'll see take-away torta stands everywhere.
> see **restaurant**

eau de toilette el agua de baño [agwa deh ban-yo]
economy class la clase turista [klaseh]
Edinburgh Edimburgo [edeemboorgo]
egg el huevo [webo], el blanquillo [blankee-yo]
eggplant la berenjena [berenHena]
either: either ... or ... o ... o ...
 either of them cualquiera de los dos [kwalk-yaira deh]
elastic el elástico
elastic band la gomita
elbow el codo
electric eléctrico
electrical appliances los electrodomésticos
electric fire la estufa eléctrica
electrician el electricista [elektreeseesta]
electricity la electricidad [elektreeseeda]
 see **voltage**
elevator el ascensor [asensor]
else: something else otra cosa

somewhere else en **o**tra parte [p**a**rteh]

•••••• DIALOGUE ••••••

would you like anything else? ¿**al**go más?
no, nothing else, thanks n**a**da más, gracias [gr**a**s-yas]

embassy la embajada [embaH**a**da]
emergency la emergencia [emairH**e**ns-ya]
this is an emergency! ¡es **u**na emergencia!
emergency exit la salida de emergencia [deh]
empty vacío [bas**ee**-o]
end el final [feen**a**l]
(verb) terminar [tairmeen**a**r]
at the end of the street al final de la calle [deh la k**a**-yeh]
when does it end? ¿cuándo term**i**na? [kw**a**ndo]
engaged (toilet) ocup**a**do
(telephone) comunic**a**ndo
(to be married) promet**i**do
engine (car) el mot**o**r
England Inglaterra [eenglat**ai**rra]
English inglés [eeng-l**e**s]
I'm English (man/woman) soy inglés/ingl**e**sa
do you speak English? ¿habla inglés? [**a**bla]
enjoy disfrut**a**r
to enjoy oneself divertirse [deebairt**ee**rseh]

•••••• DIALOGUE ••••••

how did you like the film? ¿le gustó la película? [leh goost**o**]
I enjoyed it very much, did you enjoy it? me gustó mucho, ¿le gustó a Usted? [meh – m**oo**cho – leh – oost**eh**]

enjoyable divertido [deebairt**ee**do]
enlargement (of photo) la ampliación [ampl-yas-y**o**n]
enormous enorme [en**o**rmeh]
enough bastante [bast**a**nteh]
there's not enough no hay bastante [ī]
it's not big enough no es lo suficientemente gr**a**nde [soofees-yentem**e**nteh]
that's enough b**a**sta
entrance la entr**a**da
envelope el sobre [s**o**breh]
epileptic (adj) epil**é**ptico
equipment el equipo [ek**ee**po]
error el err**o**r
especially sobre t**o**do [s**o**breh]
essential imprescindible [eempreseend**ee**bleh]
it is essential that ... es imprescindible que ... [keh]
Europe Europa [eh-oor**o**pa]
European europeo [eh-ooropeh-o]
even incluso [eenkl**oo**so]
even if ... incluso si ...
evening (early evening) la tarde [t**a**rdeh]
(after nightfall) la noche [n**o**cheh]

this evening esta tarde/noche
in the evening por la tarde/noche
evening meal la cena [sena]
eventually finalmente [feenalmenteh], por fin [feen]
ever alguna vez [bes]

DIALOGUE

have you ever been to Monterrey? ¿estuvo alguna vez en Monterrey? [estoobo – montairray]
yes, I was there two years ago sí, estuve allí hace dos años [estoobeh a-yee aseh – an-yos]

every cada
every day todos los días [dee-as]
everyone todos
everything todo
everywhere en todas partes [part-es]
exactly! ¡exactamente! [eksaktamenteh]
exam el examen
example el ejemplo [eHemplo]
for example por ejemplo
excellent excelente [ekselenteh]
excellent! ¡estupendo!
except excepto [eksepto]
excess baggage el exceso de equipaje [ekseso deh ekeepaHeh]
exchange rate el tipo de cambio [teepo deh kamb-yo]
exciting emocionante [emos-yonanteh]
excuse me (to get past) con permiso
(to get attention) ¡por favor! [fabor]
(to say sorry) disculpe [deeskoolpeh]
exhaust (pipe) el tubo de escape [toobo deh eskapeh]
exhausted (tired) agotado
exhibition la exposición [eksposees-yon]
exit la salida
where's the nearest exit? ¿cuál es la salida más cercana? [kwal – sairkana]
expect esperar [espairar]
expensive caro
experienced con experiencia [espair-yens-ya]
explain explicar [espleekar]
can you explain that? ¿puede explicármelo? [pwedeh]
express (mail) urgente [oorHenteh]
(train) el exprés
extension (phone) extensión [estens-yon], interno [eentairno]
extension 221, please extensión doscientos veintiuno, por favor [fabor]
extension lead el alargador
extra: can we have an extra one? ¿nos puede dar otro? [pwedeh]
do you charge extra for that? ¿cobra extra para esto?
extraordinary extraordinario [ekstra-ordeenar-yo]
extremely extremadamente [estremadamenteh]

eye el **o**jo [**o**Ho]
will you keep an eye on my suitcase for me? ¿me cuida la maleta? [meh kw**ee**da]
eyebrow pencil el lápiz de cejas [l**a**pees deh s**e**Has]
eye drops el colirio [kol**ee**r-yo]
eyeglasses las gafas
eyeliner el lápiz de ojos [l**a**pees deh **o**Hos]
eye make-up remover el desmaquillador de ojos [desmakee-yad**o**r]
eye shadow la sombra de ojos

F

face la cara
factory la fábrica
Fahrenheit* Fahrenheit
faint (verb) desmayarse [desmī-y**a**rseh]
she's fainted se desmayó [seh desmī-y**o**]
I feel faint (said by man/woman) estoy mareado/mareada [mareh-**a**do]
fair la feria [f**ai**r-ya]
(adj: just) justo [H**oo**sto]
fairly bastante [bast**a**nteh]
fake (thing) la imitación [eemeetas-y**o**n]
(adj) falsificado
fake fur el piel de imitación [p-y**e**l]
fall (verb) caerse [ka-**ai**rseh]
she's had a fall se cayó [seh kī-y**o**]
fall (US: noun) el otoño [ot**o**n-yo]
in the fall en otoño
false falso [f**a**l-so]
family la familia [fam**ee**l-ya]
famous famoso
fan (electrical) el ventilador [benteelad**o**r]
(handheld) el abanico
(sports) el/la hincha [**ee**ncha]
fan belt la correa del ventilador [korr**eh**-a del benteelad**o**r]
fantastic fantástico
far lejos [l**e**Hos]

•••••• DIALOGUE ••••••

is it far from here? ¿está lejos de aquí? [deh ak**ee**]
no, not very far no, no muy lejos [mwee]
well how far? bueno, ¿qué tan lejos? [bw**e**no keh]
it's about 20 kilometres son unos veinte kilómetros

fare el pasaje [pas**a**Heh]
farm (large) la hacienda [as-y**e**nda]
(small) la finca
fashionable de moda [deh]
fast rápido
fat (person) gordo
(on meat) la grasa
father el padre [p**a**dreh]
father-in-law el suegro [sw**e**gro]
faucet la llave [la y**a**beh]
fault el defecto
sorry, it was my fault disculpe, fue culpa mía [deesk**oo**lpeh fweh]
it's not my fault no es mi

culpa
faulty defectuoso [defektw**o**so]
favourite preferido [prefair**ee**do]
fax el fax
(verb: person) mand**a**r un fax a
(document) mand**a**r por fax
February febrero [febr**ai**ro]
feel sent**i**r
I feel hot t**e**ngo cal**o**r
I feel unwell no me siento bien [meh s-y**e**nto b-yen]
I feel like going for a walk se me antoja un pas**e**o [seh meh ant**o**Ha]
how are you feeling today? ¿c**ó**mo se encuentra hoy? [enkw**e**ntra oy]
I'm feeling better me siento mejor [meH**o**r]
felt-tip (pen) el rotulad**o**r
fence la cerca [s**ai**rka]
fender la def**e**nsa
ferry el f**e**rry
festival el festival [festeeb**a**l], la fi**e**sta
fetch: I'll fetch him lo pasaré a recoger [pasar**eh** a rekoH**air**]
will you come and fetch me later? ¿vendrás a buscarme más tarde? [bendr**a**s a boosk**a**rmeh mas t**a**rdeh]
feverish con fiebre [f-y**e**breh]
few: a few **u**nos p**o**cos
a few days unos días
fiancé el novio [n**o**b-yo]
fiancée la novia [n**o**b-ya]
field el c**a**mpo
fight la pelea [pel**eh**-a]
figs los higos [**ee**gos]
fill (verb) llenar [yen**a**r]
fill in rellenar [reh-yen**a**r]
do I have to fill this in? ¿t**e**ngo que rellenar **e**sto? [keh]
fill up llenar [yen**a**r]
fill it up, please lleno, por favor [y**e**no por fab**o**r]
filling (in cake, sandwich) el relleno [reh-y**e**no]
(in tooth) el empaste [emp**a**steh]
film (movie, for camera) la película

•••••• DIALOGUE ••••••

do you have this kind of film?
¿tiene películas de este tipo? [t-yeneh – deh **e**steh t**ee**po]
yes, how many exposures? sí, ¿de cuántas f**o**tos? [kw**a**ntas]
36 tr**e**inta y seis

film processing el revelado [rebel**a**do]
filter coffee el café de filtro [kaf**eh** deh f**ee**ltro]
filter papers los papeles de filtro [pap**e**l-es]
filthy muy sucio [mw**ee** s**oo**s-yo]
find (verb) encontr**a**r
I can't find it no lo encuentro [enkw**e**ntro]
I've found it ya lo encontré [enkontr**eh**]
find out enterarse [enter**a**rseh]
could you find out for me? ¿me lo puede averiguar? [meh lo pw**e**deh abaireegw**a**r]
fine (noun) la multa [m**oo**lta]
it's fine today hoy hace buen tiempo [oy as**eh** bwen t-y**e**mpo]

•••••• DIALOGUES ••••••

how are you? ¿cómo estás?
I'm fine, thanks bien, gracias [b-yen gras-yas]

is that OK? ¿va bien así? [ba]
that's fine, thanks está bien, gracias

finger el dedo
finish (verb) terminar [tairmeenar], acabar
I haven't finished yet no he terminado todavía [eh tairmeenado todabee-a]
when does it finish? ¿cuándo termina? [kwando tairmeena]
fire el fuego [fwego]
(blaze) el incendio [eensend-yo]
fire! ¡fuego!
can we light a fire here? ¿se puede prender fuego aquí? [seh pwedeh prendair – akee]
it's on fire está ardiendo [ard-yendo]
fire alarm la alarma de incendios [deh eensend-yos]
fire brigade los bomberos [bombairos]

In the event of a fire, the number to ring is 08.

fire escape la salida de incendios [deh eensend-yos]
fire extinguisher el extintor [esteentor]
first primero [preemairo]
I was first (said by man/woman) fui el primero/la primera [fwee]
at first al principio [preenseep-yo]
the first time la primera vez [bes]
first on the left la primera a la izquierda [eesk-yairda]
first aid primeros auxilios [owkseel-yos]
first aid kit el botiquín [boteekeen]
first class (travel etc) de primera (clase) [preemaira (klaseh)]
first floor la primera planta
(US) la planta baja [baHa]
first name el nombre de pila [nombreh deh]
fish el pez [pes]
(food) el pescado
(verb) pescar
fishing village el pueblo de pescadores [pweblo deh peskador-es]
fishmonger's la pescadería [peskadairee-a]
fit (attack) el ataque [atakeh]
fit: it doesn't fit me no me viene bien [b-yeneh b-yen]
fitting room el probador
fix (repair) arreglar
(arrange) fijar [feeHar]
can you fix this? ¿puede arreglar esto? [pwedeh]
fizzy con gas
flag la bandera [bandaira]
flannel la manopla
flash (for camera) el flash
flat (noun: apartment) el

departamento
(adj) llano [yano]
I've got a flat tyre se me ponchó la llanta [seh meh – yanta]
flavour el sabor
flea la pulga
flight el vuelo [bwelo]
flight number el número de vuelo [noomairo deh]
flippers las aletas
flood la inundación [eenoondas-yon]
floor el piso
florist la florería [floraireeа-a]
flour la harina [areena]
flower la flor
flu el gripe [greepeh]
fluent: he speaks fluent Spanish domina el español [espan-yol]
fly la mosca
(verb) volar [bolar]
can we fly there? ¿podemos ir en avión? [eer en ab-yon]
fly in llegar en avión [yegar]
fly out irse en avión [eerseh]
fog la niebla [n-yebla]
foggy: it's foggy hay niebla [ī]
folk dancing el baile tradicional [bīleh tradees-yonal]
folk music la música folklórica [mooseeka]
follow seguir [segeer]
follow me sígame [seegameh]
food la comida
food poisoning la intoxicación alimenticia [eentokseekas-yon aleementees-ya]
food shop/store la tienda de alimentos [t-yenda deh], el ultramarinos [ooltramareenos]
foot* (of person, measurement) el pie [p-yeh]
on foot a pie
football (game) el fútbol
(ball) el balón
football match el partido de fútbol
for para, por
do you have something for ...? (headache/diarrhoea etc) ¿tiene algo para ...? [t-yeneh]

•••••• DIALOGUES ••••••

who's the mole poblano for? ¿para quién es el mole poblano? [k-yen]
that's for me es para mí
and this one? ¿y éste? [ee esteh]
that's for her ése es para ella [eseh – eh-ya]

where do I get the bus for Puebla? ¿dónde se toma el autobús para Puebla? [dondeh seh – pwebla]
the bus for Puebla leaves from the Zócalo el autobús para Puebla sale del Zócalo [saleh del sokalo]

how long have you been here for? ¿cuánto tiempo lleva aquí? [kwanto t-yempo yeba akee]
I've been here for two days, how about you? llevo aquí dos días, ¿y Usted? [yebo – ee oosteh]
I've been here for a week llevo aquí una semana

forehead la frente [frenteh]
foreign extranjero [estranHairo]
foreigner (man/woman) el extranjero, la extranjera
forest el bosque [boskeh]
forget olvidar [olbeedar]
I forget no me acuerdo [meh akwairdo]
I've forgotten se me olvidó [seh meh olbeedo]
fork el tenedor
(in road) la bifurcación [beefoorkas-yon]
form (document) el formulario [formoolar-yo]
formal (dress) de etiqueta [deh eteeketa]
fortnight quince días [keenseh dee-as], la quincena [keensena]
fortunately por suerte [swairteh]
forward: could you forward my mail? ¿puede enviarme el correo? [pwedeh emb-yarmeh el korreh-o]
forwarding address la nueva dirección [nweba deereks-yon]
foundation (make-up) la crema base [baseh]
fountain la fuente [fwenteh]
foyer el vestíbulo [besteeboolo]
fracture la fractura [fraktoora]
France Francia [frans-ya]
free libre [leebreh]
(no charge) gratuito [gratweeto]
is it free (of charge)? ¿es gratis?
freeway la autopista [owtopeesta]
freezer el congelador [konHelador]
French francés [frans-es]
French fries las papas fritas
frequent frecuente [frekwenteh]
how frequent is the bus to Monterrey? ¿cada cuánto tiempo hay autobús a Monterrey [kwanto t-yempo ī – montairray]
fresh fresco
fresh orange el jugo de naranja [Hoogo de naranHa]
Friday viernes [b-yairn-es]
fridge la refrigeradora [refreeHairadora]
fried frito
fried egg el huevo frito [webo]
friend (male/female) el amigo, la amiga
friendly simpático
from de [deh], desde [desdeh]
when does the next train from Guadalajara arrive? ¿cuándo llega el próximo tren de Guadalajara? [kwando yega – deh gwadalaHara]
from Monday to Friday de lunes a viernes [deh]
from next Thursday a partir del próximo jueves [parteer]

••••• DIALOGUE •••••

where are you from? ¿de dónde es Usted? [dondeh es oosteh]
I'm from Los Angeles soy de Los Angeles [anHel-es]

front la parte delantera [parteh delantaira]

in front delante [del**a**nteh]
in front of the hotel delante del hot**e**l
at the front en la parte de delante [deh]
frost la esc**a**rcha
frozen congelado [konHel**a**do]
frozen food los congel**a**dos
fruit la fr**u**ta
fruit juice el jugo de fr**u**tas [H**oo**go deh]
fry freír [freh-**ee**r]
frying pan la sart**é**n
full lleno [**y**eno]
it's full of ... est**á** lleno de ... [deh]
I'm full (said by man/woman) est**o**y lleno/llena
full board pensión complet**a** [pens-y**o**n]
fun: it was fun fue muy divertido [fweh mwee deebairt**ee**do]
funeral el funeral [foonair**a**l]
funny (strange) r**a**ro
(amusing) divertido [deebairt**ee**do]
furniture los muebles [mw**e**b-les]
further más allá [a-y**a**]
it's further down the road está más adelante [adel**a**nteh]

DIALOGUE

how much further is it to Cuernavaca? ¿cuánto f**a**lta p**a**ra Cuernavaca? [kw**a**nto – kwairnab**a**ka]
about 5 kilometres **u**nos c**i**nco kil**ó**metros

fuse el fusible [foos**ee**bleh]
the lights have fused se fundieron los pl**o**mos [seh foond-y**ai**ron]
fuse box la caja de fusibles [k**a**Ha deh foos**ee**b-les]
fuse wire el pl**o**mo
future el futuro [foot**oo**ro]
in the future en el futuro

G

gallon* el gal**ó**n
game (cards etc) el jue**g**o [Hw**e**go]
(match) el part**i**do
(meat) la caza [c**a**sa]
garage (for fuel) la gasolinera [gasoleen**ai**ra]
(for repairs) el taller (de reparaciones) [ta-y**ai**r (deh reparas-y**o**n-es)]
(for parking) el garaje [gar**a**Heh], la cochera [koch**ai**ra]

> Unless your car is a basic VW, Ford or Dodge, parts are likely to be expensive and hard to come by. Bring a basic spares kit. Tyres can suffer badly so you should carry a good spare with you. Roadside **vulcanizadoras** and **llanteros** can do temporary tyre repairs. New tyres are expensive. If you do need help look for a **taller mecánico**.
> see **petrol**

garden el jardín [Hard**ee**n]
garlic el ajo [**a**Ho]
gas el gas
(US) la gasol**i**na
see **petrol**
gas cylinder (camping gas) la b**o**mba de gas
gasoline la gasol**i**na
see **petrol**
gas permeable lenses las lentillas por**o**sas [lent**ee**-yas]
gas station la gasolinera [gasoleen**ai**ra]
see **petrol**
gate la puerta [pw**ai**rta]
(at airport) la puerta de embarque [deh emb**a**rkeh]
gay gay
gay bar el bar gay
gearbox la caja de cambios [k**a**Ha deh k**a**mb-yos]
gear lever el cambio
gears la m**a**rcha
general general [Hener**a**l]
gents (toilet) el servicio de señores [sairb**ee**s-yo deh sen-y**o**r-es]
genuine (antique etc) auténtico [owt**e**nteeko]
German (adj, language) alem**á**n
German measles la rubeola [roobeh-**o**la]
Germany Alemania [alem**a**n-ya]
get (fetch) traer [tr**a**-air]
will you get me another one, please? me trae **o**tro, por favor [meh tr**a**-eh – fab**o**r]
how do you get to ...? ¿c**ó**mo se va a ...?[seh ba]
do you know where I can get them? ¿sabe dónde las puedo conseguir? [s**a**beh d**o**ndeh las pw**e**do konseg**ee**r]

•••••• DIALOGUE ••••••

can I get you a drink? ¿puedo ofrecerle **a**lgo de beber? [pw**e**do ofres**ai**rleh – deh beb**ai**r]
no, I'll get this one – what would you like? no, yo invito – ¿qué se le antoja? [eenb**ee**to keh seh leh ant**o**Ha]
a glass of red wine una c**o**pa de v**i**no t**i**nto [deh]

get back (return) regres**a**r
get in (arrive) llegar [yeg**a**r]
get off bajarse [baH**a**rseh]
where do I get off? ¿dónde tengo que bajarme? [d**o**ndeh – keh baH**a**rmeh]
get on (to train etc) subirse [soob**ee**rseh]
get out (of car etc) bajarse [baH**a**rseh]
get up (in the morning) levantarse [lebant**a**rseh]
gift el reg**a**lo
gift shop la tienda de reg**a**los [t-y**e**nda]
gin la ginebra [Heen**e**bra]
a gin and tonic, please un gintónic, por favor [jeent**o**neek – fab**o**r]
girl la chica [ch**ee**ka], la joven [H**o**ben], la chava [ch**a**ba]
girlfriend la novia [n**o**b-ya]
give dar
can you give me some

change? ¿me da suelto? [meh]
I gave it to him se lo dí (a él) [seh]
will you give this to ...? ¿podría entregarle esto a ...? [entregarleh]

•••••• DIALOGUE ••••••

how much do you want for this? ¿cuánto vale esto? [kwanto baleh]
1,000 pesos mil pesos
I'll give you 800 le doy ochocientos [leh]

give back devolver [debolbair]
glad feliz [felees]
glass (material) el vidrio [beedr-yo]
(tumbler) el vaso [baso]
(wine glass) la copa
a glass of wine una copa de vino [deh]
glasses las gafas
gloves los guantes [gwant-es]
glue el pegamento
go (verb) ir [eer]
we'd like to go to the swimming-pool nos gustaría ir a la alberca
where are you going? ¿adónde va? [adondeh ba]
where does this bus go? ¿adónde va este autobús? [esteh]
let's go! ¡vamos! [bamos]
she's gone (left) se fue [seh fweh]
where has he gone? ¿dónde se ha ido? [dondeh seh a]
I went there last week estuve la semana pasada [estoobeh]
go away irse [eerseh]
go away! ¡lárguese! [largeh-seh]
go back (return) regresar
go down (the stairs etc) bajar [baHar]
go in entrar
go out (in the evening) salir
do you want to go out tonight? ¿quiere salir esta noche? [k-yaireh – nocheh]
go through pasar por
go up (the stairs etc) subir
goat la cabra
God Dios [d-yos]
goggles las gafas protectoras
gold el oro
golf el golf
golf course el campo de golf [deh]
good bueno [bweno]
good! ¡muy bien! [mwee b-yen]
it's no good es inútil [eenooteel]
goodbye hasta luego [asta lwego]
good evening buenas tardes [bwenas tard-es]
Good Friday el Viernes Santo [b-yairn-es]
see holiday
good morning buenos días [bwenos]
good night buenas noches [bwenas noch-es]

goose el ganso
got: we've got to ... tenemos que ... [keh]
have you got any apples? ¿tiene manzanas? [t-yeneh]
government el gobierno [gob-yairno]
gradually poco a poco
grammar la gramática
gram(me) el gramo
granddaughter la nieta [n-yeta]
grandfather el abuelo [abwelo]
grandmother la abuela [abwela]
grandson el nieto [n-yeto]
grapefruit la toronja [toronHa]
grapefruit juice el jugo de toronja [Hoogo deh]
grapes las uvas [oobas]
grass el pasto, el césped [sesped]
grateful agradecido [agradeseedo]
gravy la salsa
great (excellent) muy bueno [mwee bweno]
that's great! ¡estupendo! [estoopendo]
a great success un gran éxito [ekseeto]
Great Britain Gran Bretaña [bretan-ya]
greedy guloso
green verde [bairdeh]
green card (car insurance) la carta verde
greengrocer's la frutería [frootairee-a]
grey gris [grees]
grill la parrilla [parree-ya]
grilled a la parrilla, a la plancha
grocer's (la tienda de) abarrotes [(t-yenda deh) abarot-es]
ground el piso
on the ground en el piso
ground floor la planta baja [baHa]
group el grupo
guarantee la garantía
is it guaranteed? ¿lleva garantía? [yeva]
Guatemalan (adj) guatemalteco [gwatemalteko]
guest (man/woman) el invitado [eembeetado], la invitada
guesthouse la pensión [pens-yon]
see hotel
guide el/la guía [gee-a]
guidebook la guía
guided tour la visita con guía [beeseeta]
guitar la guitarra [geetarra]
Gulf of Mexico el Golfo
gum (in mouth) la encía [ensee-a]
gun la pistola
gym el gimnasio [Heemnas-yo]

H

hair el pelo
hairbrush el cepillo para el pelo [sepee-yo]
haircut el corte de pelo [korteh deh]
hairdresser's la peluquería

[pelookairee-a]
hairdryer el secador de pelo [deh]
hair gel el fijador (para el pelo) [feeHador]
hairgrip la horquilla [orkee-ya]
hair spray la laca
half* la mitad [meeta]
half an hour media hora [med-ya ora]
half a litre medio litro [med-yo]
about half that aproximadamente la mitad de eso [aprokseemadamenteh – deh]
half board media pensión [med-ya pens-yon]
half fare el medio boleto [med-yo], el boleto con descuento [deskwento]
half price a mitad del precio [meeta del pres-yo]
ham el jamón [Hamon]
hamburger la hamburguesa [amboorgesa]
hammer el martillo [martee-yo]
hammock la hamaca [amaka]
hand la mano
handbag el bolso
handbrake el freno de mano [deh]
handkerchief el pañuelo [pan-ywaylo]
handle (on door) el mango (on suitcase etc) el asa
hand luggage el equipaje de mano [ekeepaH-eh]
hang-gliding el ala delta
hangover la cruda [krooda]
I've got a hangover tengo cruda
happen suceder [soosedair]
what's happening? ¿qué pasa? [keh]
what has happened? ¿qué pasó?
happy contento
I'm not happy about this esto no me convence [meh konbenseh]
harbour el puerto [pwairto]
hard duro [dooro]
(difficult) difícil [deefeeseel]
hard-boiled egg el huevo duro [webo]
hard lenses las lentillas duras [lentee-yas]
hardly apenas
hardly ever casi nunca
hardware shop la ferretería [fairretairee-a], la tlapalería [tlapalairee-a]
hat el sombrero [sombrairo]
hate (verb) odiar [od-yar]
have* tener [tenair]
can I have a ...? ¿me da ...? [meh]
do you have ...? ¿tiene ...? [t-yeneh]
what'll you have? ¿qué va a tomar? [keh ba]
I have to leave now tengo que irme ahora [eermeh a-ora]
do I have to ...? ¿tengo que ...?
can we have some ...? ¿nos

pone ...? [p**o**neh]
hayfever la fiebre del heno [f-y**e**breh del **e**no]
hazelnut la avellana [abeh-y**a**na]
he* él
head la cabeza [kab**e**sa]
headache el dolor de cabeza [deh], la jaqueca [Hak**e**ka]
headlights las luces de cruce [l**oo**s-es de kr**oo**seh]
headphones los auriculares [owreekool**a**r-es]

health
The lack of sanitation in Mexico is often exaggerated, but a degree of caution is wise. Don't try anything too exotic in the first few days; avoid food that has been on display for a while and is not freshly cooked. You should also steer clear of salads, and peel fruit before eating it. Avoid raw shellfish, and don't eat anywhere that is obviously dirty (most Mexican restaurants are scrupulously clean); street stalls in particular are suspect. A bout of diarrhoea (or **turista** as it's known in Mexico), caused by the change in food and routine, affects most people to some degree, but its symptoms do pass; if they last for more than a few days, you should consult a doctor. Malaria is endemic in many parts of Mexico. It's a good idea to take malaria tablets for two weeks before you leave and continue taking them for six weeks after you return home. Two other common problems are altitude sickness and too much sun. Allow yourself time to acclimatize by taking things easy and use a strong sunscreen, wear a hat or stick to the shade. As a general rule, drink more than you would at home, and stay out of the sun at the hottest times of day.
see **water** and **mosquito**

health food shop la tienda naturista [t-y**e**nda natoor**ee**sta]
healthy sano
hear escuchar [eskooch**a**r]

•••••• DIALOGUE ••••••

can you hear me? ¿me escuchas? [meh esk**oo**chas]
I can't hear you, could you repeat that? no le escucho, ¿podría repetirlo? [leh]

hearing aid el audífono [owd**ee**fono]
heart el corazón [koras**o**n]
heart attack el infarto
heat el calor
heater (in room) la estufa (in car) la calefacción [kalefaks-y**o**n]
heating la calefacción
heavy pesado
heel (of foot) el talón

(of shoe) el tac**ó**n
could you heel these? ¿podría cambiar los tacones? [kamb-y**a**r – tak**o**n-es]
heelbar el zapatero [sapat**ai**ro]
height la alt**u**ra
helicopter el helic**ó**ptero
hello! ¡hola! [**o**la]
(answer on phone) ¡bueno! [bw**e**no]
helmet el c**a**sco
help la ayuda [ī-y**oo**da]
(verb) ayudar [ī-yood**ar**]
help! ¡soc**o**rro!
can you help me? ¿puede ayudarme? [pw**e**deh ī-yood**a**rmeh]
thank you very much for your help muchas gracias por su ayuda [m**oo**chas gr**a**s-yas]
helpful amable [am**a**bleh]
hepatitis la hepatitis [epat**ee**tees]
her*: I haven't seen her no la he visto [eh b**ee**sto]
to her a ella [**eh**-ya]
with her con ella
for her p**a**ra ella
that's her ella es
that's her towel **é**sa es su to**a**lla
herbal tea el té de hierbas [teh deh y**ai**rbas]
herbs las hierbas
here aquí [ak**ee**]
here is/are ... aquí est**á**/están ...
here you are (offering) aquí tiene [t-y**e**neh]
hers* (el) suyo [s**oo**-yo], (la) s**u**ya
that's hers es de ella [deh **eh**-ya], es suyo/suya
hey! ¡oiga! [**oy**ga]
hi! (hello) ¡hola! [**o**la]
hide (verb) esconder [eskond**air**]
high **a**lto
highchair la silla **a**lta p**a**ra bebés [s**ee**-ya – beh-b**e**s]
highway (US) la autopista [owtop**ee**sta]
hill el cerro [sairr**o**]
him*: I haven't seen him no lo he visto [eh b**ee**sto]
to him a él
with him con él
for him p**a**ra él
that's him él es
hip la cadera [kad**ai**ra]
hire (verb) alquilar [alkeel**ar**], arrend**ar**
for hire de alquiler [deh alkeel**air**]
where can I hire a bike? ¿dónde puedo alquilar **u**na bicicl**e**ta? [d**o**ndeh pw**e**do]
see rent
his*: it's his car es su c**a**rro
that's his **e**so es de él [deh], **e**so es suyo [s**oo**-yo]
history la historia [eest**o**r-ya]
hit (verb) golpear [golpeh-**a**r]
hitch-hike pedir aventón [abent**o**n], hacer autostop [as**air** owtost**o**p], pedir ráid [rīd]

Hitching into Mexico from the US is not recommended. Quite apart from the obvious safety risks, even if you get a through lift, you will need to walk or take a short bus ride across the border; otherwise it will be marked on your tourist card that you came in by car and (although it's unlikely) you may have problems when it's time to leave. Within Mexico, hitchhiking is also not recommended. Lifts are scarce, distances are vast and risks are high.

hobby el pasatiempo [pasat-**ye**mpo]
hold (verb) tener en la mano [ten**air**]
hole el agujero [agooHairo], el hoyo [**oy**-o]
holiday las vacaciones [bakas-**yo**n-es]
  on holiday de vacaciones [deh]

New Year (**Año Nuevo**) is a national holiday in Mexico, as is Christmas Day and (unofficially) the Day of the Virgin of Guadalupe on December 12th. New Year is often the occasion for family reunions, and people travel home to their place of origin to celebrate it – hence the need to book transport for this period well ahead of time. **Reyes** (January 6th: Twelfth Night) is the day when presents are exchanged, rather than Christmas Day.
Secular **Independence Day** (Sept 16) is in some ways more solemn than the religious festivals with their exuberant fervour.
El Día de los Muertos (Day of the Dead) is All Souls' Day and its eve (Nov 1-2) when offerings are made to ancestors' souls, frequently with picnics and all-night vigils on their graves. People build shrines in their homes to honour their departed relatives, but it's the cemeteries to head for if you want to see the really spectacular stuff. Sweetmeats and papier mâché statues of dressed up skeletons give the whole proceedings rather a gothic air.
The country's biggest holiday, however, is **Semana Santa**, the week leading up to Easter when there are celebrations everywhere.
Viernes Santo (Good Friday) is the biggest day; Easter Thursday and Saturday are also public holidays (**días feriados**). Many people travel to their home towns over Easter, so public transport is bursting at the seams.

home la casa
  at home (in my house) en casa

(in my country) en mi país [pa**ee**s]
we go home tomorrow regresamos a casa mañana

honest honrado [onr**a**do]

honey la miel [m-yel]

honeymoon la luna de miel [l**oo**na deh]

hood (US) el capó, el capote [kap**o**teh], el cofre [k**o**freh]

hope la esperanza [espair**a**nsa]
I hope so espero que sí [esp**ai**ro keh]
I hope not espero que no
hopefully it won't rain no lloverá, eso espero [yobair**a**]

horn (of car) el klaxon

horrible horrible [orr**ee**bleh]

horse el caballo [kab**a**-yo]

horse racing las carreras de caballos [karr**ai**ras deh kab**a**-yos]

horse riding la equitación [ekeetas-y**o**n]
I like horse riding me gusta montar a caballo [meh – kab**a**-yo]

hospital el hospital [ospeet**a**l]

hospitality la hospitalidad [ospeetaleed**a**]
thank you for your hospitality gracias por su hospitalidad [gr**a**s-yas]

hot caliente [kal-y**e**nteh]
(spicy) picante [peek**a**nteh], picoso
I'm hot tengo calor
it's hot today hoy hace calor [oy **a**seh]

hotel el hotel [ot**e**l]

> Mexican hotels may describe themselves as anything from **posadas** and **casas de huéspedes** to plain **hoteles**. The terms are used almost interchangeably, but the **casa de huéspedes** will usually be a cheaper guesthouse. Finding a room is rarely difficult; the cheaper hotels will often be concentrated round the main square (**zócalo**), or near the market, train station or bus station. The more modern and expensive hotels will either be in the more expensive districts or on the outskirts of towns, and only accessible by car. **Motel-** or **hotel-garaje** usually indicates hotels where couples go for a few hours (and where you pay by the hour), but they may still be clean and quite reasonable in price. Hotel prices have now been deregulated, so you should shop around if you can: a little gentle haggling rarely goes amiss and many places will have some less expensive rooms, so ask: **¿tiene un cuarto más barato?** Air-conditioning (**aire acondicionado**) is a feature that inflates prices. Unless it is unbearably hot and humid, a room with a single ceiling fan is generally fine.

hotel room el cuarto de hotel [kw**a**rto deh ot**e**l]
hour la hora [**o**ra]
house la casa
house wine el vino de la casa [b**ee**no deh]
see wine
hovercraft el aerodeslizador [a-airodesleesad**o**r]
how cómo
how many? ¿cuántos? [kw**a**ntos]
how do you do? ¡mucho gusto! [m**oo**cho g**oo**sto]

•••••• DIALOGUES ••••••

how are you? ¿cómo le va? [leh ba]
fine, thanks, and you? bien gracias, ¿y Usted? [b-yen gr**a**s-yas ee oost**eh**]

how much is it? ¿cuánto vale? [kw**a**nto b**a**leh]
1,000 pesos mil pesos [p**e**sos]
I'll take it me lo quedo [meh lo k**e**do]

humid húmedo [**oo**medo]
humour el humor [oom**o**r]
hungry hambriento [ambr-y**e**nto]
I'm hungry tengo hambre [**a**mbreh]
are you hungry? ¿tiene hambre? [t-y**e**neh]
hurry (verb) apurarse [apoor**a**rseh]
I'm in a hurry tengo prisa
there's no hurry no hay prisa [ī]
hurry up! ¡apúrese! [ap**oo**reseh]
hurt doler [dol**air**]
it really hurts me duele mucho [meh dw**e**leh m**oo**cho]
husband el marido
hydrofoil la hidroala [eedro-**a**la]
hypermarket el hipermercado [eepairmairk**a**do]

I

I yo
ice el hielo [y**e**lo]
with ice con hielo
no ice, thanks sin hielo, por favor [seen – fab**o**r]
ice cream el helado [el**a**do]
ice-cream cone el cucurucho [kookoor**oo**choo]
iced coffee el café helado [kaf**eh** el**a**do]
ice lolly la paleta
idea la idea [eed**eh**-a]
idiot el/la idiota [eed-y**o**ta]
if si
ignition el encendido [ensend**ee**do]
ill enfermo [enf**air**mo]
I feel ill me encuentro mal [meh enkw**e**ntro]
illness la enfermedad [enfairmed**a**]
imitation (leather etc) de imitación [deh eemeetas-y**o**n]
immediately en seguida [seg**ee**da]
important importante

[eemportanteh]
it's very important es muy importante [mwee]
it's not important no tiene importancia [t-yeneh eemportans-ya]
impossible imposible [eemposeebleh]
impressive impresionante [eempres-yonanteh]
improve mejorar [meHorar]
I want to improve my Spanish quiero mejorar mi español [k-yairo – espan-yol]
in: it's in the centre está en el centro
in my car en mi carro
in Xalapa en Xalapa [Halapa]
in two days from now en dos días más
in five minutes dentro de cinco minutos [deh]
in May en mayo
in English en inglés [eeng-les]
in Spanish en español [espan-yol]
is he in? ¿se encuentra? [seh enkwentra]
inch* la pulgada
include incluir [eenkloo-eer]
does that include meals? ¿están incluídas las comidas? [eenkloo-eedas]
is that included? ¿está incluido en el precio? [eenkloo-eedo en el pres-yo]
inconvenient inoportuno [eenoportoono]
incredible increíble [eenkreh-eebleh]
Indian (adj: from India) indio [eend-yo]
(South American: adj) indígena [eendeeHena]
(man/woman) el/la indígena
indicator el intermitente [eentairmeetenteh]
indigestion la indigestión [eendeeHest-yon]
indoor pool la alberca cubierta [albairka koob-yairta]
indoors dentro de la casa [deh]
inexpensive económico
infection la infección [eenfeks-yon]
infectious contagioso [kontaH-yoso]
inflammation la inflamación [eenflamas-yon]
informal (occasion, meeting) informal [eenformal]
(dress) de sport [deh]
information la información [eenformas-yon]
do you have any information about ...? ¿tiene información sobre ... ? [t-yeneh – sobreh]
information desk la información
injection la inyección [een-yeks-yon]
injured herido [ereedo]
she's been injured está herida
in-laws la familia política [fameel-ya]
inner tube (for tyre) la cámara de aire [deh a-eereh]

innocent inocente [eenos**e**nteh]
insect el insecto [eens**e**kto]
insect bite la picadura de insecto [deh]
do you have anything for insect bites? ¿tiene algo para la picadura de insectos? [t-y**e**neh]
insect repellent el repelente de insectos [repel**e**nteh deh]
inside dentro de [deh]
inside the hotel dentro del hotel
let's sit inside vamos a sentarnos adentro [b**a**mos]
insist insistir [eenseest**ee**r]
I insist insisto
insomnia el insomnio [eens**o**mn-yo]
instant coffee el café instantáneo [kaf**eh** eenstant**a**neh-o]
instead: give me that one instead deme ese otro [d**e**meh **e**seh]
instead of ... en lugar de ... [deh]
intersection el cruce [kr**oo**seh]
insulin la insulina [eensool**ee**na]
insurance el seguro [seg**oo**ro]
intelligent inteligente [eentelee**He**nteh]
interested: I'm interested in ... me interesa ... [meh eentair**e**sa]
interesting interesante [eenteres**a**nteh]
that's very interesting es muy interesante [mwee]
international internacional [eentairnas-yon**a**l]
interpret actuar de intérprete [actoo-**a**r deh eent**ai**rpreteh]
interpreter el/la intérprete
interval (at theatre) el intermedio [eentairm**e**d-yo]
into en
I'm not into ... no me gusta ... [meh g**oo**sta]
introduce presentar
may I introduce ...? le presento a ... [leh]
invitation la invitación [eembeetas-y**o**n]
invite invitar [eembeet**a**r]
Ireland Irlanda [eerl**a**nda]
Irish irlandés [eerland-**e**s]
I'm Irish (man/woman) soy irlandés/irlandesa
iron (for ironing) la plancha
(metal) el hierro [y**ai**rro]
can you iron these for me? ¿puede planchármelos? [pw**e**deh]
is* es, está
island la isla [**ee**sla]
it ello, lo [**eh**-yo]
it is ... es ...; está ...
is it ...? ¿es ...?; ¿está ... ?
where is it? ¿dónde está? [d**o**ndeh]
it's him es él
it was ... era ... [**ai**ra]; estaba ...
Italian (adj) italiano [eetal-y**a**no]
Italy Italia
itch el comezón [komes**o**n]
it itches me pica [meh]

J

jack (for car) el **ga**to
jacket el **sa**co
jam la mermelada [mairmel**a**da]
jammed: it's jammed se atoró [seh]
January enero [en**ai**ro]
jar el pote [p**o**teh]
jaw la mandíbula
jazz el jazz
jealous celoso [sel**o**so]
jeans los vaqueros [bak**ai**ros]
jellyfish la medusa [med**oo**sa]
jersey el jersey [Hairs**eh**]
jetty el muelle [mw**eh**-yeh]
jeweller's shop la joyería [Ho-yair**ee**-a]
jewellery las joyas [H**o**-yas]
Jewish judío [Hood**ee**-o]
job el trabajo [trab**a**Ho], el puesto [pw**e**sto]
jogging el **foo**ting
to go jogging hacer footing [as**air**]
joke el chiste [ch**ee**steh]
journey el viaje [b-y**a**Heh]
have a good journey! ¡buen viaje! [bwen]
jug la jarra [h**a**rra]
a jug of water **u**na jarra de **a**gua [deh]
juice el jugo [H**oo**go]
July julio [H**oo**l-yo]
jump (verb) brinc**ar**
jumper el jersey [Hairs**eh**]
jump leads las pinzas (para la batería) [p**ee**nsas (p**a**ra la batair**ee**-a)]
junction el cruce [kr**oo**seh]
June junio [H**oo**n-yo]
jungle la **sel**va
just (only) solamente [solam**e**nteh]
just two sólo dos
just for me sólo p**a**ra mí
just here aquí mismo [ak**ee** m**ee**smo], aquí mero [m**ai**ro]
not just now ahora no [a-**o**ra]
we've just arrived acab**a**mos de llegar [deh yeg**a**r]

K

kayak el k**a**yak
keep quedarse [ked**a**rseh]
keep the change quédese con el cambio [k**e**deseh – k**a**mb-yo]
can I keep it? ¿puedo quedármelo? [pw**e**do ked**a**rmelo]
please keep it por favor, quédeselo [fab**o**r k**e**deselo]
ketchup el catsup [kats**oo**p]
kettle el hervidor [airbeed**o**r]
key la llave [y**a**beh]
the key for room 201, please la llave del doscientos **u**no, por favor [fab**o**r]
keyring el llavero [yab**ai**ro]
kidneys los riñones [reen-y**o**n-es]
kill mat**ar**
kilo* el k**i**lo
kilometre* el kil**ó**metro
how many kilometres is it to ...? ¿cuántos kilómetros hay a ...? [kw**a**ntos – ī]

kind (nice) amable [am**a**bleh]
that's very kind es muy amable [mwee]

•••••• DIALOGUE ••••••

which kind do you want? ¿qué tipo quiere? [keh t**ee**po k-y**ai**reh]
I want this/that kind quiero este/aquel tipo [k-y**ai**ro **e**steh/ak**e**l]

king el rey [ray]
kiosk el quiosco [kee-**o**sko]
kiss el beso
(verb) besarse [bes**a**rseh]
kitchen la cocina [kos**ee**na]
kitchenette la cocina pequeña [pekw**e**n-ya]
Kleenex® el klínex®
knee la rodilla [rod**ee**-ya]
knickers los pantis
knife el cuchillo [kooch**ee**-yo]
knock (verb: on door) llamar [yam**a**r]
knock down atropellar [atropeh-y**a**r]
he's been knocked down lo atropellaron [atropeh-y**a**ron]
knock over (object) volcar [bolk**a**r]
(pedestrian) atropellar [atropeh-y**a**r]
know (somebody, a place) conocer [konos**air**]
(something) saber [sab**air**]
I don't know no sé [seh]
I didn't know that no lo sabía
do you know where I can find ...? ¿sabe dónde puedo encontrar ...? [s**a**beh d**o**ndeh pw**e**do]

•••••• DIALOGUE ••••••

do you know how this works? ¿sabe cómo funciona esto? [foons-y**o**na]
sorry, I don't know lo siento, no sé [s-y**e**nto no seh]

L

label la etiqueta [eteek**e**ta]
ladies' room, ladies' (toilet) el servicio de señoras [sairb**ee**s-yo deh sen-y**o**ras]
ladies' wear la ropa de señoras
lady la señora [sen-y**o**ra]
lager la cerveza clara [sairb**e**sa]
see beer
lagoon la laguna
lake el lago
lamb (meat) el cordero [kord**ai**ro]
lamp la lámpara
land la tierra [t-y**ai**rra]
(verb) aterrizar [aterrees**a**r]
lane (motorway) el carril
(small road) la callejuela [ka-yeh-Hw**e**la]
language el idioma [eed-y**o**ma]
language course el curso de idiomas [k**oo**rso deh]
large grande [gr**a**ndeh]
last último [**oo**lteemo]
last week la semana pasada
last Friday el viernes pasado
last night anoche [an**o**cheh]
what time is the last train to Veracruz? ¿a qué hora es el último tren para Veracruz? [keh **o**ra – bairakr**oo**s]

late tarde [t**a**rdeh]
sorry I'm late disculpe, me retrasé [deesk**oo**lpeh meh retras**eh**]
the train was late el tren se demor**ó**
we must go – we'll be late deb**e**mos irnos – llegaremos tarde [**ee**rnos – yegar**e**mos]
it's getting late se est**á** haciendo tarde [seh – as-y**e**ndo]
later más tarde [t**a**rdeh]
I'll come back later regresaré más tarde [regresar**eh**]
see you later hasta luego [**a**sta lw**e**go]
later on más tarde
latest lo último [**oo**lteemo]
by Wednesday at the latest p**a**ra el mi**é**rcoles a más tard**ar**
Latin America América [am**ai**reeka]
Latin American (adj) americano [amaireek**a**no]
(man) el (lat**i**no) americano
(woman) la (latino) americ**a**na
laugh (verb) reirse [reh-**ee**rseh]
launderette/laundromat la lavandería automática [labandair**ee**-a owtom**a**teeka]
laundry (clothes) la r**o**pa sucia [s**oo**s-ya]
(place) la lavandería [labandair**ee**-a]
lavatory el baño [b**a**n-yo]
law la ley [lay]
lawn el césped [s**e**sped]
lawyer (man/woman) el abog**a**do, la abog**a**da
laxative el laxante [laks**a**nteh]
lazy flojo [fl**o**Ho]
lead (electrical) el cable [k**a**bleh]
lead (verb) llevar [yev**a**r]
where does this lead to? ¿adónde va **e**sto? [ad**o**ndeh ba]
leaf la hoja [**o**Ha]
leaflet el folleto [fo-y**e**to]
leak (in roof) la gotera [got**ai**ra]
(gas, water) el escape [esk**a**peh]
(verb) filtrar [feeltr**a**r]
the roof leaks el tejado tiene goteras [teH**a**do t-y**e**neh got**ai**ras]
learn aprender [aprend**air**]
least: not in the least de ningu**n**a manera [deh – man**ai**ra]
at least al menos
leather (fine) la piel [p-yel]
(heavy) el cuero [kw**ai**ro]
leave (verb) irse [**ee**rseh]
I am leaving tomorrow me voy mañ**a**na [meh]
he left yesterday se fue ay**e**r [seh fweh]
may I leave this here? ¿puedo dejar esto aquí? [pw**e**do deh-H**a**r **e**sto ak**ee**]
I left my coat in the bar dejé el abrigo en el bar [deh-H**eh**]

•••••• DIALOGUE ••••••

when does the bus for Taxco leave? ¿cuándo sale el autobús para Taxco? [kw**a**ndo s**a**leh – t**a**sko]
it leaves at 9 o'clock sale a las n**ue**ve

leek el puerro [pw**ai**rro]
left izquierda [eesk-y**ai**rda]
on the left a la izquierda
to the left hacia la izquierda [**a**s-ya]
turn left dé vuelta a la izquierda [deh bw**e**lta]
there's none left no queda ninguno [k**e**da]
left-handed zurdo [s**oo**rdo]
left luggage (office) la consigna [kons**ee**gna], la paquetería [paketair**ee**-a]
leg la pierna [p-y**ai**rna]
lemon el limón
lemonade la limonada
lemon tea el té con limón [teh]
lend prestar
will you lend me your ... ? ¿podría prestarme su ...? [prest**a**rmeh]
lens (of camera) el objetivo [obHet**ee**bo]
lesbian la lesbiana [lesb-y**a**na]
less menos
less expensive menos caro
less than 10 menos de diez [deh]
less than you menos que tú [keh too]
lesson la lección [leks-y**o**n]

let (allow) dejar [deh-H**a**r]
will you let me know? ¿me tendrás al corriente? [meh – korr-y**e**nteh]
I'll let you know le avisaré [leh abeesar**eh**]
let's go for something to eat vamos a comer algo [b**a**mos a kom**air**]
let off: will you let me off at ...? ¿me deja en...? [meh d**eh**-Ha]
letter la carta
do you have any letters for me? ¿tiene cartas para mí? [t-y**e**neh]
letterbox el buzón [boos**o**n]

Bright red letterboxes (**buzones**) in the street are quite reliable, but to be absolutely certain of delivery, post your letters and packets at the post office.
see **post office**

lettuce la lechuga [lech**oo**ga]
lever la palanca
library la biblioteca [beebl-yot**e**ka]
licence el permiso
lid la tapa
lie (verb: tell untruth) mentir
lie down acostarse [akost**a**rseh], echarse [**e**charseh]
life la vida [b**ee**da]
lifebelt el salvavidas [salbab**ee**das]
lifeguard el/la socorrista
life jacket el chaleco salvavidas

[salbab**ee**das]
lift (in building) el ascensor [asens**o**r]
could you give me a lift? ¿me podría llevar? [meh – yeb**a**r]
would you like a lift? ¿quiere que lo lleve? [k-y**ai**reh keh lo y**e**beh]
light la luz [loos]
(not heavy) ligero [leeH**ai**ro]
do you have a light? (for cigarette) ¿tiene fuego? [t-y**e**neh fw**e**go]
light green verde claro [b**ai**rdeh]
light bulb el foco
I need a new light bulb necesito un foco nuevo [neses**ee**to – nw**e**bo]
lighter (cigarette) el encendedor [ensended**o**r]
lightning el relámpago
like (verb) gustar [goost**a**r]
I like it me gusta [meh]
I like going for walks me gusta pasear
I like you me gustas
I don't like it no me gusta
do you like ...? ¿le gusta ...? [leh]
I'd like a beer quisiera una cerveza [kees-y**ai**ra]
I'd like to go swimming me gustaría ir a bañarme
would you like a drink? ¿quiere beber algo? [k-y**ai**reh]
would you like to go for a walk? ¿quieres dar un paseo? [k-y**ai**r-es]
what's it like? ¿cómo es?
I want one like this quiero uno como éste [k-y**ai**ro – **e**steh]
lime la lima [l**ee**ma]
lime cordial el jarabe de lima [Har**a**beh deh]
line la línea [l**ee**neh-a]
could you give me an outside line? ¿puede darme línea? [pw**e**deh d**a**rmeh]
lips los labios [l**a**b-yos]
lip salve la crema de labios [deh]
lipstick el lápiz de labios [l**a**pees]
liqueur el licor
listen oir [o-**ee**r]
litre* el litro
a litre of white wine un litro de vino blanco [deh]
little chico
just a little, thanks un poquito, gracias [pok**ee**to gr**a**s-yas]
a little milk un poco de leche
a little bit more un poquito más
live (verb) vivir [beeb**ee**r]
we live together vivimos juntos [beeb**ee**mos H**oo**ntos]

•••••• DIALOGUE ••••••

where do you live? ¿dónde vive? [d**o**ndeh b**ee**beh]
I live in London vivo en Londres [b**ee**bo en l**o**nd-res]

lively alegre [al**e**greh], animado

liver el hígado [**ee**gado]
lizard la lagartija [lagart**ee**Ha]
loaf el pan
lobby (in hotel) el vestíbulo [best**ee**boolo]
lobster la langosta
local local
can you recommend a local wine/restaurant? ¿puede recomendarme un vino/un restaurante local? [pw**e**deh rekomend**a**rmeh]
lock la cerradura [sairrad**oo**ra]
(verb) cerrar [sairr**a**r]
it's locked está cerrado con llave [sairr**a**do kon y**a**beh]
lock in dejar encerrado [deh-H**a**r ensairr**a**do]
lock out: I've locked myself out he cerrado la puerta con las llaves dentro [eh sairr**a**do la pw**ai**rta – y**a**b-es]
locker (for luggage etc) la consigna automática [kons**ee**gna owtom**a**teeka]
lollipop la paleta
London Londres [l**o**nd-res]
long largo
how long will it take to fix it? ¿cuánto tiempo tardará en arreglarlo? [kw**a**nto t-y**e**mpo]
how long does it take? ¿cuánto tiempo lleva? [y**e**ba]
a long time mucho tiempo [m**oo**cho]
one day/two days longer un día/dos días más
long distance call la llamada de larga distancia [yam**a**da deh – deest**a**ns-ya]
look: I'm just looking, thanks sólo estoy mirando, gracias [gr**a**s-yas]
you don't look well tienes cara de enfermo [t-y**e**n-es k**a**ra deh enf**ai**rmo]
look out! ¡cuidado! [kweed**a**do]
can I have a look? ¿me deja ver? [meh d**eh**-Ha b**air**]
look after cuidar [kweed**a**r]
look at mirar
look for buscar
I'm looking for ... estoy buscando ...
look forward to: I'm looking forward to seeing it tengo muchas ganas de verlo [m**oo**chas – deh b**ai**rlo]
loose (handle etc) suelto [sw**e**lto]
lorry el camión [kam-y**o**n], el tráiler [trīlair]
lose perder [paird**air**], extraviarse [estrab-y**a**rseh]
I've lost my way me extravié [estrab-y**e**h]
I'm lost, I want to get to ... me perdí, quiero ir a ... [k-y**ai**ro eer]
I've lost my bag perdí el bolso
lost property (office) (la oficina de) objetos perdidos [(ofees**ee**na deh) obH**e**tos paird**ee**dos]
lot: a lot, lots mucho, muchos [m**oo**cho]
not a lot no mucho
a lot of people mucha gente

a lot bigger mucho mayor
I like it a lot me gusta mucho [meh g**oo**sta]
lotion la loción [los-y**o**n]
loud fuerte [fw**ai**rteh]
lounge (in house, hotel) el salón (in airport) la sala de espera [deh esp**ai**ra]
love el amor
(verb) querer [kair**air**]
I love Mexico me encanta México [meh – m**e**Heeko]
lovely encantador
low bajo [b**a**Ho]
luck la suerte [sw**ai**rteh]
good luck! ¡buena suerte! [bw**e**na]
luggage el equipaje [ekeep**a**H-eh]
luggage trolley el carrito portaequipajes [porta-ekeep**a**H-es]
lump (on body) la hinchazón [eenchas**o**n]
lunch el almuerzo [almw**ai**rso]
lungs los pulmones [poolm**o**n-es]
luxurious (hotel, furnishings) de lujo [deh l**oo**Ho]
luxury el lujo

M

machine la máquina [m**a**keena]
mad (insane) loco
(angry) furioso [foor-y**o**so]
magazine la revista [reb**ee**sta]
maid (in hotel) la camarera [kamar**ai**ra]
maiden name el nombre de soltera [n**o**mbreh deh solt**ai**ra]
mail el correo [korr**eh**-o]
is there any mail for me? ¿hay correspondencia para mí? [ī korrespond**e**ns-ya]
see post office
mailbox el buzón [boos**o**n]
see letterbox
main principal [preenseep**a**l]
main course el plato principal
main post office la oficina central de correos [ofees**ee**na sentr**a**l deh korr**eh**-os]
main road (in town) la calle principal [k**a**-yeh preenseep**a**l]
(in country) la carretera principal [karret**ai**ra]
mains (for water) la llave de paso [y**a**beh deh]
mains switch (for electricity) el interruptor de la red eléctrica [eentairroopt**o**r deh la reh]
make (brand name) la marca
(verb) hacer [as**air**]
I make it 500 pesos son quinientos pesos en total
what is it made of? ¿de qué está hecho? [deh keh est**a** **e**cho]
make-up el maquillaje [makee-y**a**Heh]
man el hombre [**o**mbreh]
manager el gerente [Hair**e**nteh]
I'd like to speak to the manager quisiera hablar con el gerente [kees-y**ai**ra abl**a**r]
manageress la gerente

mañana
You may never experience it at all, but Mexico is still a place where there are days when everything seems to go wrong – especially if it involves bureaucrats or machinery. Getting things done can be exasperating. Don't even try to fight it: it will only make things worse. The only way to survive these days is to adopt the local attitude that it will work out in the end, and in the meantime there's probably something better to do anyway. The suggestion that Mexico is in some way inefficient is, like political criticism, an idea best kept to yourself.

manual (car with manual gears) el carro de marchas [deh]
many muchos [moochos]
  not many pocos
map (city plan) el plano
  (road map, geographical) el mapa

It's always worth stocking up in advance with as many brochures and plans as you can find in **Sectur** tourist offices abroad. Tourist offices in Mexico are frequently closed or have run out.

March marzo [marso]
margarine la margarina
market el mercado [mairkado], el tianguis [t-yangees]

For bargain hunters, the weekly **mercado** (market) or **tianguis** (an Aztec word, still sometimes used) is the place to head for, particularly in smaller provincial towns and villages. By and large, markets are mainly devoted to food and everyday necessities, but most have a section devoted to crafts, and in larger towns you may find a separate crafts bazaar. In larger cities there will be both local markets and larger ones that sell more or less everything. Unless you're hopeless at bargaining, prices will always be lower in the market than in the shops.
see **bargaining**

marmalade la mermelada de naranja [mairmelada deh naranHa]
married: I'm married (said by a man/woman) estoy casado/casada
  are you married? (to a man/woman) ¿está casado/casada?
mascara el rímel
match (football etc) el partido
matches las cerillas [sairee-yas]
material (fabric) el tejido [teHeedo]
matter: it doesn't matter no importa
  what's the matter? ¿qué pasa? [keh]

mattress el colchón
May mayo [mī-yo]
may: may I have another one? ¿me da otro? [meh]
may I come in? ¿se puede? [seh pwedeh]
may I see it? ¿puedo verlo? [pwedo bairlo]
may I sit here? ¿puedo sentarme aqui? [sentarmeh akee]
maybe quizás [keesas]
mayonnaise la mayonesa [mī-yonesa]
me*: that's for me ése es para mí [eseh]
send it to me mándemelo
me too yo también [tamb-yen]
meal la comida

•••••• DIALOGUE ••••••

did you enjoy your meal? ¿te gustó la comida? [teh goosto]
it was excellent, thank you estuvo riquísima, gracias [reekeeseema gras-yas]

mean (verb) querer decir [kairair deseer]
what do you mean? ¿qué quiere decir? [keh k-yaireh]

•••••• DIALOGUE ••••••

what does this word mean? ¿qué significa esta palabra?
it means ... in English significa ... en inglés [eeng-les]

measles el sarampión [saramp-yon]
meat la carne [karneh]
mechanic el mecánico
medicine la medicina [medeeseena]
medium (adj: size) medio [med-yo]
medium-dry semi-seco
medium-rare poco hecho [echo]
medium-sized de tamaño medio [taman-yo med-yo]
meet encontrarse [encontrarseh]
(for the first time) conocerse [konosairseh]
nice to meet you encantado de conocerle [deh konosairleh]
where shall I meet you? ¿dónde nos vemos? [dondeh nos bemos]
meeting la reunión [reh-oon-yon]
meeting place el lugar de encuentro [loogar deh enkwentro]
melon el melón
men los hombres [omb-res]
mend (clothes) remendar
could you mend this for me? ¿puede arreglarme esto? [pwedeh arreglármeh]
men's toilet el servicio de hombres [sairbees-yo deh omb-res]
menswear la ropa de hombre [deh ombreh]
mention (verb) mencionar [mens-yonar]
don't mention it no hay de

qué [ī deh keh]
menu la carta
may I see the menu, please? ¿me deja ver la carta? [meh deh-Ha bair]
see **menu reader** page 239
message: are there any messages for me? ¿hay algún recado para mí? [ī]
I want to leave a message for ... quisiera dejar un recado para ... [kees-yaira deh-Har]
metal el metal
metre* el metro
Mexican (adj) mexicano [meHeekano]
(man) el mexicano
(woman) la mexicana
the Mexicans los mexicanos
Mexico México [meHeeko]

> The name of the capital city of Mexico is a source of infinite confusion to travellers. Mexico City is not a place on any Mexican map nor is it ever used by Mexicans – they call it **México** or sometimes **El D.F.** ([el deh efeh]: the **Distrito Federal** is the administrative zone that contains most of the urban areas). The country took its name from the city, and in conversation México almost always means the latter. The nation is **la República** or in speeches **la Patria** – very rarely Mexico.

Mexico City la ciudad de México [s-yooda deh], el Distrito Federal [fedairal], el D.F. [deh efeh]
microwave (oven) el (horno) microondas [(orno) meekro-ondas]
midday el mediodía [med-yodee-a]
at midday a mediodía
middle: in the middle en el centro [sentro]
in the middle of the night en las altas horas de la noche [oras deh la nocheh]
the middle one el de en medio
midnight la medianoche [med-yanocheh]
at midnight a medianoche
might: I might es posible [poseebleh]
I might not go puede que no vaya [pwedeh keh no bī-ya]
I might want to stay another day quizás decida quedarme otro día [keesas deseeda kedarmeh]
migraine la jaqueca [Hakeka]
mild (taste) suave [swabeh]
(weather) templado
mile* la milla [mee-ya]
milk la leche [lecheh]
milkshake el licuado [leekwado]
millimetre* el milímetro
minced meat el picadillo [peekadee-yo]
mind: never mind! ¡no importa!
I've changed my mind cambié

de idea [kamb-y**eh** deh eed**eh**-a]

•••••• DIALOGUE ••••••

do you mind if I open the window? ¿le importa que **a**bra la ventana? [leh eemp**o**rta keh – bent**a**na]
no, I don't mind no, no me importa [meh]

mine*: it's mine es m**í**o
mineral water el agua mineral [**a**gwa meenaira**l**], el Tehuacán® [teh-wak**a**n]
mint-flavoured con sab**o**r a m**e**nta
mints las pastillas de m**e**nta [past**ee**-yas deh]
minute el minuto [meen**oo**to]
in a minute ahorita [a-or**ee**ta]
just a minute un momento
mirror el espejo [esp**e**Ho]
Miss Señorita [sen-yor**ee**ta]
miss: I missed the bus perdí el autob**ú**s [paird**ee**]
missing: one of my ... is missing f**a**lta **u**no de mis ... [deh]
there's a suitcase missing falta **u**na mal**e**ta
mist la nebl**i**na
mistake el err**o**r
I think there's a mistake me parece que hay una equivocación [meh par**e**seh keh ī **oo**na ekeebokas-y**o**n]
sorry, I've made a mistake perd**ó**n, me equivoqué [meh ekeebok**eh**]
misunderstanding el malentend**i**do
mix-up: sorry, there's been a mix-up perd**ó**n hubo una confusión [**oo**bo **oo**na konfoos-y**o**n]
modern moderno [mod**ai**rno]
modern art gallery la galería de arte moderno [galair**ee**-a deh **a**rteh]
moisturizer la crema hidratante [eedrat**a**nteh]
moment: I won't be a moment no me t**a**rdo [meh]
monastery el monasterio [monast**ai**r-yo]
Monday lunes [l**oo**n-es]
money el dinero [deen**ai**ro]
month el mes
monument el monumento [monoom**e**nto]
(statue) la estatua [est**a**twa]
moon la l**u**na
moped el ciclomotor [seeklomot**o**r]
more* más
can I have some more water, please? me da más **a**gua, por favor [meh – fab**o**r]
more expensive/interesting más c**a**ro/interes**a**nte
more than 50 más de cincu**e**nta [deh]
more than that más que **e**so [keh]
a lot more mucho más [m**oo**cho]

•••••• DIALOGUE ••••••

would you like some more? ¿quiere más? [k-y**ai**reh]

no, no more for me, thanks no, para mí no, gracias [gras-yas]
how about you? ¿y Usted? [ee oosteh]
I don't want any more, thanks nada más, gracias

morning la mañana [man-yana]
this morning esta mañana
in the morning por la mañana
mosquito el mosquito, el zancudo [sankoodo]

> Mosquitos (called **zancudos** more often than **mosquitos**) are active at all times of the day, but are particularly prevalent in the evening. Wear long sleeves, skirts or trousers, avoid dark colours, which attract mosquitos, and put repellent on all exposed skin. Alternatively, use a mosquito coil in your room or sleep under a mosquito net. Other biting insects are bedbugs, sandflies (on beaches), and head or body lice which can be picked up from bedding and people; scorpions and snakes are more serious but rarer hazards; seek medical help if bitten, explaining: **me picó un zancudo/una víbora/un escorpión** [meh peeko oon sankoodo/oona beebora/oon eskorp-yon] (I've been bitten by a mosquito/snake/scorpion).
> see **health**

mosquito coil el espiral antimosquitos
mosquito net la red antimosquitos
mosquito repellent el repelente de mosquitos [repelenteh deh]
most: I like this one most of all éste es el que más me gusta [esteh – keh mas meh goosta]
most of the time la mayor parte del tiempo [mī-yor parteh del t-yempo]
most tourists la mayoría de los turistas [mī-yoree-a deh]
mostly generalmente [Henairalmenteh]
mother la madre [madreh]
motorbike la moto
motorboat la (lancha) motora
motorway la autopista [owtopeesta]
see **driving**
mountain la montaña [montan-ya]
in the mountains en la sierra [s-yaira]
mountaineering el montañismo [montan-yeesmo]
mountain range la sierra
mouse el ratón
moustache el bigote [beegoteh]
mouth la boca
mouth ulcer la llaga [yaga]
move: he's moved to another room se trasladó a otro cuarto [seh – kwarto]
could you move your car? ¿podría cambiar de lugar el carro? [kamb-yar deh]

could you move up a little? ¿puede correrse un poco? [pwedeh korrairseh]
where has it moved to? ¿adónde se trasladó? [adondeh seh]
movie la película [peleekoola]
movie theater el cine [seeneh]
Mr Señor [sen-yor]
Mrs Señora [sen-yora]
Ms Señorita [sen-yoreeta]
much mucho [moocho]
much better/worse mucho mejor/peor [mī-yor/peh-or]
much hotter mucho más caliente [kal-yenteh]
not (very) much no mucho
I don't want very much un poco nada más
mud el barro, el lodo
mug (for drinking) la taza [tasa]
I've been mugged me asaltaron
mum la mamá
mumps las paperas [papairas]
museum el museo [mooseh-o]

Most museums and galleries will be open from about 9 a.m. to 1 p.m. and again from 3 to 6 p.m. Many have reduced entry fees or are free on Sundays, but may open only in the morning; most are closed on Monday. Archaeological sites (**zonas arqueológicas**) are usually open right through the day.

mushrooms los champiñones [champeen-yon-es]
music la música [mooseeka]
musician el/la músico [mooseeko]
Muslim (adj) musulmán [moosoolman]
mussels los mejillones [meHee-yon-es]
must: I must tengo que [keh]
I mustn't drink alcohol no debo beber alcohol [bebair alko-ol]
mustard la mostaza [mostasa]
my* mi; (pl) mis
myself: I'll do it myself (said by man/woman) lo haré yo mismo/misma [areh]
by myself (said by man/woman) yo solo/sola

N

nail (finger) la uña [oon-ya]
(metal) el clavo [klabo]
nailbrush el cepillo para las uñas [sepee-yo – oon-yas]
nail varnish el esmalte para uñas [esmalteh]
name el nombre [nombreh]
my name's John me llamo John [meh yamo]
what's your name? ¿cómo se llama? [seh yama], ¿cuál es su nombre? [kwal – nombreh]
what is the name of this street? ¿cómo se llama esta calle?

In the Spanish-speaking world people generally use two surnames, the second of which is their mother's. In Mexico you will come across many unusual Christian names, some of them of Aztec origin (**Cuauhtémoc**, **Xóchitl**). It is also very common for people to be addressed by a title: **Licenciado** (graduate), **Maestro** (teacher), **Ingeniero** (Engineer) etc.

napkin la servilleta [sairbee-**ye**ta]
nappy el pañal [pan-y**a**l]
narrow (street) estrecho [estr**e**cho]
nasty (person) desagradable [desagrad**a**bleh]
(weather, accident) m**a**lo
national nacional [nas-yon**a**l]
nationality la nacionalidad [nas-yonaleed**a**]
natural natural [natoor**a**l]
nausea la náusea [n**ow**seh-a]
navy (blue) azul marino [as**oo**l]
near cerca [s**ai**rka]
is it near the city centre? ¿está cerca del centro? [s**e**ntro]
do you go near the Zócalo? ¿p**a**sa Usted cerca del Zócalo? [oost**eh** – s**o**calo]
where is the nearest ...? ¿dónde está el ... más cercano? [d**o**ndeh – sairk**a**no]
nearby por aquí cerca [ak**ee**]
nearly c**a**si
necessary necesario [neses**a**r-yo]
neck el cuello [kw**eh**-yo]
necklace el collar [ko-y**a**r]
necktie la corb**a**ta
need: I need ... necesito un ... [neses**ee**to]
do I need to pay? ¿necesito pag**a**r?
needle la aguja [ag**oo**Ha]
negative (film) el negativo [negat**ee**bo]
neither: neither (one) of them ninguno (de ellos) [neeng**oo**no (deh **eh**-yos)]
neither ... nor ... ni ... ni ...
nephew el sobr**i**no
net (in sport) la red
Netherlands Los Países Bajos [pa-**ee**s-es b**a**Hos]
network map el m**a**pa
never n**u**nca, jamás [Ham**a**s]

•••••• DIALOGUE ••••••

have you ever been to Mérida? ¿ha est**a**do alg**u**na vez en M**e**rida? [bes]
no, never, I've never been there no, nunca estuve [est**oo**beh]

new nuevo [nw**e**bo]
news (radio, TV etc) las noticias [not**ee**s-yas]
newspaper el periódico [pair-y**o**deeko]
newspaper kiosk el puesto de periódicos [pw**e**sto deh]
New Year el Año Nuevo [**a**n-yo nw**e**bo]
Happy New Year! ¡Feliz Año

Nuevo! [felees]
see holiday
New Year's Eve Nochevieja [nocheh-b-yeHa]
New Zealand Nueva Zelanda [nweba selanda]
New Zealander: I'm a New Zealander (man/woman) soy neozelandés/neozelandesa [neh-o-seland-es]
next próximo
the next street on the left la próxima calle a la izquierda [ka-yeh a la eesk-yairda]
at the next stop en la siguiente parada [seeg-yenteh]
next week la semana que viene [keh b-yeneh]
next to al lado de [deh]
Nicaraguan (adj) nicaraguense [neekaragwenseh]
nice (food) bueno [bweno]
(looks, view etc) lindo
(person) simpático
niece la sobrina
night la noche [nocheh]
at night de noche [deh], por la noche
good night buenas noches [bwenas noch-es]

•••••• DIALOGUE ••••••

do you have a single room for one night? ¿tiene un cuarto individual para una noche? [t-yeneh oon kwarto eendeebeedwal]
yes, madam sí, señora [sen-yora]
how much is it per night? ¿cuánto es la noche? [kwanto]
it's 3,000 pesos for one night son tres mil pesos la noche
thank you, I'll take it gracias, me la quedo [gras-yas meh la kedo]

nightclub la discoteca [deeskoteka]
nightdress el camisón
night porter el portero [portairo]
no no
I've no change no tengo cambio [kamb-yo]
there's no ... left no queda ... [keda]
no way! ¡ni hablar! [ablar]
oh no! (upset, annoyed) ¡Dios mío! [d-yos]
nobody nadie [nad-yeh]
there's nobody there no hay nadie [ī]
noise el ruido [rweedo]
noisy: it's too noisy hay demasiado ruido [ī demas-yado]
non-alcoholic sin alcohol [seen alko-ol]
none ninguno
non-smoking compartment no fumadores [foomador-es]
noon el mediodía [med-yodee-a]
no-one nadie [nad-yeh]
nor: nor do I yo tampoco
normal normal [nor-mal]
north norte [norteh]
in the north en el norte
north of Taxco al norte de Taxco [deh tasko]

North America América del norte [am**ai**reeka del n**o**rteh]
North American (man) el norteameric**a**no
(woman) la norteameric**a**na
(adj) norteamericano
northeast nordeste [nord**e**steh]
northern del norte [n**o**rteh]
Northern Ireland Irlanda del Norte [eerl**a**nda del n**o**rteh]
northwest noroeste [noro-**e**steh]
Norway Noruega [norw**e**ga]
Norwegian (adj) noru**e**go
nose la nariz [nar**ee**s]
nosebleed la hemorragia nas**a**l [emorr**a**H-ya]
not* no
no, I'm not hungry no, no t**e**ngo hambre [**a**mbreh]
I don't want any, thank you no quiero, gracias [k-y**ai**ro gr**a**s-yas]
it's not necessary no es necesario [neses**a**r-yo]
I didn't know that no lo sabía
not that one – this one ése no – éste [**e**seh – **e**steh]
note (banknote) el billete [bee-y**e**teh]
notebook el cuaderno [kwad**ai**rno]
notepaper (for letters) el pap**e**l de c**a**rta [deh]
nothing n**a**da
nothing for me, thanks p**a**ra mí nada, gracias [gr**a**s-yas]
nothing else nada más
novel la novela [nob**e**la]
November noviembre [nob-y**e**mbreh]
now ahora [a-**o**ra]
number el número [n**oo**mairo]
I've got the wrong number me equivoqué de número [meh ekeebok**eh** deh]
what is your phone number? ¿cuál es su número de tel**é**fono? [kw**a**l]
number plate la pl**a**ca
nurse (man/woman) el enfermero [enfairm**ai**ro], la enferm**e**ra
nursery slope la p**i**sta de principiantes [deh preenseep-y**a**nt-es]
nut (for bolt) la tuerca [tw**ai**rka]
nuts las nueces [nw**e**s-es]

O

o'clock: at two o'clock a las dos
occupied (US: toilet etc) ocupado [okoop**a**do]
October octubre [okt**oo**breh]
odd (strange) extraño [ekstr**a**n-yo]
of de [deh]
off (lights) apag**a**do
it's just off calle Corredera está cerca de calle Corred**e**ra [s**ai**rka deh k**a**-yeh]
we're off tomorrow nos vamos mañ**a**na [b**a**mos]
offensive (language, behaviour) ofensivo [ofens**ee**bo]
office (place of work) la oficina [ofees**ee**na]
officer (said to policeman) señor oficial [sen-y**o**r ofee-sy**a**l]

often a men**u**do
not often p**o**cas veces [b**e**s-es]
how often are the buses? ¿c**a**da cuándo p**a**sa el cami**ó**n? [kw**a**ndo]
oil el aceite [as**ay**teh]
ointment la pom**a**da
OK bueno [bw**e**no]
are you OK? ¿est**á** bien? [b-yen]
is that OK with you? ¿le parece bien? [leh par**e**seh]
is it OK to ...? ¿se puede ...? [seh pw**e**deh]
that's OK thanks (it doesn't matter) est**á** bien, gracias [gr**a**s-yas]
I'm OK (nothing for me) p**a**ra mí n**a**da
(I feel OK) me siento bien [meh s-y**e**nto]
is this train OK for ...? ¿este tren va a...? [**e**steh – ba]
I said I'm sorry, OK? ya pedí disculpas ¿okey? [deesk**oo**lpas ok**ay**]
old viejo [b-y**e**Ho]

•••••• DIALOGUE ••••••

how old are you? ¿cuántos años tiene? [kw**a**ntos **a**n-yos t-y**e**neh]
I'm twenty-five tengo veinticinco años
and you? ¿y Usted? [ee oost**eh**]

old-fashioned pas**a**do de m**o**da [deh]
old town (old part of town) el barrio antiguo [b**a**rr-yo ant**ee**gwo]
in the old town en el barrio antiguo
olive la aceituna [asayt**oo**na], la oliva [ol**ee**ba]
black/green olives las aceit**u**nas n**e**gras/verdes [b**ai**rd-es]
olive oil el aceite de oliva [as**ay**teh deh ol**ee**ba]
omelette la tortilla de huevo [tort**ee**-ya deh w**e**bo]
on en
on the street/beach en la c**a**lle/pl**a**ya
is it on this road? ¿est**á** en **e**sta calle?
on the plane en el avi**ó**n
on Saturday el s**á**bado
on television en la t**e**le
I haven't got it on me no lo traigo [trīgo]
this one's on me (drink) **é**sta me t**o**ca a mí [meh]
the light wasn't on la luz no est**a**ba prend**i**da
what's on tonight? ¿qué p**o**nen **e**sta n**o**che? [keh]
once (one time) **u**na vez [bes]
at once (immediately) en seguida [seg**ee**da]
one* uno [**oo**no], **u**na
the white one el bl**a**nco, la bl**a**nca
one-way: a one-way ticket to ... un boleto de ida p**a**ra ... [deh **ee**da]
onion la cebolla [seb**o**-ya]
only s**ó**lo
only one sólo **u**no

it's only 6 o'clock son sólo las seis
I've only just got here acabo de llegar [deh yegar]
on/off switch el interruptor [eentairrooptor]
open (adj) abierto [ab-yairto]
(verb) abrir [abreer]
when do you open? ¿a qué hora abre? [keh ora abreh]
I can't get it open no puedo abrirlo [pwedo]
in the open air al aire libre [īreh leebreh]
opening times el horario [orar-yo]
open ticket el boleto abierto [ab-yairto]
opera la ópera
operation (medical) la operación [opairas-yon]
operator (telephone: man/woman) el operador, la operadora

> For the international operator (for collect calls), dial 09.

opposite: the opposite direction el sentido contrario
the bar opposite el bar de enfrente [deh enfrenteh]
opposite my hotel enfrente de mi hotel
optician el óptico
or o
orange (fruit) la naranja [naranHa]
(colour) (color) naranja
orange juice (fresh) el jugo de naranja [Hoogo deh]
(fizzy, diluted) el refresco de naranja
orchestra la orquesta [orkesta]
order: can we order now? (in restaurant) ¿podemos pedir ya?
I've already ordered, thanks ya pedí, gracias [gras-yas]
I didn't order this no pedí esto
out of order averiado [abair-yado], fuera de servicio [fwaira deh sairbees-yo]
ordinary corriente [korr-yenteh]
other otro
the other one el otro
the other day el otro día
I'm waiting for the others estoy esperando a los demás
do you have any others? ¿tiene otros? [t-yeneh]
otherwise de otra manera [deh – manaira]
our* nuestro [nwestro], nuestra; (pl) nuestros, nuestras
ours* (el) nuestro, (la) nuestra
out: he's out no está
three kilometres out of town a tres kilómetros de la ciudad
outdoors fuera de casa [fwaira deh]
outside ... fuera de ...
can we sit outside? ¿podemos sentarnos fuera?
oven el horno [orno]
over: over here por aquí [akee]

over there por allá [a-**ya**]
over 500 más de quinientos [deh]
it's over se acabó [seh]
overcharge: you've overcharged me me cobró de más [meh – deh]
overcoat el abrigo
overlook: I'd like a room overlooking the courtyard quiero un cuarto que da al patio [k-y**ai**ro oon kw**a**rto keh da]
overnight (travel) toda la noche [n**o**cheh]
overtake adelantarse a [adelant**a**rseh]
owe: how much do I owe you? ¿cuánto le debo? [kw**a**nto leh]
own: my own ... mi propio ... [pr**o**p-yo]
are you on your own? (to a man/woman) ¿está solo/sola?
I'm on my own (said by man/woman) estoy solo/sola
owner (man/woman) el propietario [prop-yet**a**r-yo], la propietaria

P

Pacific Ocean el Océano Pacífico [os**eh**-ano]
pack: a pack of ... un paquete de ... [pak**e**teh deh]
(verb) hacer las maletas [as**air**]
a pack of cigarettes una cajetilla de cigarros [kaHet**ee**-ya deh seeg**a**rros]
package (parcel) el paquete [pak**e**teh]
package holiday el paquete
packed lunch la bolsa con la comida
packet: a packet of cigarettes una cajetilla de cigarros [kaHet**ee**-ya deh seeg**a**rros]
padlock el candado
page (of book) la página [p**a**Heena]
could you page Mr ...? ¿podría llamar al Señor (por altavoz) ...? [yam**a**r – altab**o**s]
pain el dolor
I have a pain here me duele aquí [meh dw**e**leh ak**ee**]
painful doloroso
painkillers los analgésicos [anal**H**eseekos]
paint la pintura
painting el cuadro [kw**a**dro]
pair: a pair of ... un par de ... [deh]
Pakistani (adj) paquistaní [pakeestan**ee**]
palace el palacio [pal**a**s-yo]
pale pálido
pale blue azul claro [as**oo**l]
pan la olla [**o**-ya]
panties (underwear: women's) las bragas, los pantis
pants (underwear: men's) los calzones [kals**o**n-es]
(women's) las bragas
(US: trousers) los pantalones [pantal**o**n-es]
pantyhose las pantimedias

[panteem**e**d-yas]
paper el papel
(newspaper) el periódico [pair-y**o**deeko]
a piece of paper un pedazo de papel [ped**a**so deh]
paper handkerchiefs los klínex®
parcel el paquete [pak**e**teh]
pardon (me)? (didn't understand/hear) ¿mande? [m**a**ndeh]
parents: my parents mis padres [p**a**d-res]
parents-in-law los suegros [sw**e**gros]
park el parque [p**a**rkeh]
(verb) estacionar [estas-yon**a**r]
can I park here? ¿puedo estacionarme aquí? [pw**e**do estas-yon**a**rmeh ak**ee**]

parking
Parking restrictions in cities are complicated and foreigners are easy pickings for traffic police, who usually remove one or both licence plates in lieu of giving a ticket (retrieving them can be an expensive and time-consuming business). Since theft is a real threat, it's worth paying extra for a hotel with secure parking. There are now increasing numbers of multi-storey car parks (**estacionamientos**), often under or around the central square. Here your car will be fairly secure, though it is wise to leave nothing inside it.

parking lot el estacionamiento [estas-yonam-y**e**nto]
part la parte [p**a**rteh]
partner (boyfriend, girlfriend etc) el compañero [kompan-y**ai**ro], la compañera
party (group) el grupo
(political) el partido
(celebration) la fiesta
pass (in mountains) el paso
passenger (man/woman) el pasajero [pasaH**ai**ro], la pasajera
passport el pasaporte [pasap**o**rteh]

Citizens of most Western countries (France and South Africa are exceptions) do not require a visa to enter Mexico as tourists for less than 90 days. What they do need is a valid passport and a tourist card (or **FMT – Folleto de Migración Turística**). Tourist cards are free and, if flying direct, you should be able to pick one up on the plane, through a travel agent or at a Mexican consulate. It is preferable to obtain a card in advance as it may be difficult to get one from border officials. Don't lose the blue copy of your tourist card, given back to you after immigration inspection. You are legally required to carry it at all times and must hand it in when leaving Mexico.

past*: **in the past** antiguamente [anteegwamenteh]
just past the information office justo después de la oficina de información [Hoosto despwes deh]
path el camino
pattern el dibujo [deebooHo]
pavement la acera [asaira]
on the pavement en la acera
pavement café el café terraza [kafeh terrasa]
pay (verb) pagar
can I pay, please? me pasa la cuenta, por favor [meh – kwenta por fabor]
it's already paid for ya está pagado

•••••• DIALOGUE ••••••

who's paying? ¿quién paga? [k-yen]
I'll pay pago yo
no, you paid last time, I'll pay no, Usted pagó la última vez, pago yo [oosteh – oolteema bes]

pay phone el teléfono público [poobleeko], la caseta telefónica
peaceful tranquilo [trankeelo]
peach el durazno [doorasno]
peanuts los cacahuates [kakawat-es]
pear la pera [paira]
peas los chícharos [cheecharos]
peculiar extraño [ekstran-yo]
pedestrian crossing el paso de peatones [peh-aton-es]
pedestrian precinct la calle peatonal [ka-yeh peh-atonal]
peg (for washing) la pinza [peensa]
(for tent) la estaca
pen la pluma [plooma]
pencil el lápiz [lapees]
penfriend (male/female) el amigo/la amiga por correspondencia [korrespondens-ya]
penicillin la penicilina [peneeseeleena]
penknife la navaja [nabaHa]
pensioner el jubilado [Hoobeelado], la jubilada
people la gente [Henteh]
the other people in the hotel los otros huéspedes en el hotel [wesped-es]
too many people demasiada gente [demas-yada]
pepper (spice) la pimienta [peem-yenta]
(vegetable) el pimiento
peppermint (sweet) el dulce de menta [doolseh deh]
per: **per night** por noche [nocheh]
how much per day? ¿cuánto es por día? [kwanto]
per cent por ciento [s-yento]
perfect perfecto [pairfekto]
perfume el perfume [pairfoomeh]
perhaps quizás [keesas]
perhaps not quizás no
period (of time) el período [pairee-odo]
(menstruation) la regla

perm la permanente [pairmanenteh]
permit el permiso [pairmeeso]
person la persona [pairsona]
personal stereo el walkman® [wolkman]
Peruvian (adj) peruano [peroo-ano]
petrol la gasolina

> Petrol can be a problem: the government oil company Pemex has a monopoly and sells two types of petrol: **nova** (leaded) and **magna sin** (unleaded) which cost about the same as regular unleaded north of the border. Often, however, **nova** is the only type available; it's very dirty and is quick to foul up any car with a highly-tuned engine or anything designed to run on unleaded petrol. Two new brands called **nova plus** and **extra plus** have been introduced but are not easy to come by. **Diesel** is also available.

petrol can la lata de gasolina [deh]
petrol station la gasolinera [gasoleenaira]
pharmacy la farmacia [far-mas-ya]

> For minor medical problems, head for the green cross and the **farmacia** signs. Pharmacists are usually knowledgeable and helpful, and many also speak some English. They can sell medicines over the counter which would only be available on prescription at home.

phone el teléfono
(verb) llamar por teléfono [yamar]

> Local phone calls are cheap, and most hotels will let you call locally for free. Coin-operated phones, even those that seem to be in a terrible state, usually work for local calls. Internal long-distance calls can be made from any reasonably new coin-operated phone, but these are far more expensive. Public phones are blue for long-distance, or orange for local (and operator-connected) calls only. On both, you lift the receiver, insert coins (check for the dialling tone: some have a button to get the tone) then dial. Some take phonecards, available from telephone offices and stores near the phones that use them. Currently there are two types of card, which won't work in the same telephones. Many newer phones say they accept credit cards but in practice they usually don't. Slightly more expensive and reliable are **casetas telefónicas**. They can →

be simply shops or bars with public phones, indicated by a sign outside, or they can be specialist phone and fax places displaying a blue and white **Larga Distancia** sign. **Casetas telefónicas** are also found at almost every bus station and airport. You're connected by an operator, who gives you the bill afterwards. Wherever you make them from, international calls are very expensive, particularly from hotels. The least bad rates are from public call boxes using a phonecard. You may prefer to call collect (**por cobrar**), which you can do from any public phone by dialling the international operator (09), or have a calling card that offers service from Mexico.

phone book la guía telefónica [gee-a]
phone box la caseta telefónica
phonecard la tarjeta de teléfono [tarHeta deh]
phone number el número de teléfono [noomairo deh]
photo la foto
excuse me, could you take a photo of us? ¿le importaría sacarnos una foto? [leh]
phrasebook el libro de frases [deh fras-es]
piano el piano [p-yano]
pickpocket el/la carterista [kartaireesta]
pick up: will you come and pick me up? ¿pasarás a recogerme? [rekoHairmeh]
picnic el picnic
picture el cuadro [kwadro]
pie (meat) la empanada
(fruit) la tarta
piece el pedazo [pedaso]
a piece of ... un pedazo de ... [deh]
pig el chancho, el cerdo [sairdo]
pill la píldora
I'm on the pill estoy tomando la píldora
pillow la almohada [almo-ada]
pillow case la funda (de almohada) [foonda (deh)]
pin el alfiler [alfeelair]
pineapple la piña [peen-ya]
pineapple juice el jugo de piña [Hoogo deh]
pink rosa
pipe (for smoking) la pipa [peepa]
(for water) el tubo [toobo]
pipe cleaners los limpiapipas [leemp-yapeepas]
pity: it's a pity! ¡qué pena! [keh]
pizza la pizza
place el lugar [loogar]
at your place en tu casa
at his place en su casa
plain el llano [yano]
(not patterned) liso

plane el avión [ab-y**o**n]
by plane en avión
plant la pl**a**nta
plaster cast la escayola [eskī-y**o**la]
plasters las tir**i**tas
plastic pl**á**stico
(credit cards) las tarjetas de crédito [tarHetas deh kr**e**deeto]
plastic bag la b**o**lsa de plástico
plate el pl**a**to
platform la vía [b**ee**-a]
which platform is it for Puebla, please? ¿de qué vía sale el tren para Puebla, por favor? [deh keh b**ee**-a s**a**leh – pw**e**bla por fab**o**r]
play (in theatre) la **o**bra
(verb) jugar [Hoog**a**r]
(instrument) toc**a**r
playground el patio de recreo [p**a**t-yo deh rekr**eh**-o]
pleasant agradable [agrad**a**bleh]
please por favor [fab**o**r]
yes please sí, por favor
could you please ...? ¿podría hacer el favor de ...? [as**air** – deh]
please don't no, por favor
pleased: pleased to meet you (said by man/woman) encant**a**do/encant**a**da de conocerle [deh konos**air**leh]
pleasure: my pleasure es un gusto [g**oo**sto]
plenty: plenty of ... mucho ... [m**oo**cho]
there's plenty of time ten**e**mos mucho tiempo [t-y**e**mpo]
that's plenty, thanks es suficiente, gracias [soofees-y**e**nteh gr**a**s-yas]
pliers los alicates [aleek**a**t-es]
plug (electrical) el enchufe [ench**oo**feh]
(for car) la bujía [booH**ee**-a]
(in sink) el tap**ó**n
plumber el plomero [plom**ai**ro]
p.m. de la tarde [deh la t**a**rdeh]
poached egg el huevo escalf**a**do [w**e**bo]
pocket el bolsillo [bols**ee**-yo]
point: two point five dos c**o**ma c**i**nco
there's no point no vale la pena [b**a**leh]
points (in car) los plat**i**nos
poisonous venenoso [benen**o**so]
police la policía [polees**ee**-a]
call the police! ¡llame a la policía! [y**a**meh]

Mexican police are no better or worse than any others, but they are very badly paid and it is quite usual to have to bribe or tip them. It is common to be accused of some minor traffic violation and be asked to pay an on-the-spot fine. Sometimes these are open to negotiation. These small bribes are known as **mordidas** and they may also be extracted by border officials or bureaucrats. In general, if the amount is small, it's better to pay up and avoid any direct →

confrontation, particularly with the police. More common than the **mordida** is the **propina** (tip), a payment that is made on your initiative. There is no need to do this but often it helps to speed bureaucracy. In the event of an emergency, phone 06 for the police.

policeman el (agente de) policía [aHenteh deh]
police station la comisaría de policía
policewoman la policía
polish el betún [betoon]
polite educado [edookado]

politics
There's plenty of political discussion in Mexico, but unless you're sure you know who you're talking to, it's safest to keep your opinions guarded. Praising the bravery of the opposition in the presence of a local PRI bigwig just could land you in trouble. And almost anywhere, ciriticism of the country by a local is fine, but if it's an outsider talking even the most jaded of Mexicans is likely to find a core of outraged patriotism.

polluted contaminado
pony el poney
pool (for swimming) la alberca [albairka]
poor (not rich) pobre [pobreh]
(quality) de baja calidad [deh baHa kaleeda]
pop music la música pop [mooseeka]
pop singer el/la cantante de música pop [kantanteh deh]
population la población [poblas-yon]
pork la carne de chancho [karneh deh chancho]
port (for boats) el puerto [pwairto]
(drink) el Oporto
porter (in hotel) el portero [portairo]
portrait el retrato
posh (restaurant) de lujo [deh looHo]
possible posible [poseebleh]
is it possible to ...? ¿es posible ...?
as ... as possible lo más ... posible
post (mail) el correo [korreh-o]
(verb) echar al correo
could you post this for me? ¿podría echarme esto al correo? [echarmeh]

postal service
Mexican postal services are reasonably efficient. Airmail to Mexico should arrive within a few days, but may take a couple of weeks to get anywhere remote. Post offices are open →

Monday to Friday 9 a.m. to 6 p.m. and Saturday 9 a.m. to noon. Poste restante letters should be addressed to **Lista de Correos** at the **Correo Central** (the main post office in any town). All mail that arrives is displayed on a list updated daily, but held for two weeks only. Anything sent abroad by airmail should have an airmail stamp (**por avión**) on it or it is liable to go surface. Sending packages and parcels out of the country is difficult and regulations vary. Take your parcel and its contents (unsealed) to any post office and they'll set you on your way. Many stores will send parcels for you, which is a great deal easier.

postbox el buzón [booso**n**]
postcard la postal [pos-t**a**l]
postcode el código postal
poster el póster [p**o**stair], el cartel
poste restante la lista de Correos [l**ee**sta deh korr**eh**-os]
post office el correo [korr**eh**-o]
potato la papa
potato chips (US) las patatas fritas (de bolsa) [deh]
pots and pans los cacharros de cocina [deh kos**ee**na], las ollas [**o**-yas]
pottery (objects) la cerámica [sair**a**meeka]
pound* (money, weight) la libra
power cut el apagón
power point la toma de corriente [deh korr-y**e**nteh]
practise: I want to practise my Spanish quiero practicar el español [k-y**ai**ro – espan-y**o**l]
prawns las gambas
prefer: I prefer ... prefiero ... [pref-y**ai**ro]
pregnant embarazada [embaras**a**da]
prescription (for chemist) la receta [res**e**ta]
see **pharmacy**
present (gift) el regalo
president (of country) el/la presidente [preseed**e**nteh]
pretty lindo
it's pretty expensive es bastante caro [bast**a**nteh]
price el precio [pr**e**s-yo]
priest el sacerdote [sasaird**o**teh]
prime minister (man/woman) el primer ministro [preem**ai**r], la primera ministra
printed matter los impresos
priority (in driving) la preferencia [prefair**e**ns-ya]
prison la cárcel [k**a**rsel]
private privado [preeb**a**do], particular [parteekool**a**r]
private bathroom el baño privado [b**a**n-yo]
probably probablemente [prob**a**bleh-m**e**nteh]
problem el problema
no problem! ¡con mucho gusto! [m**oo**cho g**oo**sto]

program(me) el programa
promise: I promise lo prometo
pronounce: how is this pronounced? ¿cómo se pronuncia esto? [seh pronoons-ya]
properly (repaired, locked etc) bien [b-yen]
protection factor (of suntan lotion) el factor de protección [deh proteks-yon]
Protestant (adj) protestante [protestanteh]
public convenience los servicios públicos [sairbees-yos poobleekos]
public holiday el día feriado [dee-a fer-yado]
pudding (dessert) el postre [postreh]
pull jalar [Halar]
pullover el suéter [swetair]
puncture la ponchadura
purple morado
purse (for money) el monedero [monedairo]
(US: handbag) el bolso
push empujar [empoo-Har]
pushchair la sillita de ruedas [see-yeeta deh rwedas]
put poner [ponair]
where can I put ...? ¿dónde pongo ...? [dondeh]
could you put us up for the night? ¿podría alojarnos esta noche? [aloHarnos – nocheh]
pyjamas el pijama [peeHama]
pyramid la pirámide [peerameedeh]

Q

quality la calidad [kaleeda]
(personal) la cualidad [kwaleeda]
quarantine la cuarentena [kwarentena]
quarter la cuarta parte [kwarta parteh]
quayside: on the quayside en el muelle [mweh-yeh]
question la pregunta [pregoonta]
queue la cola
quick rápido [rapeedo]
that was quick sí que ha sido rápido [keh a]
what's the quickest way there? ¿cuál es el camino más directo? [kwal – deerekto]
fancy a quick drink? ¿se te antoja una copa? [seh teh antoHa]
quickly rápidamente [rapeedamenteh]
quiet (place, hotel) tranquilo [trankeelo]
(person) callado [ka-yado]
quiet! ¡cállese! [ka-yeseh]
quite (fairly) bastante [bastanteh]
(very) muy [mwee]
that's quite right eso es cierto [s-yairto]
quite a lot bastante

R

rabbit el conejo [kon**e**Ho]
race (for runners, cars) la carrera [karr**ai**ra]
racket (tennis etc) la raqueta [rak**e**ta]
radiator (of car, in room) el radiador [rad-yad**o**r]
radio la radio [r**a**d-yo]
on the radio por radio
raft la b**a**lsa
rail: by rail en tren
railway el ferrocarr**i**l
rain la lluvia [y**oo**b-ya]
in the rain bajo la lluvia [b**a**Ho]
it's raining est**á** lloviendo [yob-y**e**ndo]
raincoat el impermeable [eempairmeh-**a**bleh]
rape la violación [b-yolas-y**o**n]
rare (uncommon) p**o**co com**ú**n
(steak) (muy) p**o**co hecho [mwee – **e**cho]
rash (on skin) la erupción cutánea [airoops-y**o**n koot**a**neh-a]
raspberry la frambuesa [frambw**e**sa]
rat la r**a**ta
rate (for changing money) el tipo de cambio [t**ee**po deh k**a**mb-yo]
rather: it's rather good es bastante bueno [bast**a**nteh bw**e**no]
I'd rather ... prefiero ... [pref-y**ai**ro]
razor la maquinilla de afeitar [makeen**ee**-ya deh afayt**a**r]
(electric) la máquina de afeitar eléctrica [m**a**keena]
razor blades las hojas de afeitar [**o**Has]
read leer [leh-**air**]
ready prepar**a**do
are you ready? (to man/woman) ¿est**á**s l**i**sto/l**i**sta?
I'm not ready yet (said by man/woman) aún no est**oy** listo/lista [a-**oo**n]

•••••• DIALOGUE ••••••

when will it be ready? ¿cuándo estar**á** listo? [kw**a**ndo]
it should be ready in a couple of days estará listo en un par de días

real verdadero [bairdad**ai**ro], auténtico [owt**e**nteeko]
really realmente [reh-alm**e**nteh]
that's really great eso es estup**e**ndo
really? (doubt) ¿no puede ser? [pw**e**deh s**air**]
(polite interest) ¿de veras? [deh b**ai**ras]
rear lights las calaveras [kalab**ai**ras]
rearview mirror el (espejo) retrovisor [esp**e**Ho retrobees**o**r]
reasonable (prices etc) mod**e**sto
receipt el recibo [res**ee**bo]

It is wise to ask for a receipt (**un recibo**) for any goods that you buy, especially mechanical or electrical items, since you may be asked for them by Customs officials. Remember to keep receipts for fairly new items such as cameras that you have brought into the country with you.

recently recientemente [res-yentem**e**nteh], recién [res-y**e**n]
reception la recepción [reseps-y**o**n]
at reception en la recepción
reception desk la recepción
receptionist el/la recepcionista [reseps-yon**ee**sta]
recognize reconocer [rekonos**air**]
recommend: could you recommend ...? ¿puede Usted recomendar ...? [pw**e**deh oost**eh**]
record (music) el disco [d**ee**sko]
red rojo [r**o**Ho]
red wine el vino tinto [b**ee**no t**ee**nto]
refund la devolución [deboloos-y**o**n]
can I have a refund? ¿puede devolverme el dinero? [pw**e**deh debolb**air**meh el deen**air**o]
region la zona [s**o**na], la región [reH-y**o**n]
registered: by registered mail por correo certificado [korr**eh**-o sairteefeek**a**do]
registration number el número de placa [n**oo**mairo deh]
relatives los parientes [par-y**e**nt-es]
religion la religión [releeH-y**o**n]
remember: I don't remember no recuerdo [rekw**air**do]
I remember recuerdo
do you remember? ¿recuerda?
rent (for apartment etc) la renta, el arriendo [arr-y**e**ndo]
(verb) rentar, arrendar, alquilar [alkeel**a**r]
to/for rent se alquila [seh alk**ee**la]

•••••• DIALOGUE ••••••

I'd like to rent a car quisiera rentar un carro [kees-y**ai**ra]
for how long? ¿por cuánto tiempo? [kw**a**nto t-y**e**mpo]
two days dos días
this is our range ésta es nuestra selección [nw**e**stra seleks-y**o**n]
I'll take the ... me quedo con el ... [meh k**e**do]
is that with unlimited mileage? ¿es con kilometraje ilimitado? [keelometr**a**Heh]
it is sí
can I see your licence please? ¿me deja ver su carnet, por favor? [meh d**eh**-Ha bair soo karn**eh** por fab**o**r]
and your passport y su pasaporte [ee soo pasap**o**rteh]

is insurance included? ¿va incluido el seguro? [ba eenkloo-**ee**do]
yes, but you pay the first 50,000 pesos sí, pero Usted paga los primeros cincuenta mil pesos [p**ai**ro oost**eh** p**a**ga los preem**ai**ros]
can you leave a deposit of ...? ¿puede dejar un enganche de ...? [pw**e**deh deh-H**a**r oon eng**a**ncheh deh]

rented car el carro rentado
repair (verb) arreglar
can you repair it? ¿puede arreglarlo? [pw**e**deh]
repeat repetir
could you repeat that? ¿puede repetir eso? [pw**e**deh]
reservation la reservación [resairbas-y**o**n]
I'd like to make a reservation quisiera hacer reservación [kees-y**ai**ra as**ai**r]

•••••• DIALOGUE ••••••

I have a reservation tengo cuarto reservado [kw**a**rto resairb**a**do]
yes sir, what name please? sí, señor, ¿a nombre de quién, por favor? [sen-y**o**r a n**o**mbreh deh k-y**e**n por fab**o**r]

reserve reservar [resairb**a**r]

•••••• DIALOGUE ••••••

can I reserve a table for tonight? ¿puedo reservar una mesa para esta noche? [pw**e**do – n**o**cheh]
yes madam, for how many people? sí, señora, ¿para cuántos? [sen-y**o**ra – kw**a**ntos]
for two para dos
and for what time? ¿y para qué hora? [ee p**a**ra keh **o**ra]
for eight o'clock para las ocho
and could I have your name please? ¿me deja su nombre, por favor? [meh d**eh**-Ha soo n**o**mbreh por fab**o**r]
see **alphabet** for spelling

rest: I need a rest necesito un descanso [neses**ee**to]
the rest of the group el resto del grupo [gr**oo**po]
restaurant el restaurante [restowr**a**nteh]

Basic meals are served at **restaurantes**, but you can get breakfast, snacks and often full meals at **cafeterías** too. There are take-out and fast-food places serving sandwiches, **tortas** (filled rolls), and **tacos** (soft, rolled **tortillas** with a filling) as well as more international-style food. In addition you'll find establishments serving nothing but fruit drinks (**licuados**) and fruit salads (usually identified by a sign saying **Jugos y Licuados**), and street stalls dishing out everything from **tacos** to orange juice to ready-made crisp vegetable salads sprinkled with chilli, salt and lime. Just about every market in the country has a cooked food section too, and these are invariably the →

cheapest places to eat. In the big cities and resorts, of course, there are international restaurants too: pizzas and Chinese food are ubiquitous.

You can eat a full meal in a restaurant at any time of day, but you'd do well to adopt the local habit of taking your main meal at lunchtime, since this is when **comidas corridas** (set meals, varied daily) are served, from around 1-5 p.m. You can find these in the cheaper **cocina económica** or **comedor** where it is likely to be all that is available. In more expensive places, the same thing may be known as the **menú del día** or **menú turístico** and you may have to ask for it specifically.

restaurant car el coche-comedor [k**o**cheh komed**o**r]
rest room el baño [b**a**n-yo], los servicios [sairb**ee**s-yos]
see **toilet**
retired: I'm retired est**o**y jubilado/jubil**a**da [Hoobeel**a**do]
return (ticket) el boleto de ida y vuelta [deh **ee**da ee bw**e**lta]
see **ticket**
reverse charge call la llamada por cobr**a**r [yam**a**da]
reverse gear la m**a**rcha atr**á**s
revolting asqueroso [askair**o**so]
rib la costilla [kost**ee**-ya]
rice el arroz [arr**o**s]
rich rico [r**ee**ko]
ridiculous ridículo [reed**ee**koolo]
right (correct) corr**e**cto
(not left) der**e**cho
you were right ten**í**a razón [ras**o**n]
that's right es cierto [s-y**ai**rto]
this can't be right **e**sto no puede ser [pw**e**deh sair]
right! ¡bueno! [bw**e**no]
is this the right road for ...? ¿es éste el cam**i**no p**a**ra ...? [**e**steh]
on the right a la der**e**cha
turn right dé vuelta a la derecha [deh bw**e**lta]
right-hand drive con el volante a la derecha [bol**a**nteh]
ring (on finger) el anillo [an**ee**-yo]
I'll ring you te llamaré [teh yamar**eh**]
ring back volver a llamar [bolb**ai**r a yam**a**r]
ripe (fruit) mad**u**ro
rip-off: it's a rip-off es **u**na est**a**fa
rip-off prices los precios exagerados [pr**e**s-yos eksaHair**a**dos]
risky arriesgado [arr-yesg**a**do]
river el r**í**o
road la carretera [karret**ai**ra]
is this the road for ...? ¿es **é**sta la carretera p**a**ra ...?
down the road calle abajo [k**a**-yeh ab**a**Ho]
road accident el accidente de tr**á**nsito [akseed**e**nteh deh]

road map el m**a**pa de carreter**a**s
roadsign la señal de tr**á**fico [sen-y**a**l deh]
rob: I've been robbed! ¡me rob**a**ron! [meh]
rock la r**o**ca
(music) el rock
on the rocks (with ice) con hielo [y**e**lo]
rodeo la charreada [charreh-**a**da]
roll (bread) el bolillo [bol**ee**-yo]
roof el tejado [teH**a**do]
roof rack la b**a**ca
room el cuarto [kw**a**rto]
in my room en mi cuarto

•••••• DIALOGUE ••••••

do you have any rooms? ¿tiene cuarto? [t-y**e**neh]
for how many people? ¿p**a**ra cuántas personas? [kw**a**ntas pairs**o**nas]
for one/for two para **u**no/dos
yes, we have rooms free sí, ten**e**mos cuartos libres [l**ee**b-res]
for how many nights will it be? ¿p**a**ra cuántas noches? [n**o**ch-es]
just for one night para **u**na noche sólo [n**o**cheh]
how much is it? ¿cuánto es? [kw**a**nto]
... with bathroom and ... without bathroom ... con baño y ... sin baño [b**a**n-yo ee ... seen]
can I see a room with bathroom? ¿me enseña un cuarto con baño? [meh ens**e**n-ya]
OK, I'll take it me lo quedo [meh lo k**e**do]

room service el servicio de cuarto [sairb**ee**s-yo deh]
rope la cuerda [kw**ai**rda]
rosé (wine) el vino ros**a**do [b**ee**no]
roughly (approximately) approximadamente [–m**e**nteh]
round: it's my round me t**o**ca [meh]
roundabout (for traffic) la glorieta [glor-y**e**ta]
round trip ticket el bol**e**to de ida y vuelta [deh **ee**da ee bw**e**lta]
see **ticket**
route la ruta [r**oo**ta]
what's the best route? ¿cuál es la mejor ruta? [kw**a**l es la meH**o**r]
rubber (material) el hule [**oo**leh]
(eraser) la g**o**ma de borr**a**r
rubber band la gom**i**ta
rubbish (waste) la bas**u**ra
(poor quality goods) las porquerías [porkair**ee**-as]
rubbish! (nonsense) ¡babosadas!
rucksack la moch**i**la
rude grosero [gros**ai**ro]
rug (mat) la alf**o**mbra, el tapete [tap**e**teh]
(blanket) la cobija [kob**ee**Ha], la m**a**nta, la fraz**a**da [fras**a**da]
ruins las ruinas [rw**ee**nas]
rum el ron

rum and Coke® la cub**a**ta (de ron)
run (verb: person) correr [korr**air**]
how often do the buses run? ¿c**a**da cuánto p**a**san los cami**o**nes? [kwanto]
I've run out of money se me acab**ó** el dinero [seh meh – deen**air**o]
rush hour la hora p**i**co [**o**ra]

S

sad triste [tr**ee**steh]
saddle (for horse) la silla de mont**a**r [s**ee**-ya deh]
(on bike) el sillín [see-y**ee**n]
safe seguro [seg**oo**ro]
safety pin el seguro
sail la vela [b**e**la]
sailboard el windsurf
sailboarding el windsurf
salad la ensal**a**da
salad dressing el aliño p**a**ra la ensalada [al**ee**n-yo]
sale: for sale se vende [seh b**e**ndeh]
salmon el salmón [sal-m**o**n]
salt la sal
same: the same el m**i**smo, la m**i**sma
the same as this igual a **é**ste [eegw**a**l a **e**steh]
the same again, please **o**tro igual, por favor [fab**o**r]
it's all the same to me me da igual [meh]
sand la arena [ar**eh**-na]
sandals los guaraches [war**a**ch-es]
sandwich el sandwich [s**a**ndweech], la t**o**rta
sanitary napkin/towel la compr**e**sa
sardines las sard**i**nas
Saturday s**á**bado
sauce la s**a**lsa
saucepan la olla [**o**-ya]
saucer el platillo [plat**ee**-yo]
sauna la sauna [s**ow**na]
sausage la salch**i**cha
say: how do you say ... in Spanish? ¿c**ó**mo se dice ... en español? [seh d**ee**seh en espan-y**o**l]
what did he say? ¿qué dijo? [keh d**ee**Ho]
I said ... dije ... [d**ee**Heh]
he said ... dijo ...
could you say that again? ¿podría repet**i**rlo?
scarf (for neck) la buf**a**nda
(for head) el pañuelo [pan-yw**e**lo]
scenery el paisaje [pīs**a**Heh]
schedule (US) el horario [or**ar**-yo]
scheduled flight el vuelo regular [bw**e**lo regool**ar**]
school la escuela [eskw**e**la]
scissors: a pair of scissors las tijeras [teeH**ai**ras]
scotch el wh**i**sky
Scotch tape® el scotch, el D**u**rex®
Scotland Escocia [esk**o**s-ya]
Scottish escocés [eskos-**e**s]
I'm Scottish (man/woman) soy

escocés/escocesa
scrambled eggs los huevos revueltos [webos rebweltos]
scratch el rasguño [rasgoon-yo]
scream chillar [chee-yar]
screw el tornillo [tornee-yo]
screwdriver el destornillador [destornee-yador]
sea el mar
  by the sea junto al mar [Hoonto]
seafood los mariscos
seafood restaurant la marisquería [mareeskairee-a]
seafront el paseo marítimo [paseh-o mareeteemo]
  on the seafront en la playa [plī-ya]
seagull la gaviota [gab-yota]
search for (verb) buscar
seashell la concha marina
seasick: I feel seasick (said by man/woman) estoy mareado/mareada [mareh-ado]
  I get seasick me mareo [meh mareh-o]
seaside: by the seaside en la playa [plī-ya]
seat el asiento [as-yento]
  is this seat taken? ¿está ocupado este asiento? [esteh]
seat belt el cinturón de seguridad [seentooron deh segooreeda]
sea urchin el erizo de mar [aireeso]
seaweed el alga
secluded apartado
second (adj) segundo
  (of time) el segundo
  just a second! ¡un momentito!
second class (travel) de segunda clase [segoonda klaseh]
secondhand usado [oosado]
see ver [bair]
  can I see? ¿puedo ver? [pwedo]
  have you seen ...? ¿ha visto ...? [a beesto]
  I saw him this morning lo vi esta mañana [bee]
  see you! ¡hasta luego! [asta lwego]
  I see (I understand) entiendo [ent-yendo]
self-service autoservicio [owtosairbees-yo]
sell vender [bendair]
  do you sell ...? ¿vende ...? [bendeh]
Sellotape® el scotch, el Durex®
send enviar [emb-yar], mandar
  I want to send this to England quiero enviar esto a Inglaterra [k-yairo]
senior citizen el jubilado, [Hoobeelado], la jubilada
separate separado
  a separate room un cuarto aparte [aparteh]
separated: I'm separated (said by man/woman) estoy separado/separada
separately (pay, travel) por separado

September septiembre [set-yembreh]
septic séptico
serious serio [sair-yo]
(illness) grave [grabeh]
service charge el servicio [sairbees-yo]
service station la estación de servicio [estas-yon deh]
serviette la servilleta [sairbee-yeta]
set menu el menú [menoo], la comida corrida
several varios [bar-yos]
sew coser [kosair]
could you sew this back on? ¿podría coserme esto? [kosairmeh]
sex el sexo
sexy sexy
shade: in the shade a la sombra
shallow (water) poco profundo
shame: what a shame! ¡que pena! [keh]
shampoo el champú
a shampoo and set un lavado y marcado [labado ee]
share (verb) compartir
sharp (knife) afilado
(taste) ácido [aseedo]
(pain) agudo
shattered (very tired) agotado
shaver la máquina de afeitar [makeena deh afaytar]
shaving foam la espuma de afeitar
shaving point el enchufe (para la máquina de afeitar) [enchoofeh – makeena]
shawl el rebozo [reboso]
she* ella [eh-ya]
is she here? ¿está (ella) aquí? [akee]
sheet (for bed) la sábana
shelf la estantería [estantairee-a]
shellfish los mariscos
sherry el jerez [Her-es]
ship el barco
by ship en barco
shirt la camisa
shit! ¡mierda! [m-yairda]
shock el susto
I got an electric shock me dio un choque eléctrico [meh – chokeh]
shock-absorber el amortiguador [amorteegwador]
shocking chocante [chokanteh]
shoes los zapatos [sapatos]
a pair of shoes un par de zapatos [deh]
shoelaces las agujetas [a-ooHetas]
shoe polish el betún
shoe repairer's la zapatería [sapatairee-a]
shop la tienda [t-yenda]

It's difficult to generalize about opening hours in Mexico. Shops tend to keep long hours, say from 9 a.m. to 8 p.m., though some places still close for a **siesta**, usually between 1 and 3 p.m., but sometimes longer.

shopping: I'm going shopping voy de **c**o**mpras** [boy deh]
shopping centre el centro comercial [s**e**ntro komairs-y**a**l]
shop window el escaparate [eskapar**a**teh]
shore la orilla [or**ee**-ya]
short (time, journey) c**o**rto
(person) bajo [b**a**Ho]
it's only a short distance queda bastante cerca [k**e**da bast**a**nteh s**ai**rka]
shortcut el atajo [at**a**Ho]
shorts los pantalones cortos [pantal**o**n-es]
should: what should I do? ¿que hago? [keh **a**go]
he shouldn't be long no debe tardar [d**e**beh]
you should have told me me lo hubieras dicho [meh oob-y**ai**ras]
shoulder el hombro [**o**mbro]
shout (verb) gritar
show (in theatre) el espectáculo [espekt**a**koolo]
could you show me? ¿me lo enseña? [meh lo ens**e**n-ya]
shower (in bathroom) la regadera [regad**ai**ra]
(of rain) el chubasco [choob**a**sko]
with shower con baño [b**a**n-yo]
shower gel el gel de baño [Hel deh]
shut (verb) cerrar [sairr**a**r]
when do you shut? ¿a qué hora cierran? [keh **o**ra s-y**ai**rran]
when do they shut? ¿a qué hora cierran?
they're shut está cerrado [sairr**a**do]
I've shut myself out cerré y dejé la llave dentro [sairr**eh** ee deh-H**eh** la y**a**beh]
shut up! ¡cállese! [k**a**-yeseh]
shutter (on camera) el obturador
(on window) la contraventana [kontrabent**a**na]
shy tímido [t**ee**meedo]
sick (ill) enfermo [enf**ai**rmo]
I'm going to be sick (vomit) voy a devolver [boy a debolb**ai**r]
side el lado
the other side of town al otro lado de la ciudad [deh la s-yood**a**]
sidelights los pilotos, las calaveras [kalab**ai**ras]
side salad la ensalada aparte [ap**a**rteh]
side street la callejuela [ka-yeh-Hw**e**la]
sidewalk la banqueta [bank**e**ta]
sight: the sights of ... los lugares de interés de ... [loog**a**r-es deh eentair-**e**s]
sightseeing: we're going sightseeing vamos a hacer un recorrido turístico [b**a**mos a as**air** oon]
sightseeing tour el recorrido turístico
sign (notice) el letrero [letr**ai**ro]
(roadsign) la señal de tráfico [sen-y**a**l deh]

signal: he didn't give a signal no hizo ninguna señal [**ee**so]
signature la firma [f**ee**rma]
signpost el letrero [letr**ai**ro]
silence el silencio [seel**e**ns-yo]
silk la seda
silly tonto
silver la plata
silver foil el papel de aluminio [aloom**ee**n-yo]
similar parecido [pares**ee**do]
simple (easy) sencillo [sens**ee**-yo]
since: since yesterday desde ayer [d**e**sdeh ī-y**ai**r]
since I got here desde que llegamos aquí [keh yeg**a**mos ak**ee**]
sing cantar
singer el/la cantante [kant**a**nteh]
single: a single to ... un boleto de ida para ... [deh **ee**da]
I'm single (said by man/woman) soy soltero/soltera [solt**ai**ro]
single bed la cama individual [eendeebeedw**a**l]
single room el cuarto individual [kw**a**rto]
single ticket el boleto de ida [deh **ee**da]
sink (in kitchen) el fregadero [fregad**ai**ro]
sister la hermana [airm**a**na]
sister-in-law la cuñada [koon-y**a**da]
sit: can I sit here? ¿puedo sentarme aquí? [pw**e**do sent**a**rmeh ak**ee**]
is anyone sitting here? ¿está ocupado este asiento? [**e**steh as-y**e**nto]
sit down sentarse [sent**a**rseh]
sit down! ¡siéntese! [s-y**e**nteseh]
size el tamaño [tam**a**n-yo]
(of clothes) la talla [t**a**-ya]
skin la piel [p-yel]
skin-diving el buceo [boos**eh**-o]
skinny flaco
skirt la falda
sky el cielo [s-y**e**lo]
sleep (verb) dormir
did you sleep well? ¿dormiste bien? [dorm**ee**steh b-yen]
I need a good sleep necesito dormir bien [neses**ee**to]
sleeper (on train) el coche-cama [k**o**cheh k**a**ma]
sleeping bag la bolsa de dormir [deh]
sleeping car el coche-cama [k**o**cheh-k**a**ma]
sleeping pill la pastilla para dormir [past**ee**-ya]
sleepy: I'm feeling sleepy tengo sueño [sw**e**n-yo]
sleeve la manga
slide (photographic) la diapositiva [d-yaposeet**ee**ba]
slip (under dress) la funda [f**oo**nda]
slippery resbaladizo [resbalad**ee**so]
slow lento
slow down! ¡cálmese! [k**a**lmeseh]
slowly: could you say it slowly?

¿podría decirlo despacio? [deseerlo despas-yo]
very slowly muy lento [mwee]
small chico
smell: it smells! (smells bad) ¡apesta!
smile (verb) sonreir [sonreh-eer]
smoke el humo [oomo]
do you mind if I smoke? ¿le importa que fume? [leh – keh foomeh]
I don't smoke no fumo
do you smoke? ¿fuma?
snack la comida ligera [leeHaira]
snake la culebra, la víbora [beebora]
sneeze (verb) estornudar
snorkel el tubo de buceo [toobo deh booseh-o]
snow la nieve [n-yebeh]
it's snowing está nevando [nebando]
so: it's so good es tan bueno [bweno]
not so fast no tan de prisa [deh preesa]
so am I yo también [tamb-yen]
so do I yo también
so-so más o menos
soaking solution (for contact lenses) el líquido preservador [leekeedo presairbador]
soap el jabón [Habon]
soap powder el jabón en polvo [em polbo]
sober sobrio [sobr-yo]
sock el calcetín [kalseteen]
socket (electrical) el enchufe [enchoofeh]
soda (water) la soda
sofa el sofá
soft (material etc) suave [swabeh]
soft-boiled egg el huevo pasado por agua [webo – agwa]
soft drink el refresco
soft lenses las lentes blandas [lent-es]
sole (of shoe, of foot) la suela [swela]
could you put new soles on these? ¿podría cambiarles las suelas? [kamb-yarl-es]
some: can I have some water? ¿me da agua? [meh]
can I have some rolls? ¿me da unos bolillos?
can I have some? ¿me da unos?
somebody, someone alguien [alg-yen]
something algo
something to drink algo de beber [deh bebair]
sometimes a veces [bes-es]
somewhere en alguna parte [parteh]
son el hijo [eeHo]
song la canción [kans-yon]
son-in-law el yerno [yairno]
soon dentro de poco [deh]
I'll be back soon no me tardo [meh]
as soon as possible lo antes posible [ant-es poseebleh]
sore: it's sore me duele [meh

dweleh]
sore throat el dolor de garganta [deh]
sorry: (I'm) sorry disculpe [deeskoolpeh]
sorry? (didn't understand) ¿mande? [mandeh]
sort: what sort of ...? ¿qué clase de ...? [keh klaseh deh]
soup la sopa
sour (taste) ácido [aseedo]
south el sur [soor]
in the south al sur
South Africa Sudáfrica
South African (adj) sudafricano
I'm South African (man/woman) soy sudafricano/sudafricana
South America América del Sur [amaireeka]
South American (adj) sudamericano
(man/woman) el sudamericano, la sudamericana
southeast el sudeste [sood-esteh]
southwest el sudoeste [soodo-esteh]
souvenir el recuerdo [rekwairdo]
Spain España [espan-ya]
Spaniard (man/woman) el español [espan-yol], la española
Spanish español
spanner la llave inglesa [yabeh]
spare parts los repuestos [repwestos], las refacciones [refaks-yon-es]
spare tyre la llanta de repuesto [yanta deh]
sparkplug la bujía [booHee-a]
speak hablar [ablar]
do you speak English? ¿habla inglés? [abla eeng-les]
I don't speak ... no hablo ... [ablo]

DIALOGUE

can I speak to Pablo? ¿puedo hablar con Pablo? [pwedo]
who's calling? ¿quién le llama? [k-yen leh yama]
it's Patricia soy Patricia
I'm sorry, he's not in, can I take a message? lo siento, no está, ¿quiere dejar recado? [s-yento – k-yaireh deh-Har]
no thanks, I'll call back later no gracias, llamaré más tarde [gras-yas yamareh mas tardeh]
please tell him I called por favor, dígale que llamé [fabor deegaleh keh yameh]

speciality la especialidad [espes-yaleeda]
spectacles las gafas
speed la velocidad [beloseeda]
speed limit el límite de velocidad [leemeeteh deh]
speedometer el velocímetro [beloseemetro]
spell: how do you spell it? ¿cómo se escribe? [seh eskreebeh]
see alphabet
spend gastar
spider la araña [aran-ya]
spin-dryer la secadora
splinter la astilla [astee-ya]

spoke (in wheel) el r**a**dio [r**a**d-yo]
spoon la cuch**a**ra
sport el dep**o**rte [dep**o**rteh]
sprain: I've sprained my ... me torcí el ... [meh tors**ee**]
spring (season) la primavera [preemab**aira**]
(of car, seat) el resorte [res**o**rteh]
square (in town) la plaza [pl**a**sa]
main square el zócalo [s**o**kalo]
stairs la escalera [eskal**aira**]
stale (bread) d**u**ro
(food) pas**a**do
stall: the engine keeps stalling el mot**o**r se p**a**ra c**a**da r**a**to [seh]
stamp la estampilla [estamp**ee**-ya], el timbre [t**ee**mbreh]

•••••• DIALOGUE ••••••

a stamp for England, please **u**na estampilla p**a**ra Inglat**e**rra, por favor [fab**o**r]
what are you sending? ¿qué es lo que envía? [keh – emb**ee**-a]
this postcard **e**sta post**a**l

Stamps are sold at post offices (**el correo**) and in some shops. If you send items from post offices you may have them franked (**franqueado**) and you can also send registered mail (**certificado**). Parcels should always be posted from the post office; letters and postcards can be mailed at a red post box (**buzón**).

standby el vuelo standby [bw**e**lo]
star la estrella [estr**eh**-ya]
(in film) el/la protagon**i**sta
start el principio [preens**ee**p-yo]
(verb) comenzar [komens**a**r]
when does it start? ¿cuándo comienza? [kw**a**ndo com-y**e**nsa]
the car won't start el c**a**rro no arr**a**nca
starter (of car) el mot**o**r de arranque [arr**a**nkeh]
(food) la entr**a**da
starving: I'm starving me muero de hambre [meh mw**ai**ro deh **a**mbreh]
state (country) el est**a**do
the States (USA) los Est**a**dos Unidos [oon**ee**dos]
station la estación de ferrocarr**i**l [estas-y**o**n deh fairrokarr**ee**l]
statue la estatua [est**a**twa]
stay: where are you staying? ¿dónde est**á** alojado? [d**o**ndeh – aloH**a**do]
I'm staying at ... (said by man/woman) estoy aloj**a**do/aloj**a**da en ...
I'd like to stay another two nights me gustaría quedarme dos noches más [meh – ked**a**rmeh – n**o**ch-es]
steak el filete [feel**e**teh]
steal rob**a**r
my bag has been stolen me rob**a**ron el b**o**lso [meh]
steep (hill) empin**a**do,

escarpado
steering la dirección [deereks-y**o**n]
step: on the steps en las escaleras [eskal**ai**ras]
stereo el estéreo [est**ai**reh-o]
sterling la libra esterlina [estairl**ee**na]
steward (on plane) el auxiliar de vuelo [owkseel-y**a**r deh bw**e**lo]
stewardess la azafata [asaf**a**ta]
sticking plaster la tirita
still: I'm still waiting sigo esperando
is he still there? ¿sigue ahí? [s**ee**geh a-**ee**]
keep still! ¡quédese quieto! [k**e**deseh k-y**e**to]
sting: I've been stung algo me ha picado [meh a]
stockings las medias [m**e**d-yas]
stomach el estómago
stomach ache el dolor de estómago [deh]
stone (rock) la piedra [p-y**e**dra]
stop (verb) parar
please, stop here (to taxi driver etc) pare aquí, por favor [p**a**reh ak**ee** por fab**o**r]
do you stop near ...? ¿para cerca de ...? [s**ai**rka deh]
stop doing that! ¡deje de hacer eso! [d**eh**-Heh deh as**ai**r]
stopover la escala
storm la tormenta
straight: it's straight ahead todo recto
a straight whisky un whisky solo
straightaway en seguida [seg**ee**da]
strange (odd) extraño [estr**a**n-yo]
stranger (man/woman) el forastero [forast**ai**ro], la forastera
I'm a stranger here no soy de aquí [deh ak**ee**]
strap la correa [korr**eh**-a]
strawberry la fresa, la frutilla [froot**ee**-ya]
stream el arroyo [arr**o**-yo]
street la calle [k**a**-yeh]
on the street en la calle
streetmap el plano de la ciudad [deh la s-yood**a**]
string la cuerda [kw**ai**rda]
strong fuerte [fw**ai**rteh]
stuck atascar
the key's stuck la llave se atascó [y**a**beh seh]
student el/la estudiante [estood-y**a**nteh]

> **stupid**
> Don't call people **estúpido** – it seems a natural translation from the English stupid, and travellers tend to use it unthinkingly, but in Mexico it's a far stronger word and can cause serious offence.

subway (US) el metro
see **bus**
suburb el suburbio [soob**oo**rb-yo]
suddenly de repente [deh

repenteh]
suede el ante [anteh]
sugar el azúcar [asookar]
suit el traje [traHeh]
it doesn't suit me (jacket etc) no me queda bien [meh keda b-yen]
it suits you te queda muy bien [teh – mwee]
suitcase la maleta
summer el verano [bairano]
in the summer en verano
sun el sol
in the sun al sol
out of the sun a la sombra
sunbathe tomar el sol
sunblock (cream) la crema protectora, el filtro solar
sunburn la quemadura de sol [kemadoora deh]
sunburnt quemado [kemado]
Sunday domingo
sunglasses las gafas de sol [deh]
sun lounger la tumbona
sunny: it's sunny hace sol [aseh]
sunroof (in car) el techo corredizo [korredeeso]
sunset la puesta del sol [pwesta]
sunshade la sombrilla [sombree-ya]
sunshine la luz del sol [loos]
sunstroke la insolación [eensolas-yon]
suntan el bronceado [bronseh-ado]
suntan lotion la loción bronceadora [los-yon bronseh-adora]
suntanned bronceado [bronseh-ado]
suntan oil el aceite bronceador [asayteh]
super fabuloso
supermarket el supermercado [soopairmairkado]
supper la cena [sena]
supplement (extra charge) el suplemento [sooplemento]
sure: are you sure? ¿está seguro?
sure! ¡por supuesto! [soopwesto]
surfboard la tabla de surf [deh soorf]
surfing el surfing
surname el apellido [apeh-yeedo]
swearword la grosería [grosairee-a]
sweater el suéter [swetair]
sweatshirt la sudadera [soodadaira]
Sweden Suecia [swes-ya]
Swedish (adj) sueco [sweko]
sweet (dessert) el postre [postreh]
(adj: taste) dulce [doolseh]
sweetcorn el elote [eloteh]
sweets los dulces [dools-es]
swelling el hinchazón [eenchason]
swim (verb) bañarse [ban-yarseh]
I'm going for a swim voy a bañarme [boy a ban-yarmeh]
let's go for a swim vamos a

bañarnos [b**a**mos a ban-y**a**rnos]
swimming costume el traje de baño [tr**a**Heh deh b**a**n-yo]
swimming pool la alberca [alb**ai**rka]
swimming trunks el traje de baño [tr**a**Heh deh b**a**n-yo]
switch el interruptor [eentairoopt**o**r]
switch off apagar
switch on prender [prend**ai**r]
swollen hinchado [eench**a**do]

T

table la mesa
a table for two una mesa para dos
tablecloth el mantel
table tennis el ping-pong
table wine el vino de mesa [b**ee**no deh]
tailback (of traffic) la caravana de carros [karab**a**na deh]
tailor el sastre [s**a**streh]
take (lead) tomar
(accept) aceptar [asept**a**r]
can you take me to the airport? ¿me lleva al aeropuerto? [meh y**e**ba al īropw**ai**rto]
do you take credit cards? ¿acepta tarjetas de crédito? [as**e**pta tarH**e**tas deh kr**e**deeto]
fine, I'll take it me llevo éste [meh y**e**bo **e**steh]
can I take this? (leaflet etc) ¿puedo llevarme esto? [pw**e**do yeb**a**rmeh]
how long does it take? ¿cuánto tarda? [kw**a**nto]
it takes three hours tarda tres horas [**o**ras]
is this seat taken? ¿está ocupado este asiento? [**e**steh as-y**e**nto]
a hamburger to take away una hamburguesa para llevar [yeb**a**r]
can you take a little off here? (to hairdresser) ¿puede quitarme un poco de aquí? [pw**e**deh keet**a**rmeh – deh ak**ee**]
talcum powder el talco
talk (verb) platicar
tall alto
tampons los tampones [tamp**o**n-es]
tan el bronceado [bronseh-**a**do]
to get a tan broncearse [bronseh-**a**rseh]
tank (in car) el depósito [dep**o**seeto]
tap la llave [y**a**beh]
tape (for cassette) la cinta [s**ee**nta]
(sticky) la cinta adhesiva [ades**ee**ba]
tape measure la cinta métrica
tape recorder la grabadora
taste el sabor
can I taste it? ¿puedo probarlo? [pw**e**do]
taxi el taxi, el colectivo [kolekt**ee**bo]
will you get me a taxi? ¿me consigue un taxi? [meh kons**ee**geh]

where can I find a taxi? ¿dónde encuentro un taxi? [d**o**ndeh enkw**e**ntro]

•••••• DIALOGUE ••••••

to the airport/to the Sol Hotel please al aeropuerto/al hotel Sol, por favor [īropw**ai**rto/al ot**e**l – fab**o**r]
how much will it be? ¿cuánto va a ser? [kw**a**nto ba a sair]
1,000 pesos mil pesos
that's fine, right here, thanks está bien aquí mismo, gracias [b-yen ak**ee** m**ee**smo gr**a**s-yas]

Taxis can be good value, but beware of rip-offs. Unless you're confident that the meter is working, fix a price before you get in. In the big cities, there may be tables of fixed prices posted at prominent spots. At almost every airport and some of the biggest bus stations, you'll find a booth selling vouchers for the official taxis and even though these might cost more than a regular cab, it's worth it for the extra security. Never accept a ride in any kind of unofficial or unmarked taxi. In bigger towns and cities, **combis**, **colectivos** or **peseros** offer a faster and perhaps less crowded alternative to city buses. These are minibuses, vans or large saloon cars that run along a fixed route to set destinations, and will pick up and drop off wherever you like along the way. You pay the driver for the distance travelled.

taxi-driver el/la taxista
taxi rank la parada de taxis [deh]
tea (drink) el té [teh]
  tea for one/two please un té/dos tés, por favor [fab**o**r]

Tea is often available, and you may well be offered a cup at the end of a meal. Usually it's some kind of herbal tea like **manzanilla** (camomile) or **yerbabuena** (mint). Non-herbal teas are not easy to find, though more expensive restaurants may offer other specialist teas like Earl Grey. Tea is always served without milk.

teabags las bolsas de té [deh]
teach: could you teach me? ¿podría enseñarme? [ensen-y**a**rmeh]
teacher (primary: man/woman) el maestro [ma-**e**stro], la maestra
  (secondary) el profesor, la profesora
team el equipo [ek**ee**po]
teaspoon la cucharita
tea towel el trapo de cocina [deh kos**ee**na]
teenager el/la adolescente [adoles**e**nteh]

telegram el telegr**a**ma
telephone el tel**é**fono
see **phone**
television la televisi**ó**n [telebees-y**o**n]
tell: could you tell him ...? ¿podría decirle ...? [des**ee**rleh]
temperature (weather) la temperatura [tempairat**oo**ra]
(fever) la fiebre [f-y**e**breh]
temple el t**e**mplo
tennis el t**e**nis
tennis ball la pel**o**ta de tenis [deh]
tennis court la c**a**ncha de tenis
tennis racket la raqueta de tenis [rak**e**ta]
tent la tienda de campaña [t-y**e**nda deh kamp**a**n-ya], la c**a**rpa
term (at university, school) el trimestre [treem**e**streh]
terminus (rail) la terminal [tairmeen**a**l]
terrible mal**í**simo
terrific fabuloso [faboolo**s**o]
than* que [keh]
smaller than más pequeño que [pek**e**n-yo]
thanks, thank you gracias [gr**a**s-yas]
thank you very much muchas gracias [m**oo**chas]
thanks for the lift gracias por traerme [tra-**ai**rmeh]
no thanks no gracias

•••••• DIALOGUE ••••••
thanks gracias
that's OK, don't mention it no hay de qué [ī deh keh]

that: that man ese hombre [**e**seh **o**mbreh]
that woman esa mujer [mooH**air**]
that one ése [**e**seh]
I hope that ... espero que ... [esp**ai**ro keh]
that's nice (clothes, souvenir etc) qué l**i**ndo
is that ...? ¿es ése ...?
that's it (that's right) **eso es**
the* el, la; (pl) los, las
theatre el teatro [teh-**a**tro]
their* su; (pl) sus [soos]
theirs* su, sus; (pl) suyos [s**oo**-yos], **suyas**; de ellos [deh **eh**-yos], de **e**llas
them* (things) los, las
(people) les
for them p**a**ra ellos/ellas [**eh**-yos/**eh**-yas]
with them con ellos/ellas
I gave it to them se lo di a ellos/ellas [seh]
who? – them ¿quiénes? – ellos/ellas [k-y**e**n-es]
then luego [lw**e**go]
there allí [a-y**ee**]
over there allá [a-y**a**]
up there allá arr**i**ba
is/are there ...? ¿hay ...? [ī]
there is/are ... hay ...
there you are (giving something) aquí tiene [ak**ee** t-y**e**neh]

thermometer el termómetro [tairmometro]
Thermos flask® el termo [tairmo]
these: these men estos hombres
these women estas mujeres
can I have these? ¿me puedo llevar éstos? [meh pwedo yebar]
they* (male) ellos [eh-yos]
(female) ellas [eh-yas]
thick grueso [groo-eso]
(stupid) bruto
thief (man/woman) el ladrón, la ladrona
thigh el muslo
thin flaco
thing la cosa
my things mis cosas [mees]
think pensar
(believe) creer [kreh-air]
I think so creo que sí [kreh-o keh]
I don't think so no creo
I'll think about it lo pensaré [pensareh]
third party insurance el seguro contra terceros [tairsairos]
thirsty: I'm thirsty tengo sed [seh]
this: this man este hombre [esteh]
this woman esta mujer
this one éste/ésta [esteh]
this is my wife le presento a mi mujer [leh]
is this ...? ¿es éste/ésta ...?
those: those men aquellos hombres [akeh-yos]
those women aquellas mujeres [akeh-yas]
which ones? – those ¿cuáles? – aquéllos/aquéllas [kwal-es]
thread el hilo [eelo]
throat la garganta
throat pastilles las pastillas para la garganta [pastee-yas]
through a través de [trav-es deh]
does it go through ...? (train, bus) ¿pasa por ...?
throw (verb) echar, aventar [abentar]
throw away (verb) tirar, botar
thumb el pulgar
thunderstorm la tormenta
Thursday jueves [Hweb-es]
ticket el boleto

•••••• DIALOGUE ••••••

a return to Tijuana un boleto de ida y vuelta a Tijuana [deh eeda ee bwelta a teeHwana]
coming back when? ¿cuándo piensa regresar? [kwando p-yensa]
today/next Tuesday hoy/el martes que viene [oy/el mart-es keh b-yeneh]
that will be 2,000 pesos son dos mil pesos

ticket office (bus, rail) la taquilla [takee-ya], la boletería [boletairee-a]
tide la marea [mareh-a]
tie (necktie) la corbata
tight (clothes etc) ajustado [aHoostado]
it's too tight me viene estrecho [meh b-yeneh]

tights las pantimedias [panteemed-yas]
till la caja [kaHa]
time* el tiempo [t-yempo]
what's the time? ¿qué hora es? [keh ora]
this time esta vez [bes]
last time la última vez [oolteema]
next time la próxima vez
four times cuatro veces [bes-es]
timetable el horario [orar-yo]
tin (can) la lata, el bote [boteh]
tinfoil el papel de aluminio [aloomeen-yo]
tin-opener el abrelatas
tiny minúsculo [meenooskoolo]
tip (to waiter etc) la propina

> Tips are hardly ever added to bills, and the amount is entirely up to you: in cheap places it's customary just to leave a small amount of loose change; expensive places tend to expect their full 12 per cent. It is not standard practice to tip cab drivers.

tired cansado
I'm tired (said by a man/woman) estoy cansado/cansada
tissues los klínex®
to: to Puebla/London a Puebla/Londres
to Mexico/England a México/Inglaterra
to the post office a la oficina de Correos

toast (bread) la tostada
today hoy [oy]
toe el dedo del pie [p-yeh]
together juntos [Hoontos]
we're together (in shop etc) estamos juntos
can we pay together? ¿podemos pagar todo junto, por favor? [fabor]
toilet el baño [ban-yo], los servicios [sairbees-yos]
where is the toilet? ¿dónde están los servicios? [dondeh]
I have to go to the toilet tengo que ir al baño [keh]

> Public toilets in Mexico are almost always filthy, and there's never any paper (though someone may sell it outside). They're known usually as **baños** (literally: bathrooms), **excusados**, **sanitarios** or **servicios**. The most common signs are **damas** (ladies) and **caballeros** (gentlemen), though you may find the more confusing **señoras** (women) and **señores** (men).

toilet paper el papel higiénico [eeH-yeneeko]
tomato el jitomate [Heetomateh]
tomato juice el jugo de jitomate [Hoogo deh]
tomato ketchup el catsup
tomorrow mañana [man-yana]
tomorrow morning mañana por la mañana

the day after tomorrow pasado mañana
toner (for skin) el tonificador facial [fas-yal]
tongue la lengua [lengwa]
tonic (water) la tónica
tonight esta noche [nocheh]
tonsillitis las anginas [anHeenas]
too (excessively) demasiado [demas-yado]
(also) también [tamb-yen]
too hot demasiado caliente [kal-yenteh]
too much demasiado
me too yo también
tooth el diente [d-yenteh], la muela [mwela]
toothache el dolor de muelas [deh]
toothbrush el cepillo de dientes [seepee-yo deh d-yent-es]
toothpaste la pasta de dientes
top: on top of ... encima de ... [enseema deh], arriba de
at the top en la parte de arriba [parteh]
at the top of ... en la parte más alta de ...
top floor el último piso [oolteemo]
topless topless
torch la linterna [leentairna]
total el total [tot-al]
tour la excursión [eskoors-yon]
is there a tour of ...? ¿hay recorrido de ...? [ī – deh]
tour guide el/la guía turístico [gee-a]
tourist el/la turista
tourist information office la oficina de información turística [ofeeseena deh eenformas-yon]

> The Mexican Government Ministry of Tourism (**Secretaría de Turismo**, abbreviated to **Sectur**) has helpful offices throughout the world. In Mexico, you'll find tourist offices (sometimes called **turismos**) in virtually every town, some run by Sectur and others run by state and municipal authorities.

tour operator la agencia de viajes [aHens-ya deh b-yaH-es]
towards hacia [as-ya]
towel la toalla [to-a-ya]
town la ciudad [s-yooda]
in town en el centro [sentro]
just out of town a la salida de la ciudad
town centre el centro de la ciudad [sentro deh la s-yooda]
town hall el ayuntamiento [ī-yoontam-yento]
toy el juguete [Hoogeteh]
track (US) la vía [bee-a]
tracksuit el chandal
traditional tradicional [tradees-yonal]
traffic el tránsito, la circulación [seerkoolas-yon]
traffic jam el embotellamiento [emboteh-yam-yento]

traffic lights el sem**á**foro
trailer (for carrying tent etc) el rem**o**lque [rem**o**lkeh]
(US: caravan) la carav**a**na [karab**a**na]
trailer park el c**a**mping
train el tren
by train en tren

• • • • • • DIALOGUE • • • • • •

is this the train for ...? ¿es éste el tren p**a**ra ...? [**e**steh]
sure sí, ex**a**cto
no, you want that platform there no, tiene que ir a aquella vía [t-y**e**neh keh eer a ak**eh**-ya b**ee**-a]

Rail travel is on the whole cheaper than the bus, but much slower, infrequent and rarely on time. In general, trains are only recommended in Northern and Central Mexico, though there are lines to the south. There are two main classes on Mexican trains; the standard of first class (**primera**) may vary, but you will at least be guaranteed a seat. There is also a more expensive and more luxurious **primera especial**, and the still more comfortable trains of the **servicio estrella**. You can also book a sleeping berth (**camarín**) or a sleeping compartment (**alcoba**) on all these trains. The second class carriages (**segunda**) are much cheaper, but also very crowded and often →

extremely uncomfortable. Local trains – **locales** (slow trains) or **autovías** – will usually be second class, while **rápidos** (faster trains with limited stops) are often first class only. Seats must be reserved for first class and sleepers, as far in advance as possible; second-class tickets can only be bought on the day of departure and seats cannot be reserved.

trainers (shoes) los tr**á**iner [tr**ī**nair]
train station la estación de ferrocarril [estas-y**o**n deh fairokar**ee**l]
tram el tranvía [tramb**ee**-a]
translate traducir [tradoos**ee**r]
could you translate that? ¿podría traducir **e**so?
translation la traducción [tradooks-y**o**n]
translator (man/woman) el traduct**o**r, la traduct**o**ra
trashcan el bote de la bas**u**ra [b**o**teh deh]
travel (verb) viajar [b-yaH**a**r]
we're travelling around and**a**mos de paseo [deh pas**eh**-o]
travel agent's la agencia de viajes [aH**e**ns-ya deh b-y**a**H-es]
traveller's cheque el cheque de viajero [ch**e**keh deh b-yaH**ai**ro]
see **cheque**
tray la bandeja [band**e**Ha]

tree el **á**rbol
tremendous trem**e**ndo
trendy de m**o**da [deh]
trim: just a trim please (to hairdresser) c**ó**rtemelo s**ó**lo un p**o**co, por favor [fab**o**r]
trip (excursion) la excursi**ó**n [eskoors-y**o**n]
I'd like to go on a trip to ... me gustar**í**a hacer **u**na excursi**ó**n a ... [meh – as**air**]
trolley el carr**i**to
trouble probl**e**mas [probl**e**mas]
I'm having trouble with ... t**e**ngo probl**e**mas con ...
sorry to trouble you disc**u**lpe la mol**e**stia [deesk**oo**lpeh]
trousers los pantal**o**nes [pantal**o**n-es]
true ci**e**rto [s-y**air**to]
that's not true no es ci**e**rto
trunk (US) la caju**e**la [kaнw**e**la]
trunks (swimming) el tr**a**je de b**a**ño [tr**a**нeh deh b**a**n-yo]
try (verb) intent**a**r
can I try it? ¿p**ue**do intent**a**rlo yo? [pw**e**do]
try on: can I try it on? ¿p**ue**do prob**á**rmelo?
T-shirt la camis**e**ta, la play**e**ra [plī-y**ai**ra]
Tuesday m**a**rtes [m**a**rt-es]
tuna el bon**i**to
tunnel el t**ú**nel [t**oo**nel]
turn: turn left/right tu**e**rce a la izqui**e**rda/der**e**cha [tw**air**seh]
turn off: where do I turn off? ¿d**ó**nde doy vu**e**lta? [d**o**ndeh doy bw**e**lta]
can you turn the heating off? ¿p**ue**de apag**a**r la calefacci**ó**n? [pw**e**deh – kalefaks-y**o**n]
turn on: can you turn the heating on? ¿p**ue**de pon**e**r la calefacci**ó**n? [pon**air**]
turning (in road) el desv**í**o [desb**ee**-o]
TV la t**e**le [t**e**leh]
tweezers las p**i**nzas [p**ee**nsas]
twice dos v**e**ces [b**e**s-es]
twice as much el d**o**ble [d**o**bleh]
twin beds las c**a**mas gem**e**las [Hem**e**las]
twin room el cu**a**rto con dos c**a**mas [kw**a**rto]
twist: I've twisted my ankle me torc**í** el tob**i**llo [meh tors**ee** el tob**ee**-yo]
type el t**i**po [t**ee**po]
a different type of ... **o**tro t**i**po de ... [deh]
typical t**í**pico [t**ee**peeko]
tyre la ll**a**nta [y**a**nta]

U

ugly f**e**o [f**eh**-o]
UK el R**e**ino Un**i**do [r**ay**no oon**ee**do]
ulcer la **ú**lcera [**oo**lsaira]
umbrella el par**a**guas [par**a**gwas]
uncle el t**í**o
unconscious inconsci**e**nte [eenkons-y**e**nteh]
under (in position) deb**a**jo de [deb**a**Ho deh]

(less than) **menos** de
underdone (meat) p**o**co hecho [**e**cho]
underground (railway) el m**e**tro see **bus**
underpants los calz**o**nes [kals**o**n-es]
understand: I understand lo entiendo [ent-y**e**ndo]
I don't understand no entiendo
do you understand? ¿entiende Usted? [ent-y**e**ndeh oost**eh**]
unemployed desemplead**o** [desempleh-**a**do]
unfashionable fuera de m**o**da [fw**ai**ra deh]
United States los Est**a**dos Unidos [oon**ee**dos]
university la universid**a**d [ooneebairseed**a**]
unleaded petrol la gasol**i**na sin pl**o**mo [seen]
unlimited mileage sin límite de kilometraje [l**ee**meeteh deh keelometr**a**Heh]
unlock abrir [abr**ee**r]
unpack deshacer las mal**e**tas [desas**air**]
until hasta que [**a**sta keh]
unusual p**o**co común [kom**oo**n]
up arr**i**ba
up there allá arriba [a-y**a**]
he's not up yet (not out of bed) todavía no se ha levantado [todab**ee**-a no seh a lebant**a**do]
what's up? (what's wrong?) ¿qué p**a**sa? [keh]
upmarket (restaurant, hotel etc) de lujo [deh l**oo**Ho]
upset stomach el mal del estómago
upside down al revés [reb-**e**s], b**o**ca abajo [ab**a**Ho]
upstairs arr**i**ba
urgent urgente [oorH**e**nteh]
Uruguayan (adj) uruguayo [ooroogwī-yo]
us*: with us con nos**o**tros/ nos**o**tras
for us p**a**ra nos**o**tros/ nos**o**tras
USA EE.UU., Est**a**dos Unidos [oon**ee**dos]
use (verb) emplear [empleh-**a**r]
may I use ...? ¿me permite ...? [meh perm**ee**teh]
useful útil [**oo**teel]
usual de costumbre [deh kost**oo**mbreh]
the usual (drink etc) lo de siempre [s-y**e**mpreh]

V

vacancy: do you have any vacancies? (hotel) ¿tiene cu**a**rtos libres? [t-y**e**neh kw**a**rtos l**ee**b-res]
see **room**
vacation las vacaciones [bakas-y**o**n-es]
see **holiday**
vaccination la vac**u**na [bak**oo**na]
vacuum cleaner la aspirad**o**ra
valid (ticket etc) válido [b**a**leedo]

how long is it valid for? ¿hasta cuándo tiene validez? [**a**sta kwando t-y**e**neh baleed-**e**s]
valley el valle [b**a**-yeh]
valuable (adj) valioso [bal-y**o**so]
can I leave my valuables here? ¿puedo dejar aquí mis objetos de valor? [pw**e**do deh-H**ar** ak**ee** mees obH**e**tos deh bal**or**]
value el valor
van la camioneta [kam-yon**e**ta]
vanilla vainilla [bīn**ee**-ya]
a vanilla ice cream un helado de vainilla [el**a**do deh]
vary: it varies depende [dep**e**ndeh]
vase el florero [flor**ai**ro]
veal la ternera [tairn**ai**ra]
vegetables las verduras [baird**oo**ras]
vegetarian (man/woman) el vegetariano [beHetar-y**a**no], la vegetariana
vending machine la máquina vendedora [m**a**keena bended**o**ra]
Venezuelan (adj) venezolano [benesol**a**no]
very muy [mwee]
very little for me muy poquito para mí [pok**ee**to]
I like it very much me gusta mucho [meh g**oo**sta m**oo**cho]
vest (under shirt) la camiseta
via por
video el video [beed**eh**-o]
view la vista [b**ee**sta]
villa el chalet [chal**eh**]
village el pueblo [pw**e**blo]
vinegar el vinagre [been**a**greh]
vineyard el viñedo [been-y**e**do]
visa la visa
visit (verb) visitar [beeseet**ar**]
I'd like to visit Guanajuato me gustaría conocer Guanajuato [konos**air** gwanaHw**a**to]
vital: it's vital that ... es imprescindible que ... [eempreseend**ee**bleh keh]
vodka el vodka [b**o**dka]
voice la voz [bos]
volcano el volcán [bolk**a**n]
voltage el voltaje [bolt**a**Heh]

The supply is 110 volts AC, with simple two-flat-pin rectangular plugs. Travellers from Europe and Australasia should bring an adaptor.

vomit vomitar [bomeet**ar**]
vulture el zopilote [sopeel**o**teh]

W

waist la cintura [seent**oo**ra]
waistcoat el chaleco
wait esperar [espair**ar**]
wait for me espéreme [esp**ai**remeh]
don't wait for me no me espere [meh esp**ai**reh]
can I wait until my wife/partner

gets here? ¿puedo esperar hasta que llegue mi mujer/ compañero? [pwedo – asta keh yegeh]
can you do it while I wait? ¿puede hacerlo ahora mismo? [pwedeh asairlo a-ora]
could you wait here for me? ¿puede esperarme aquí? [espairarmeh akee]
waiter el mesero [mesairo]
waiter! ¡señor! [sen-yor]
waitress la mesera [mesaira]
waitress! ¡señorita! [sen-yoreeta]
wake: can you wake me up at 5.30? ¿podría despertarme a las cinco y media? [despairtarmeh]
wake-up call la llamada para despertar [yamada]
Wales Gales [gal-es]
walk: is it a long walk? ¿se tarda mucho caminando? [seh – moocho]
it's only a short walk está cerca [sairka]
I'll walk iré caminando [eereh]
I'm going for a walk voy a dar una vuelta [boy – bwelta]
Walkman® el walkman® [wolkman]
wall (inside) la pared [pareh]
(outside) el muro
wallet la cartera [kartaira]
wander: I like just wandering around me gusta caminar sin rumbo fijo [meh goosta – seen roombo feeHo]
want: I want a ... quiero un/una ... [k-yairo]
I don't want ... no quiero ninguno/ninguna ...
I want to go home quiero irme a casa [eermeh]
I don't want to no quiero
he wants to ... quiere ... [k-yaireh]
what do you want? ¿qué quiere? [keh]
ward (in hospital) el pabellón [pabeh-yon]
warm caliente [kal-yenteh]
I'm very warm tengo mucho calor [moocho]
was*: it was ... era ... [aira]; estaba ...
wash (verb) lavar [labar]
can you wash these? ¿puede lavar estos? [pwedeh]
washer (for bolt etc) el fregadero [fregadairo]
washhand basin el lavabo [lababo]
washing (clothes) la ropa sucia [soos-ya]
washing machine la lavadora [labadora]
washing powder el detergente [detairHenteh]
washing-up liquid el (detergente) lavavajillas [lababaHee-yas]
wasp la avispa [abeespa]
watch (wristwatch) el reloj

[rel**o**H]
will you watch my things for me? ¿puede cuidarme mis c**o**sas? [pw**e**deh kweed**a**rmeh mees]
watch out! ¡cuidado! [kweed**a**do]
watch strap la correa [korr**eh**-a]
water el agua [**a**gwa]
may I have some water? ¿me da un p**o**co de agua? [meh – deh]

You should stick to bottled or distilled water, which is available everywhere: **Tehuacán** is the most common label, and is used as a general term for mineral water; **con gas** is fizzy and **sin gas** is still. Virtually every hotel will have a supply of drinking water either in the hotel room or in the corridor. Remember that ice may be made of unpurified water and that raw vegetables and salads may also have been washed in it, and this can be risky for visitors. You can buy water purification tablets at most pharmacies.

waterproof (adj) impermeable [eempairmeh-**a**bleh]
waterskiing el esquí acuático [esk**ee** akw**a**teeko]
wave (in sea) la **o**la
way: it's this way es por aquí [ak**ee**]
it's that way es por allí [a-y**ee**]
is it a long way to ...? ¿queda lejos ...? [k**e**da l**eh**-Hos]
no way! ¡de ningu**n**a manera! [deh – man**ai**ra]

DIALOGUE

could you tell me the way to ...? podría indicarme el cam**i**no a ...? [eendeek**a**rmeh]
go straight on until you reach the traffic lights s**i**ga r**e**cto hasta llegar al sem**á**foro [**a**sta yeg**a**r]
turn left tuerce a la izqui**e**rda [tw**ai**rseh]
take the first on the right tome la prim**e**ra a la der**e**cha [t**o**meh]
see where

we* nosotros, nos**o**tras
weak d**é**bil
weather el tiempo [t-y**e**mpo]

DIALOGUE

what's the weather going to be like? ¿qué tiempo va a hacer? [keh – ba a as**ai**r]
it's going to be fine va a hacer bueno [bw**e**no]
it's going to rain va a llover [yob**ai**r]
it'll brighten up later despejará más tarde [despeh-Har**a** mas t**a**rdeh]

wedding la b**o**da
wedding ring el anillo de

casado [anee-yo]
Wednesday miércoles [m-yairkol-es]
week la semana
a week (from) today dentro de una semana [deh]
a week (from) tomorrow dentro de una semana a partir de mañana [man-yana]
weekend el fin de semana [feen deh]
at the weekend el fin de semana
weight el peso
weird extraño [ekstran-yo]
weirdo: he's a weirdo es un tipo raro [teepo]
welcome: welcome to ... bienvenido a ... [b-yenbeneedo]
you're welcome (don't mention it) no hay de qué [ī deh keh]
well: I don't feel well no me siento bien [meh s-yento b-yen]
she's not well no se siente bien [seh s-yenteh]
you speak English very well habla inglés muy bien [abla eeng-les mwee]
well done! ¡bravo! [brabo]
this one as well éste también [esteh tamb-yen]
well well! (surprise) ¡ándale, pues! [andaleh pwes]

• • • • • • DIALOGUE • • • • • •

how are you? ¿cómo le va? [leh ba]
very well, thanks muy bien, gracias [mwee b-yen gras-yas]
– and you? – ¿y Usted? [ee oosteh]

well-done (meat) bien hecho [b-yen echo]
Welsh galés [gal-es]
I'm Welsh (man/woman) soy galés/galesa
were*: we were estábamos; éramos [airamos]
you were estaban; eran [airan]
they were estaban; eran
west el oeste [o-esteh], el occidente [okseedenteh]
in the west en el oeste
West Indian (adj) antillano [antee-yano]
wet mojado [moHado]
what? ¿qué? [keh]
what's that? ¿qué es eso?
what should I do? ¿qué hago? [a-go]
what a view! ¡qué vista!
what number bus is it? ¿qué número de camión es ese? [noomairo deh – eseh]
wheel la rueda [rweda]
wheelchair la silla de ruedas [see-ya deh rwedas]
when? ¿cuándo? [kwando]
when we get back cuando regresamos
when's the train/ferry?

¿cuándo es el tren/ferry?
where? ¿dónde? [dondeh]
I don't know where it is no sé dónde está [seh]

•••••• DIALOGUE ••••••

where is the cathedral? ¿dónde está la catedral?
it's over there está por ahí [a-ee]
could you show me where it is on the map? ¿puede enseñarme en el mapa dónde está? [pwedeh ensen-yarmeh]
it's just here está aquí mero [akee mairo]
see way

which: which bus? ¿qué camión? [keh]

•••••• DIALOGUE ••••••

which one? ¿cuál? [kwal]
that one ese [eseh]
this one? ¿éste? [esteh]
no, that one no, aquél [akel]

while: while I'm here ya que estoy aquí [keh estoy akee]
whisky el whisky
white blanco
white wine el vino blanco [beeno]
who? ¿quién? [k-yen]
who is it? ¿quién es?
the man who ... el hombre que... [keh]
whole: the whole week toda la semana
the whole lot todo
whose: whose is this? ¿de quién es esto? [deh k-yen]
why? ¿por qué? [keh]
why not? ¿por qué no?
wide ancho
wife la mujer [mooHair], la esposa
will*: will you do it for me? ¿puede hacer esto por mí? [pwedeh asair]
wind el viento [b-yento]
window (of house) la ventana [bentana]
(of ticket office, vehicle) la ventanilla [bentanee-ya]
near the window cerca de la ventana [sairka deh]
in the window (of shop) en el escaparate [eskaparateh]
window seat el asiento junto a la ventana [as-yento Hoonto a la bentana]
windscreen el parabrisas
windscreen wiper el limpiaparabrisas [leemp-ya-parabreesas]
windsurfing el windsurf
windy: it's very windy hace mucho viento [aseh moocho b-yento]
wine el vino [beeno]
can we have some more wine? ¿podría traernos más vino? [tra-airnos]

Wine is not seen a great deal, although Mexico does produce a fair number of perfectly good ones. You're safest sticking to →

the brand names like **Hidalgo** or **Domecq**, or those from Baja California which in many cases have borrowed techniques and winemakers from the US. **El vino de casa** (house wine) would normally be a Mexican wine; make sure you are not given a French wine or a Spanish one, both of which are likely to be very expensive.

wine list la lista de vinos [l**ee**sta deh b**ee**nos]
winter el invierno [eemb-y**ai**rno]
in the winter en invierno
winter holiday las vacaciones de invierno [bakas-y**o**n-es deh]
wire el alambre [al**a**mbreh] (electric) el cable eléctrico [k**a**bleh]
wish: best wishes sal**u**dos
with con
I'm staying with ... est**oy** en c**a**sa de ... [deh]
without sin [seen]
witness el/la testigo [test**ee**go]
will you be a witness for me? ¿acepta ser mi testigo? [as**e**pta sair]
woman la mujer [mooH**air**]

women
Women travellers, especially blonde ones, can expect to be the almost constant butt of comments from Mexican men. Try to remember that these are rarely meant to be offensive (they are 'compliments') and that, unless your Spanish is good enough to reply with a tirade of abuse, they are best ignored completely. Male companions tempted to intervene in a 'gentlemanly' manner should think twice: this is a direct challenge to the macho male, and likely to raise the stakes considerably.

wonderful estupendo [estoop**e**ndo]
won't*: it won't start no arr**a**nca
wood (material) la madera [mad**ai**ra]
woods (forest) el bosque [b**o**skeh]
wool la l**a**na
word la pal**a**bra
work el trabajo [trab**a**Ho]
it's not working no funciona [foons-y**o**na]
I work in ... trabajo en ...
world el mundo [m**oo**ndo]
worry: I'm worried (said by man/woman) est**oy** preocupado/preocup**a**da [preh-okoop**a**do]
worse: it's worse es peor [peh-**o**r]
worst el peor
worth: is it worth a visit? ¿vale

la **pe**na visitarlo? [b**a**leh – beese**e**tarlo]
would: would you give this to ...? ¿le puede dar **e**sto a ...? [leh pw**e**deh]
wrap: could you wrap it up? ¿me lo envuelve? [meh lo embw**e**lbeh]
wrapping paper el pap**e**l de envolver [deh embolb**air**]
wrist la muñeca [moon-y**e**ka]
write escribir [eskreeb**ee**r]
could you write it down? ¿puede escrib**í**rmelo? [pw**e**deh]
how do you write it? ¿c**ó**mo se escribe? [seh eskr**ee**beh]
writing paper el pap**e**l de escrib**i**r
wrong: it's the wrong key no es **é**sa la llave [y**a**beh]
this is the wrong train **é**ste no es el tren [**e**steh]
the bill's wrong la cuenta est**á** equivocada [kw**e**nta – ekeebok**a**da]
sorry, wrong number perdone, me equivoqué de número [paird**o**neh meh ekeebok**eh** deh n**oo**mairo]
there's something wrong with ... le pasa **a**lgo a ... [leh]
what's wrong? ¿qué pasa? [keh]

X

X-ray la radiografía [rad-yograf**ee**-a]

Y

yacht el yate [y**a**teh]
yard* (courtyard) el p**a**tio
year el año [**a**n-yo]
yellow amarillo [amar**ee**-yo]
yes sí
yesterday ayer [ī-y**air**]
yesterday morning ayer por la mañana [man-y**a**na]
the day before yesterday anteayer [anteh-ī-y**air**]
yet

•••••• DIALOGUE ••••••

is it here yet? ¿est**á** aquí ya? [ak**ee**]
no, not yet no, todavía no [todab**ee**-a]
you'll have to wait a little longer yet tendr**á** que esperar un poquito más [keh espair**ar** oon pok**ee**to]

yobbo el hampón [amp**o**n]
yoghurt el yogur [yog**oo**r]
you* (fam, sing) tú [too]
(pol, sing) Usted [oost**eh**]
(pol, pl) Ustedes [oost**e**d-es]
this is for you **e**sto es p**a**ra tí/Usted
with you cont**i**go/con Usted

There are two words for 'you' in Spanish. You use **Usted** if you are talking to someone older, or someone you don't know. You say **tu** when the person you are speaking to is a friend or a family member, or someone younger than yourself. In the plural, Mexicans use **Ustedes**, whoever they are speaking to.

young joven [H**o**ben]
your* (fam, sing) tu; (pl) tus [toos]
(pol, sing) su; (pl) sus [soos]
yours* (fam, sing) tuyo [t**oo**-yo], tuya
(pol, sing) suyo [s**oo**-yo], suya; de Usted [deh oost**eh**]
youth hostel el albergue juvenil [alb**ai**rgeh Hooben**ee**l]

Z

zero cero [s**ai**ro]
zip el cierre [s-y**ai**rreh]
could you put a new zip in? ¿podría cambiar el cierre? [kamb-y**a**r]
zip code el código postal [pos-t**a**l]
zoo el zoo(lógico) [zo(l**o**Heeko)]

Spanish-English

COLLOQUIAL SPANISH

The following are words you might well hear. Some of them you wouldn't ever want to use and you shouldn't be tempted to use any of the stronger ones unless you are sure of your audience.

¡ándale pues! [**a**ndaleh pwes] go on then!, OK!
¡bien! [b-yen] good!
cabrón m bastard
¡carajo! [kar**a**Ho] Christ!, shit!
chingar to fuck
¡chinga tu madre! fuck off!
coger [koH**air**] to fuck
¡Dios mío! [d-yos m**ee**-o] my God!
¿dónde carajos? [d**o**ndeh] where in hell?
¡está padre! it's great!
¡hijo de la chingada! [**ee**Ho] son of a bitch!
¡híjole! [**ee**Holeh] hell!, damn!
joder [Hod**air**] to screw up
¡lárguese! [l**a**rgeseh] go away!
¡lo jodiste! [Hod**ee**steh] you screwed up!
mamón! idiot!
mano pal, buddy
marica m, maricón m queer
mariposa f butterfly; fairy, pansy
me pega la gana I feel like it
me vale (madre) [m**a**dreh] I don't give a shit
¡mierda! [m-y**air**da] shit!
¡ni modo! well, what can you do?
no le hace [leh **a**seh] don't worry about it
¡oiga! [**oy**ga] listen here!; excuse me!
¡órale! [**o**raleh] go on then!, get on with it!
pinche [p**ee**ncheh] bloody, lousy
pocho americanized (used to refer to americanized Mexican)
¡qué chingadera! [keh cheengad**air**a] what a fuck-up!
¡qué desmadre! [keh desm**a**dreh] what a mess!
¿qué húbole? [keh **oo**boleh] how's it going?
¡qué va! [ba] no way!
un chingo de [deh] loads of

A

a to; at; per; from
abajo [ab**a**Ho] downstairs; down below
abarrotes: tienda de abarrotes f [t-y**e**nda deh abarr**o**t-es] grocer's, dry goods store
abierto [ab-y**ai**rto] open
abierto de ... a ... open from ... to ...
abierto las 24 horas del día open 24 hours
abogada f, **abogado** m lawyer
abonos mpl season tickets
aborrezco [aborr**e**sko] I hate
ábrase aquí open here
ábrase en caso de emergencia open in case of emergency
abrazo m [abr**a**so] embrace
abrebotellas m [abrebot**eh**-yas] bottle-opener
abrelatas m tin-opener
abrigo m coat
abrigo de pieles [deh p-y**e**l-es] fur coat
abril m April
abrir to open
abróchense los cinturones fasten your seatbelts
abuela f [abw**e**la] grandmother
abuelo m grandfather
abuelos mpl grandparents
aburrido boring; bored
aburrirse [aboorr**ee**rseh] to be bored; to get bored
acabar to finish
acabo de ... [deh] I have just ...
acantilado m cliff
acceso a ... access to ...
acceso a la vía to the trains
acceso playa to the beach
accidente m [akseed**e**nteh] accident
tener un accidente [ten**ai**r] to have an accident
accidente de carro [deh] car accident
accidente de montaña [mont**a**n-ya] mountaineering accident
accidente de tránsito road accident
accidente en cadena [kad**e**na] pile-up
acelerador m [aselairad**o**r] accelerator, gas pedal
acelerar [aselair**a**r] to accelerate
acento m [as**e**nto] accent
aceptar [asept**a**r] to accept
acera f [as**ai**ra] pavement, sidewalk
acerca de [as**ai**rka deh] about, concerning
acero m [as**ai**ro] steel
acetona f [aset**o**na] nail polish remover
ácido (m) [**a**seedo] sour; acid
acompañar [akompan-y**a**r] to accompany
le acompaño en el sentimiento my condolences
acondicionador de pelo m [akondees-yonad**o**r deh] hair conditioner
aconsejar [akonseh-H**a**r] to advise

acordarse [akord**a**rseh] to remember
acostar to put to bed; to lay down
acostarse [akost**a**rseh] to lie down; to go to bed
al acostarse when you go to bed
actriz f [aktr**ee**s] actress
acuerdo m [akw**ai**rdo] agreement
estoy de acuerdo [deh] I agree
de acuerdo OK
adaptador m adaptor
adelantado: por adelantado [adelant**a**do] in advance
adelantarse a [–**a**rseh] to overtake
además de [deh] besides, as well as
adentro inside
adolescente m/f [adoles**e**nteh] teenager
aduana f [adw**a**na] Customs
aduanero m [adwan**ai**ro] Customs office
aerodeslizador m [a-airo-desleesad**o**r] hovercraft
aerolínea f [a-airol**ee**neh-a] airline
aeropuerto m [a-airopw**ai**rto] airport
afeitarse [afayt**a**rseh] to shave
aficionada f [afees-yon**a**da], **aficionado** m fan, enthusiast
afortunadamente [–m**e**nteh] fortunately
afueras fpl [afw**ai**ras] suburbs
agarrar to hold, to grasp; to catch; to take
agencia f [aH**e**ns-ya] agency
agencia de viajes [deh b-y**a**H-es] travel agency
agenda f [aH**e**nda] diary
agítese antes de usar(se) shake before use
agosto m August
agradable [agrad**a**bleh] pleasant
agradar to please
agradecer [agrades**ai**r] to thank
agradecido [agrades**ee**do] grateful
agradezco [agrad**e**sko] I thank
agresivo [agres**ee**bo] aggressive
agricultor m farmer
agua f [**a**gwa] water
agua de colonia [deh kol**o**n-ya] eau de toilette
aguantar: no aguanto ... [agw**a**nto] I can't stand ...
agua potable [pot**a**bleh] drinking water
águila ratonera f [**a**geela] buzzard
aguja f [ag**oo**Ha] needle
agujero m [agooH**ai**ro] hole
agujetas fpl [a-ooH**e**tas] shoelaces
ahora [a-**o**ra] now
ahorita [a-or**ee**ta] right away; soon; just a moment ago
aire m [īreh] air
aire acondicionado [akondees-yon**a**do] air-conditioning
ajedrez m [aHed-r**e**s] chess
ajustado [aHoost**a**do] tight
ala f wing
alambre m [al**a**mbreh] wire

alambre de púa [deh p**oo**-a] barbed wire
alarma f alarm
dar la señal de alarma [sen-y**a**l deh] to raise the alarm
alberca f [alb**ai**rka] swimming pool
albergue juvenil [alb**ai**rgeh Hooben**ee**l] youth hostel
alcoba f bedroom; sleeping compartment
alcohómetro m Breathalyzer®
alegre [al**e**greh] happy
alegro: me alegro I'm pleased; I'm pleased to hear it
alemán German
Alemania f [alem**a**n-ya] Germany
alérgico a [al**ai**rHeeko] allergic to
aletas fpl flippers
alfiler m [alfeel**ai**r] pin
alfombra f rug, carpet
algo something
algodón m cotton; cotton wool, absorbent cotton
algo más something else
alguien [**a**lg-yen] somebody; anybody
algún some; any
alguno someone; anyone; one; any one
alianza f [al-y**a**nsa] wedding ring
alimentos mpl groceries, foodstuffs
allá: más allá [a-y**a**] further (on)
allí [a-y**ee**] there
almacén m [almas**e**n] department store; warehouse
almohada f [almo-**a**da] pillow
almuerzo m [almw**ai**rso] lunch
alojamiento m [aloHam-y**e**nto] accommodation
alojamiento y desayuno [desī-y**oo**no] bed and breakfast
alpinismo m mountaineering
alquilar [alkeel**a**r] to rent; to hire
alquiler m [alkeel**ai**r] rental
alquiler de barcos boat hire
alquiler de bicicletas [beeseekl**e**tas] cycle hire
alquiler de carros car rental
alquiler de esquís [esk**ee**s] water-ski hire
alquiler de tablas surfboard hire
alquileres rentals
alrededor (de) [deh] around
alta costura f haute couture, high fashion
alto (m) stop sign; high; tall
¡alto! stop!
en lo alto at the top
altura f altitude; height
altura máxima maximum headroom
aluminio m aluminium
amable [am**a**bleh] kind;
si fuera tan amable [fw**ai**ra] if you wouldn't mind
amamantar to breastfeed
amanecer m [amanes**ai**r] sunrise, daybreak
¿cómo amaneciste? how did

you sleep?
amargo bitter
amarillo [amareeyo] yellow
ambos both
ambulancia f [amboolans-ya] ambulance
América f [amaireeka] Latin America
América del Norte [norteh] North America
América del Sur South America
americana (f), **americano** (m) Latin American
amiga f friend, **amigo** m friend
amor m love
hacer el amor [asair] to make love
amortiguador m [amorteegwador] shock-absorber
amperio m [ampair-yo] amp
ampliación f [amplee-as-yon] enlargement
amplio broad; loose-fitting
ampolla f [ampo-ya] blister
analgésico m [analHeseeko] painkiller
análisis clínicos mpl clinical tests
anaranjado [anaranHado] orange (colour)
ancho (m) width, breadth; wide; loose
anchura f width, breadth
¡ándale pues! [andaleh pwes] go on then!, OK!
andaluz [andaloos] Andalusian
andar to walk; to move; to work
andinismo m mountaineering
anémico anaemic
anestesia f [anestes-ya] anaesthetic
anfiteatro m [anfeeteh-atro] amphitheatre
Angeles Verdes mpl [angel-es baird-es] breakdown service
angina (de pecho) f [anHeena] angina
anginas fpl tonsillitis
anillo m [aneeyo] ring
anoche [anocheh] last night
anochecer m [anochesair] nightfall, dusk
anochece [anocheseh] it's getting dark
ante m [anteh] suede
anteayer [anteh-ī-yair] the day before yesterday
antepasado m ancestor
antes de [ant-es deh] before
antes de entrar dejen salir let passengers off first
antes de que [keh] before
anticipo m [anteeseepo] advance
anticonceptivo m [anteekonsepteebo] contraceptive
anticongelante m [anteekonHelanteh] antifreeze
anticuado [anteekwado] out of date
anticuario m [anteekwar-yo] antiques dealer
antigüedades: una tienda de antigüedades [t-yenda deh anteegwedad-es] an antique shop

antiguo [ant**ee**gwo] old; ancient
antihistamínico m [antee-eestam**ee**neeko] antihistamine
Antillas fpl [ant**ee**-yas] the West Indies
antipático unpleasant, nasty
anulado cancelled
anular to cancel
añadir [an-yad**ee**r] to add
año m [**a**n-yo] year
Año Nuevo m [nw**e**bo] New Year
día de Año Nuevo m [d**ee**-a deh] New Year's Day
¡feliz Año Nuevo! [fel**ee**s] Happy New Year!
apagar to switch off
apagón m power cut
apague el motor switch off your engine
apague las luces switch off your lights
aparato m device
aparatos electrodomésticos electrical appliances
aparecer [apares**air**] to appear
aparezco [apar**e**sko] I appear
apasionante [apas-yon**a**nteh] thrilling
apellido m [apeh-y**ee**do] surname
apenado sorry; embarrassed, shy
apenarse [–**a**rseh] to be ashamed, to be embarrassed
apenas scarcely
apenas ... (cuando) [kw**a**ndo] hardly ... when
son las seis apenas it's only just six o'clock
apetecer: me apetece [meh apet**e**seh] I feel like
apetito m appetite
apodo m nickname
apoplejía f [apopleH**ee**-a] stroke; fit
aprender [aprend**air**] to learn
aprensivo [aprens**ee**bo] fearful, apprehensive
apriete botón para cruzar press button to cross
aprovechar [aprobech**a**r] to take advantage of
¡que aproveche! [keh aprob**e**cheh] enjoy your meal!
aproximadamente [–m**e**nteh] about
apto para mayores de 14 años y menores acompañados authorized for those over 14 and young people accompanied by an adult
apto para mayores de 18 años for adults only
apto para todos los públicos suitable for all
apurado in a hurry
apurarse [–**a**rseh] to rush, to hurry
¡apúrate! [ap**oo**rateh] hurry up!
aquel [ak**e**l] that
aquél that (one)
aquella [ak**eh**-ya] that
aquélla that (one)
aquellas [ak**eh**-yas] those
aquéllas those (ones)

aquellos [ak**eh**-yos] those
aquéllos those (ones)
aquí [ak**ee**] here
aquí tiene [t-y**e**neh] here you are
araña f [ar**a**n-ya] spider
arañazo m [aran-y**a**so] scratch
árbol m tree
ardor de estómago m [deh] heartburn
área de servicios m [**a**reh-a deh serb**ee**s-yos] service area, motorway services
arena f [ar**eh**-na] sand
aretes mpl [ar**e**t-es] earrings
argentino (m) [arHent**ee**no] Argentine; Argentinian
armario m cupboard
armería f [armair**ee**-a] gunsmith's
aro m ring
arqueología f [arkeh-oloH**ee**-a] archaeology
arrancar to pull out, to tear out; to start up
arranque m [arr**a**nkeh] ignition
arreglar to mend; to sort out, to arrange
arrendar [arrend**a**r] to rent; to hire
se arrienda to rent, for hire
arriba up; upstairs; on top
arroyo m stream
arte m [**a**rteh] art
artesanía f crafts
artículos de artesanía mpl [deh] arts and crafts
artículos de boda wedding presents
artículos de deporte [dep**o**rteh] sports goods
artículos de limpieza [leemp-yesa] household cleaning products
artículos de piel [p-yel] leather goods
artículos de playa [plī-ya] beachwear
artículos de viaje [b-y**a**Heh] travel goods
artículos escolares [eskol**a**r-es] schoolwear
artículos para el bebé [beh-b**eh**] babywear
artista m/f artist
artritis f arthritis
ascensor m [asens**o**r] lift, elevator
asegurar to insure
aseos mpl [as**eh**-os] toilets, rest rooms
así like this; like that
asiento m [as-y**e**nto] seat
así que so (that)
asma m asthma
aspiradora f vacuum cleaner
asqueroso [askair**o**so] disgusting
astigmático long-sighted
asustado afraid
asustar to frighten
atacar to attack
atajo m [at**a**Ho] shortcut
ataque m [at**a**keh] attack
ataque al corazón [koras**o**n] heart attack
atención [atens-y**o**n] please note

¡atención! take care!, caution!
atención al tren beware of trains
ateo [at**eh**-o] atheist
aterrizaje m landing
aterrizaje forzado emergency landing
aterrizar [atairrees**ar**] to land
atletismo m athletics
atorado stuck
atorarse [ator**ar**seh] to get stuck
atracar to assault; to hold up
atracciones turísticas fpl [atraks-y**o**n-es] tourist attractions
atraco a mano armada m hold-up
atractivo [atrakt**ee**bo] attractive
atrás at the back; behind
¡atrás! get back!
la parte de atrás [p**a**rteh deh] the back
está más atrás it's further back
años atrás [**a**n-yos] years ago
atrasado late
atraso m delay
atravesar [atrabes**ar**] to cross
atravieso [atrab-y**e**so] I cross
atreverse [atreb**air**seh] to dare
atropellar [atropeh-y**ar**] to knock down
atroz [atr**o**s] dreadful
audífono m [owd**ee**fono] hearing aid
aun [own] even
aún [a-**oo**n] still; yet
aunque [**ow**nkeh] although
auto m [**ow**to] car
autobús m [owtob**oo**s] coach, long distance bus
auto-estopista m/f [owto-estop**ee**sta] hitch-hiker
automóvil m [owtom**o**beel] car
autopista f [owtop**ee**sta] motorway, freeway, highway
autopista de cuota [deh kw**o**ta] toll motorway/highway
auto-servicio m [owto-sairb**ee**s-yo] self-service
autostop: hacer autostop [as**air** owtost**o**p] to hitchhike
autovía f [owtob**ee**-a] slow, local train
avenida f [aben**ee**da] avenue
aventar [abent**ar**] to throw
aventón: pedir aventón [abent**o**n] to hitch a lift
avergonzado [abairgons**a**do] ashamed
avería f [abair**ee**-a] breakdown
averiarse [abair-y**ar**seh] to break down
avión m [ab-y**o**n] aeroplane, airplane
por avión by air
avisar [abees**ar**] to inform
aviso m [ab**ee**so] advertisement; notice
aviso a los señores pasajeros passenger information
avispa f [ab**ee**spa] wasp
ayer [ī-y**air**] yesterday
ayer por la mañana [man-y**a**na] yesterday morning
ayer por la tarde [t**a**rdeh] yesterday afternoon

ayuda f [ī-y**oo**da] help
ayudar [ī-yood**ar**] to help
ayuntamiento m [ī-yoontam-y**e**nto] town hall
azotea f [asot**eh**-a] roof
azteca [ast**e**ka] Aztec
azul (m) [as**oo**l] blue
azul claro light blue
azul marino navy blue

B

baca f roof rack
bache m [b**a**cheh] hole in the road
bahía f [ba-**ee**-a] bay
bailar [bīl**ar**] to dance
ir a bailar to go dancing
baile m [b**ī**leh] dance; dancing
¡bajan! [b**a**Han] next stop please!, people getting off!
bajar [baH**ar**] to go down
bajar de [deh] to get off
bajar la velocidad [beloseed**a**] to slow down
bajarse (de) [baH**a**rseh (deh)] to get off
bajeño [baH**e**n-yo] from/of Baja California
Bajío m [baH**ee**-yo] Baja California
bajo [b**a**Ho] low; short; under; underneath
balacera f [balas**ai**ra] exchange of fire
balanceo m [balans**eh**-yo] wheel-balancing
balcón m balcony
balón m ball
balonmano m handball
balsa f raft
banco m bank; bench
bandeja f [band**e**Ha] tray
bandera f [band**ai**ra] flag
bandido m bandit
banqueta f [bank**e**ta] pavement, sidewalk
bañador m [ban-yad**o**r] swimming costume
bañarse [ban-y**a**rseh] to go swimming; to have a bath/ shower
bañera f [ban-y**ai**ra] bathtub
baño m [b**a**n-yo] bathroom; toilet, rest room; bath
baños mpl toilets, rest room
baraja f [bar**a**Ha] pack of cards
barato cheap, inexpensive
barba f chin; beard
barbacoa f barbecue; barbecued meat
barbería f [barbair**ee**-a] barber's shop
barbero m [barb**ai**ro] barber
barco m boat
barco de remo [deh] rowing boat
barco de vela [b**e**la] sailing boat
barcos para alquilar boats to rent
barra de labios f [deh l**a**b-yos] lipstick
barrio m [b**a**rr-yo] district, area
básquet m [b**a**sket] basketball
bastante [bast**a**nteh] enough; quite; very
bastante más quite a lot

more
basura f rubbish, garbage
bata f dressing gown
bate m [b**a**teh] bat
batería f [batair**ee**-a] battery; drum kit
batería de cocina [deh kos**ee**na] pots and pans
bautismo m [bowt**ee**smo] christening
bebé m [beh-b**eh**] baby
beber [beb**air**] to drink
béisbol m [b**ay**sbol] baseball
Belice [bel**ee**seh] Belize
bello [b**eh**-yo] beautiful
besar to kiss
beso m kiss
betún m [bet**oo**n] shoe polish
biblioteca f [beebl-yot**e**ka] library; bookcase
bicicleta f [beeseekl**e**ta] bicycle
bien [b-yen] well
¡bien! good!
bien ... bien ... either ... or ...
o bien ... o bien ... either ... or ...
bienes mpl [b-y**e**n-es] possessions
¡bienvenido! [b-yenben**ee**do] welcome!
bifurcación f [beefoorkas-y**o**n] fork
bigote m [beeg**o**teh] moustache
billete m [bee-y**e**teh] banknote, (US) bill
blanco (m) white
blusa f blouse
boca f mouth
boda f wedding
bodega f wine cellar
boleador m [boleh-ad**o**r] shoeshine boy
boletería f ticket office
boleto m ticket
boleto de ida [deh **ee**da] single ticket, one-way ticket
boleto de ida y vuelta [ee bw**e**lta] return ticket, round trip ticket
bolígrafo m ballpoint pen
bolsa f bag; stock exchange
bolsa de dormir [deh] sleeping bag
bolsa de plástico plastic bag
bolsa de viaje [b-y**a**Heh] travel bag
bolsillo m [bols**ee**-yo] pocket
bolso m handbag, (US) purse
bomba f bomb
bomba de gas [deh] camping gas cylinder
bomberos mpl [bomb**ai**ros] fire brigade
bordado embroidered
borracho drunk
bosque m [b**o**skeh] forest
bota f boot
botanas fpl snacks
botar to throw away
botella f [bot**eh**-ya] bottle
botiquín m [boteek**ee**n] first-aid kit
botón m button
botón desatascador coin return button
boxeo m [boks**eh**-o] boxing
boya f buoy
bracero m [bras**ai**ro] migrant

labourer from Mexico to the US
bragas fpl pants, panties
brazo m [br**a**so] arm
bricolaje m [breekol**a**Heh] DIY, do-it-yourself
brillar [bree-y**a**r] to shine
brincar to jump
brisa f breeze
británico British
brocha de afeitar f [deh afayt**a**r] shaving brush
broche m [br**o**cheh] brooch
bronce m [br**o**nseh] bronze
bronceado (m) [bronseh-**a**do] suntan; suntanned
bronceador m [bronseh-ad**o**r] suntan oil/lotion
bronquitis f [bronk**ee**tees] bronchitis
brújula f [br**oo**Hoola] compass
bruto stupid
bucear [booseh-**a**r] to skin-dive
buceo m [boos**eh**-o] skin-diving
buenas noches [bw**e**nas n**o**ch-es] goodnight
buenas tardes [t**a**rd-es] good evening
bueno [bw**e**no] good; good-natured; hello
buenos días [d**ee**-as] good morning
bufanda f scarf
bufete m [boof**e**teh] lawyer's office
bujía f [booH**ee**-a] spark plug
bulto m package; lump, swelling
burro m donkey
buscar to look for
busqué [boosk**eh**] I looked for
butacas fpl stalls
buzón [boos**o**n] letter box, postbox, mailbox

C

c/ street
c/c current account
caballeros mpl [kaba-y**ai**ros] gents, men's rest room
caballo m [kab**a**-yo] horse
cabaña f [kab**a**n-ya] beach hut
cabello m [kab**eh**-yo] hair
cabeza f [kab**e**sa] head
cabida ... personas capacity ... people
cabina telefónica f telephone booth, phone box
cable m [k**a**bleh] wire
cable de extensión m [deh ekstens-y**o**n] extension lead
cabra f goat
cabrón m bastard
cachetada f slap in the face
cacto m cactus
cada every
cada vez (que) [b**e**s (keh)] every time (that)
cadena f chain
cadera f [kad**ai**ra] hip
caduca ... expires ...
caer [ka-**air**] to fall
caerse [ka-**ai**rseh] to fall over, to fall down
café [kaf**eh**] coffee; café
cafetera f [kafet**ai**ra] coffee pot
cafetería f [kafetair**ee**-a] bar-

type restaurant
caída f [ka-**ee**da] fall
caimán m [kīm**a**n] alligator
caja f [k**a**Ha] cash desk, till; cashier
caja de ahorros [deh a-**o**rros] savings bank
caja de cambios [k**a**mb-yos] gearbox
cajera f [kaH**ai**ra], **cajero** m cashier
cajero automático [owtom**a**teeko] cashpoint, automatic teller, ATM
cajeta f [kaH**e**ta] fudge
cajetilla f [kaHet**ee**-ya] packet, (US) pack
cajuela f [kaHw**e**la] boot (of car), (US) trunk
calambre m [kal**a**mbreh] cramp
calcetines mpl [kalset**ee**n-es] socks
calculadora f calculator
calefacción f [kalefaks-y**o**n] heating
calefacción central [sentr**a**l] central heating
calendario m [–d**a**r-yo] calendar
calidad f [kaleed**a**] quality
caliente [kal-y**e**nteh] hot
calle f [k**a**-yeh] street
calle comercial [komairs-y**a**l] shopping street
calle de sentido único one-way street
callejón m [ka-yeh-H**o**n] lane, alley
callejón sin salida cul-de-sac, dead end
calle peatonal [peh-aton**a**l] pedestrianized street
calle principal [preenseep**a**l] main street
callo m [k**a**-yo] corn (on foot)
calmante m [kalm**a**nteh] tranquillizer
calor m heat
hace calor [**a**seh] it's warm/hot
calvo [k**a**lbo] bald
calza: ¿qué número calza? [keh n**oo**mairo k**a**lsa] what is your shoe size?
calzada f [kals**a**da] street
calzada deteriorada poor road surface
calzada irregular uneven surface
calzados shoe shop
calzones mpl [kals**o**n-es] underpants
cama f bed
cama de campaña [deh kamp**a**n-ya] campbed
cama individual [eendeebeedw**a**l] single bed
cama matrimonial [matreemon-y**a**l] double bed
cámara f camera; inner tube
cámara fotográfica camera
camarín m sleeping berth
camarote m [kamar**o**teh] cabin
cambiar [kamb-y**a**r] to change
cambiarse (de ropa) [kamb-y**a**rseh (deh)] to get changed
cambio m [k**a**mb-yo] change; exchange; exchange rate
cambio de divisas [deh

deebeesas] currency exchange
cambio de moneda currency exchange
cambio de sentido take filter lane to exit and cross flow of traffic
camellón m [kameh-y**o**n] central reservation
caminar to walk; to work
camino m path
camino cerrado (al tráfico) road closed to (traffic)
camino privado private road
camión m [kam-y**o**n] bus
camioneta f [kam-yon**e**ta] van
camisa f shirt
camiseta f T-shirt; vest
camisón m nightdress
campana f bell
campechano from/of Campeche
campesino m peasant farmer
camping m camping; campsite; caravan site, trailer park
campo m countryside; pitch; court; field
campo de deportes [deh dep**o**rtes] sports field
campo de futból football ground
campo de golf golf course
canadiense (m/f) [kanad-y**e**nseh] Canadian
cancelado [kansel**a**do] cancelled; stamped
cancelar [kansel**a**r] to cancel; to stamp
cancha f court; pitch
canción f [kans-y**o**n] song
canguro m/f baby-sitter
canoa f canoe; skiff
canoso greying; grey
cansado tired
cantar to sing
cantina f bar
canto m song; singing
caña f [k**a**n-ya] sugar cane; sugar cane liquor
caña de pescar [deh] fishing rod
cañería f [kan-yair**ee**-a] pipes
cañon m [kan-y**o**n] canyon
capaz: ser capaz (de) [sair kap**a**s (deh)] to be able (to); to be capable (of)
capazo m [kap**a**so] carry-cot
capilla f [kap**ee**-ya] chapel
capitalina f, **capitalino** m person who lives in the capital city
capitán m captain
capó(t) m bonnet (of car), (US) hood
cara f face
carácter m [kar**a**ktair] character; nature
tiene mal carácter [t-y**e**neh] he's got a bad temper
¡carajo! [kar**a**Ho] Christ!, shit!
¿dónde carajos? [d**o**ndeh] where in hell?
caravana f caravan, (US) trailer
carburador m carburettor
cárcel f [k**a**rsel] prison
carey m [kar**ay**] tortoiseshell
Caribe: el Caribe [kar**ee**beh] the Caribbean

caricaturas fpl cartoons
cariño m [kar**ee**n-yo] love; affection
carnet de identidad m [deh eedenteed**a**] identity card
carnet de chofer m [chof**air**] driving licence
carnicería f [karneesair**ee**-a] butcher's
caro expensive
carpa f large tent, marquee
carpintería f [karpeentair**ee**-a] joiner's, carpenter's
carrera f [karr**air**a] race; career
carreras de caballos mpl [deh kab**a**-yos] horse racing
carrete m [karr**e**teh] film (for camera)
carretera f [karret**air**a] main road
carretera cortada road blocked, road closed
carretera de circunvalación by-pass
carretera de doble carril two-lane road
carril m lane
carrito m trolley; cart; pushchair
carrito de niño [deh n**ee**n-yo] pushchair
carrito portaequipajes [porta-ekeep**a**H-es] baggage trolley
carro m car
carrocería f [karrosair**ee**-a] bodywork
carro-comedor m buffet car, restaurant car
carro rentado m rented car
carta f letter; menu
cartel m poster
cartelera de espectáculos f [kartel**air**a deh] entertainments guide
cartera f [kart**air**a] briefcase; wallet
carterista m pickpocket
cartero m postman, mailman
cartón m cardboard; carton
casa f house
  en casa at home
  en casa de Juan [deh] at Juan's
  está en su casa make yourself at home
casa de cambio f [k**a**mb-yo] bureau de change
casa de huéspedes [deh w**e**sped-es] guesthouse
casa de socorro emergency first-aid centre
casado married
casarse [kas**a**rseh] to get married
cascada f waterfall
caseta telefónica phone box, phone booth
casete f [kas**e**t] cassette
casi almost
caso m case
  en caso de que [deh keh] in case
caso urgente [oorH**e**nteh] emergency
caspa f dandruff
castaño (m) [kast**a**n-yo] sweet chestnut; brown
castigar to punish

castigo m punishment
castillo m [kast**ee**-yo] castle
casualidad: de casualidad [deh kaswaleed**a**] by chance
catarro: tengo catarro I've got a cold
católico (m) Catholic
catorce [kat**o**rseh] fourteen
causa f [k**ow**sa] cause
cauteloso [kowtel**o**so] cautious; careful
cayó [kī-y**o**] he/she fell
caza f [k**a**sa] hunting
cazadora f [kasad**o**ra] bomber jacket, blouson jacket
cazar [kas**a**r] to hunt
cazuela [kasw**e**la] f casserole; saucepan
ceda el paso give way
ceja f [s**e**Ha] eyebrow
celos: tener celos [ten**ai**r s**e**los] to be jealous
celoso [sel**o**so] jealous
cementerio m [sement**air**-yo] cemetery
cena f [s**e**na] dinner
cenar to have dinner
cenicero m [senees**ai**ro] ashtray
cenote m [sen**o**teh] deep pool used for ceremonial purposes by the Mayas
central camionera f [sentr**a**l kam-yon**ai**ra] main bus station
central de autobuses [deh owtob**oo**s-es] main bus station
central telefónica telephone exchange
centro m [s**e**ntro] centre
centro ciudad [s-yood**a**] city/town centre
centro comercial [komairs-y**a**l] shopping centre
centro deportivo sports centre
centro de salud [deh sal**oo**] health centre
centro urbano city/town centre
ceñido [sen-y**ee**do] tight-fitting
cepillo m [sep**ee**-yo] brush
cepillo de dientes [deh d-y**e**nt-es] toothbrush
cepillo de pelo hairbrush
cera f [s**ai**ra] wax
cerámica f [sair**a**meeka] pottery; ceramics
cerca de [s**ai**rka deh] near
cerilla f [sair**ee**-ya] match
cero [s**ai**ro] zero
cerrada f [sairr**a**da] cul-de-sac
cerrado [sairr**a**do] closed
cerrado por defunción closed due to bereavement
cerrado por descanso del personal closed for staff holidays
cerrado por obras/reforma/vacaciones closed for alterations/renovation/holidays
cerradura f [sairrad**oo**ra] lock
cerramos los ... we close on ...
cerrar [sairr**a**r] to close
cerrar con llave [y**a**beh] to lock
cerrojo m [sairr**o**Ho] bolt
certificado m [sairteefeek**a**do] certificate; registered letter
cervecería f [sairbesair**ee**-a] bar specializing in beer

césped m [s**e**sped] lawn
cesta f [s**e**sta] basket
cesto de la compra m [s**e**sto deh] shopping basket
chabacano m apricot
chaleco m [chal**e**ko] waistcoat, (US) vest
chaleco salvavidas [salbab**ee**das] life-jacket
chalet m [chal**eh**] villa
chalupa f dugout
chamarra f woollen jacket; waistcoat, (US) vest
champú m shampoo
changarro m small store
chapapote m [chapap**o**teh] tar; pitch
chaparro very small
chaparrón m shower; downpour
chaqueta f [chak**e**ta] cardigan; jacket
charcutería f [charkootair**ee**-a] delicatessen
charlar to chat
charreada f [charreh-**a**da] horse-riding display, rodeo
charro m horseman
chato snub-nosed
chava f [ch**a**ba] girl
chavo m boy
checar to check
cheque de viajero m [ch**e**keh deh b-yaH**ai**ro] travellers' cheque
chequera f [chek**ai**ra] cheque book
chiapaneco [ch-yapan**e**ko] from/of Chiapas
chica f girl
chicle m [ch**ee**kleh] chewing gum
chico m boy
chiflar to whistle
chilango from/of Mexico City
chileno (m) Chilean
chillar [chee-y**a**r] to shout, to scream
chinampa f man-made island
chinche m drawing pin; bug
chingadera: ¡qué chingadera! [keh cheengad**ai**ra] what a fuck-up!
chingar to fuck
¡chinga tu madre! [m**a**dreh] fuck off!
chingo: un chingo de [deh] loads of
chino (m) Chinese
chiste m [ch**ee**steh] joke
chocar con to run into
chocolate con leche m [chokol**a**teh kon l**e**cheh] milk chocolate
chofer m [chof**air**] driver
choque m [ch**o**keh] crash; clash
chorros: a chorros loads
chubasco m sudden short shower
chubasquero m [choobask**ai**ro] cagoule
churrasco m roast meat
Cía. company
cicatriz f [seekatr**ee**s] scar
ciclismo m [seekl**ee**smo] cycling
ciclista m/f [seekl**ee**sta] cyclist
ciego [s-y**e**go] blind
cielo m [s-y**e**lo] sky
cien [s-yen] hundred

ciencia f [s-y**e**ns-ya] science
ciento ... [s-y**e**nto] a hundred and ...
cierre m [s-y**ai**rreh] zip, zipper
cierren las puertas close the doors
cierro [s-y**ai**rro] I close
cigarro m [seeg**a**rro] cigarette
cinco [s**ee**nko] five
cincuenta [seen-kw**e**nta] fifty
cine m [s**ee**neh] cinema, movie theater
cinta f [s**ee**nta] tape; ribbon
cintura f [seent**oo**ra] waist; waist measurement
cinturón m [seentoor**o**n] belt
cinturón de seguridad [deh segooreed**a**] seat belt
circo m [s**ee**rko] circus
circulación f [seerkoolas-y**o**n] traffic; circulation
circule despacio drive slowly
circule por la derecha keep to your right
círculo m [s**ee**rkoolo] circle
circunvalación f [seerkoonbalas-y**o**n] ring road
cita f [s**ee**ta] appointment
ciudad f [s-yood**a**] town, city
claro clear; light
¡claro! of course!
clase f [kl**a**seh] class
clausurar [klowsoor**a**r] to close down
clavado de acantilado m [klab**a**do] cliff-diving
clavo m [kl**a**bo] nail; clove
claxon m [kl**a**kson] horn
clima m climate
climatizado [kleemateess**a**do] air-conditioned
clínica f hospital; clinic
cobija f [kob**ee**Ha] rug, blanket
cobrar to charge; to earn
cobre m [k**o**breh] copper
cocer [kos**ai**r] to boil
coche-cama m sleeper, sleeping car
cochecito m [koches**ee**to] pram
coche-comedor m [k**o**cheh komed**o**r] dining car
cocina f [kos**ee**na] kitchen
cocinar [koseen**a**r] to cook
cocinera f [koseen**ai**ra], **cocinero** m cook
código de la circulación m highway code
código postal m [pos-t**a**l] postcode, zip code
codo m elbow
coger [koH**ai**r] to fuck
cojo m [k**o**Ho] person with a limp
cola f tail; queue
hacer cola to queue
colcha f bedspread
colchón m mattress
colchoneta inflable f [eenfl**a**bleh] air mattress
colección f [koleks-y**o**n] collection
colectivo m [kolekt**ee**bo] collective taxi
colegio m [kol**e**H-yo] school
collar m [ko-y**a**r] necklace
colocar to place, to put
colonia f [kol**o**n-ya] urban district

color m colour
columna vertebral f spine
comadre f [kom**a**dreh] godmother
combi m collective taxi, minibus
combustible m [komboost**ee**bleh] fuel
comedor m dining room
comenzar [komens**a**r] to begin
comer [kom**air**] to eat
comerciante m [komairs-y**a**nteh] shopkeeper; dealer
comicios mpl [kom**ee**s-yos] elections
comida f lunch; food; meal
comidas para llevar [y**e**var] take-away meals, meals to go
comienzo (m) [kom-y**e**nso] I begin; beginning
comisaría f police station
como as; like
¿cómo está? how are you?
¿cómo le va? [leh ba] how are things?
como quieras [k-y**ai**ras] it's up to you
compact m compact disc
compadre m [komp**a**dreh] godfather
compañera f [kompan-y**ai**ra] girlfriend
compañero m mate; boyfriend
compañía f [kompan-y**ee**-a] company
compañía aérea [a-**ai**reh-a] airline
comparar to compare
compartir to share
completamente [–m**e**nteh] completely
completo full; no vacancies
complicado complicated
compra: hacer la compra [as**air**] to do the shopping
compramos a ... buying rate ...
comprar to buy
compras: ir de compras [eer deh] to go shopping
compresa m sanitary towel, sanitary napkin
comprimido efervescente m soluble tablet
comprimidos mpl tablets
computadora f computer
comunicando engaged, busy, occupied
con with
concha f shell
concierto m [kons-y**ai**rto] concert
condenar to sentence
condición: a condición de que [kondees-y**o**n deh keh] on condition that
condón m condom
confección f [konfeks-y**o**n] clothing industry
confecciones fpl [konfeks-y**o**n-es] ready-to-wear clothes
conferencia internacional f [konfair**e**ns-ya eentairnas-yon**a**l] international call
conferencia interurbana long-distance call
confesar to admit; to confess
confirmar to confirm

confitería f [konfeetair**ee**-a] sweetshop, candy store
conforme [konf**o**rmeh] as
estar conforme to agree
congelado [konHel**a**do] frozen
congelador m [konHelad**o**r] freezer
congelados mpl [konHel**a**dos] frozen foods
conjunto m [konH**oo**nto] group; band
conmigo with me
conmoción cerebral f [konmos-y**o**n sairebr**a**l] concussion
conmover [konmob**air**] to move
conmutadora f switchboard
conocer [konos**air**] to know
conozco [kon**o**sko] I know
conque [konk**eh**] so, so then
consentido spoiled
consérvese en lugar fresco store in a cool place
consigna f [kons**ee**gna] left luggage, baggage check
consigna automática [owtom**a**teeka] left luggage lockers, baggage lockers
consigo with himself; with herself; with yourself; with themselves; with yourselves
constar: me consta I can confirm
consulado m consulate
consulta médica surgery, doctor's office
consúmase antes de ... best before ...
contacto: ponerse en contacto con to contact
contado: pagar al contado to pay cash
contador m, **contadora** f accountant
contagioso [kontaH-y**o**so] contagious
contaminado polluted
contar to count; to tell
contener [konten**air**] to contain
contenido m contents
contento happy
contestar to reply, to answer
contigo with you
continuación: a continuación [konteenwas-y**o**n] then, next; below
continuar [konteenw**a**r] to continue
contra against
contradecir [kontrades**ee**r] to contradict
contraindicaciones fpl contraindications
contraventanas fpl [kontrabent**a**nas] shutters
control de pasaportes m passport control
convalecencia f [konbales**e**ns-ya] convalescence
convencer [konbens**air**] to persuade
copa f wine glass
coquetear [koketeh-**a**r] to flirt
corazón m [koras**o**n] heart
corbata f tie, necktie
cordillera f [kordee-y**ai**ra] mountain range
cordones mpl [kord**o**n-es] shoelaces

correa del ventilador f [korr**eh**-a del benteelad**o**r] fan belt
correo m [korr**eh**-o] post, mail; post office
correo aéreo [a-**ai**reh-o] airmail
correo central [sen-tr**a**l] main post office
correo terrestre [tairr**e**streh] surface mail
correo urgente [oorH**e**nteh] express
correr [korr**air**] to run
correspondencia f [–d**e**ns-ya] transfer, change
hacer correspondencia en ... to change (trains/buses) at ...
corrida de toros f [deh] bullfight
corriente peligrosa dangerous current
corrimiento de tierras danger: landslides
cortadura f cut
cortar to cut
cortarse [kort**a**rseh] to cut oneself
cortauñas m [korta-**oo**n-yas] nail clippers
corte de pelo m [k**o**rteh deh] haircut
corte y confección [ee konfeks-y**o**n] dressmaking
cortina f curtain
corto short; short of money
cosa f thing
coser [kos**air**] to sew
costa f coast
costar to cost
costilla f [kost**ee**-ya] rib
costumbre f [kost**oo**mbreh] custom
costurera f [kostoor**ai**ra] seamstress
cráneo m [kr**a**neh-o] skull
crédito m credit; unit(s)
creer [kreh-**air**] to believe
crema f cream
crema base [b**a**seh] foundation cream
crema de belleza [deh beh-y**e**sa] cold cream
crema hidratante [eedrat**a**nteh] moisturizer
crema limpiadora [leemp-yad**o**ra] cleansing cream
creyó [kreh-y**o**] he/she believed
criticar to criticize
cruce m [kr**oo**seh] crossroads; junction, intersection; crossing
cruce de ciclistas danger: cyclists crossing
cruce de ganado danger: cattle crossing
crucero m [kroos**ai**ro] cruise
cruda f hangover
cruzar [kroos**a**r] to cross
Cruz Roja f [kroos r**o**Ha] Red Cross
cuaderno m [kwad**ai**rno] notebook
cuadra f [kwadra] block
está a dos cuadros it's two blocks away
cuadrado [kwadr**a**do] square
cuadro m [kw**a**dro] painting
de cuadros [deh] checked
cual [kwal] which; who;

¿cuál? which?
¿cuándo? [kwando] when?
¿cuánto? [kwanto] how much?
en cuanto ... as soon as ...
¡cuánto lo lamento! I'm so sorry!
¿cuántos? how many?
cuarenta [kwarenta] forty
cuartel m [kwartell] barracks
cuartilla f [kwartee-ya] writing paper
cuarto (m) [kwarto] quarter; fourth; room
cuarto con dos camas twin room
cuarto de baño [ban-yo] bathroom
cuarto de estar sitting room
cuarto de hora [deh ora] quarter of an hour
cuarto doble [dobleh] double room
cuarto individual [eendeebeedwal] single room
cuarto piso fourth floor, (US) fifth floor
cuate m [kwateh] friend, pal; twin
cuatro [kwatro] four
cuatrocientos [kwatros-yentos] four hundred
cubierta f [koob-yairta] deck
cubierto (m) covered; overcast; menu
cubiertos mpl cutlery
cubo m [koobo] bucket; cube
cubo de la basura [deh] dustbin, trashcan
cucaracha f cockroach
cuchara f spoon
cucharilla f [koocharee-ya] teaspoon
cuchillería f [koochee-yairee-a] cutlery
cuchillo m [koochee-yo] knife
cuelgue, espere y retire la tarjeta hang up, wait and remove card
cuello m [kweh-yo] neck; collar
cuenta f [kwenta] bill, (US) check; account
cuenta corriente [korr-yenteh] current account
cuentas fpl beads
cuento m [kwento] tale
cuerda f [kwairda] rope; string
cuero m [kwairo] leather
cuerpo m [kwairpo] body
cuesta (f) [kwesta] it costs; slope
cuesta abajo/arriba [abaHo] downhill/uphill
cueva f [kweba] cave
cuidado (m) [kweedado] take care; look out; care
cuidado con ... caution ...
cuidado con el escalón mind the step
cuidado con el perro beware of the dog
cuidar [kweedar] to look after; to nurse
culebra f snake
culpa f fault, blame; guilt
es culpa mía it's my fault
culturismo m body building
cumplas: ¡que cumplas muchos más! many happy returns!

cumpleaños m [koompleh-**a**n-yos] birthday
cuna f cot, (US) crib
cuneta f gutter
cuñada f [koon-y**a**da] sister-in-law
cuñado m [koon-y**a**do] brother-in-law
cuota m [kw**o**ta] contribution; membership fee; motorway toll
cura m priest
curado cured; drunk; smoked
curar to cure; to heal
curarse [koor**a**rseh] to heal up
curva f [k**oo**rba] bend; curve
curva peligrosa dangerous bend
cuyo [k**oo**-yo] whose; of which

D

D. (Don) Mr.
damas fpl draughts, (US) checkers; ladies' toilet, ladies' room
danés [dan-**e**s] Danish
danza f [d**a**nsa] dancing; dance
danzón m [dans**o**n] popular Mexican dance
dañar [dan-y**a**r] to damage
dañarse la espalda [dan-y**a**rseh] to hurt one's back
daños mpl [d**a**n-yos] damage(s)
dar to give
dar el visto bueno a [bw**e**no] to approve
dcha. (derecha) right
de [deh] of; from
de dos metros de alto two metres high
debajo de [deb**a**Ho deh] under
deber (m) [deb**air**] to have to; to owe; duty
deberes mpl [deb**air**-es] homework
débil weak
decepción f [deseps-y**o**n] disappointment
decepcionado [deseps-yon**a**do] disappointed
decidir [deseed**ee**r] to decide
décimo [d**e**seemo] tenth
decir [des**ee**r] to say; to tell
declaración f [deklaras-y**o**n] declaration; statement
declarar to declare, to state
dedo m finger
dedo del pie [p-yeh] toe
defectuoso [defektw**o**so] faulty
dejar [deh-H**a**r] to leave; to let
dejar de beber [deh beb**air**] to stop drinking
delante de [del**a**nteh] in front of
delantera f [delant**air**a] front (part)
delantero front; foward
la parte delantera [p**a**rteh] the front (part)
Delegación de Servicios Migratorios f Immigration Department
demás: los demás the others, the rest
demasiado [demas-y**a**do] too much
demasiados too many

democracia f [demokr**a**s-ya] democracy
demora f delay
demorar: ¿cuánto demora? [kw**a**nto] how long does it take?
dentadura postiza f [post**ee**sa] dentures
dentista m/f dentist
dentro (de) [deh] inside
dentro de dos semanas in two weeks' time
dentro de poco soon
departamento m apartment
departamento amueblado [amwebl**a**do] furnished apartment
departamento sin amueblar [amwebl**a**r] unfurnished apartment
depende [dep**e**ndeh] it depends
dependienta f [–y**e**nta], **dependiente** m [–y**e**nteh] shop assistant
deporte m [dep**o**rteh] sport
deportista m/f sportsman/sportswoman
deportivo [deport**ee**bo] sports
deportivos mpl trainers
depósito m tank; deposit
deprimido depressed
derecha f right
a la derecha (de) on the right (of)
derecho: todo derecho straight ahead
derribar to pull down, to demolish
derrota f defeat
desacuerdo m [desakw**ai**rdo] disagreement
desagradable [–d**a**bleh] unpleasant
desaparecer [–res**air**] to disappear
desaparecido m victim of illegal arrest
desarmador m screwdriver
desastre m [des**a**streh] disaster
desayunar [desī-yoon**a**r] to have breakfast
desayuno m [desī-y**oo**no] breakfast
descansar to rest
descanso m interval
descarado cheeky
descarrilarse to be derailed
descolgar el aparato lift receiver
descomponerse [deskompon**ai**rseh] to break down
descompostura breakdown, mechanical problem
descompuesto [deskompw**e**sto] broken; broken down
descubierto [deskoob-y**ai**rto] discovered; uncovered
descubrir to discover; to uncover
descuelgue el auricular lift the receiver
descuento [deskw**e**nto] discount
descuidado [deskweed**a**do] careless
¡descuide! [deskw**ee**deh] don't worry about it!

desde [d**e**sdeh] since
desde luego [lw**e**go] of course
desde que [keh] since
desear [deseh-**ar**] to want; to wish
¿qué desea? [keh des**eh**-a] what can I do for you?
desembarcadero m [desembarkad**ai**ro] quay
desempleado (m) [desempleh-**a**do] unemployed person; unemployed
desempleo m [desempl**eh**-o] unemployment
desfile m [desf**ee**leh] procession
desfile de modas fashion show
desgracia: por desgracia [desgr**a**s-ya] unfortunately
desgraciadamente [–dam**e**nteh] unfortunately
deshacer las maletas [des-as**air**] to unpack
desierto m [des-y**ai**rto] desert
desinfectante m [–t**a**nteh] disinfectant
desmadre m [desm**a**dreh] chaos; mess
¡qué desmadre! [keh desm**a**dreh] what a mess!
desmaquillarse [desmakee-y**a**rseh] to remove one's make-up
desmayarse [desmī-y**a**rseh] to faint
desnudo naked
desnutrición f [desnootrees-y**o**n] malnutrition
desobediente [desobed-y**e**nteh] disobedient
desodorante m [–r**a**nteh] deodorant
desordenado untidy
desorientarse [desor-yent**a**rseh] to lose one's way
despachador automático m [owtom**a**teeka] ticket machine
despacho de petróleo m [deh petr**o**leh-o] store selling paraffin and oil for heating
despacio [desp**a**s-yo] slowly
despedida f farewell
despedirse [desped**ee**rseh] to say goodbye
despegar to take off
despegue m [desp**eh**-geh] take-off
despejado [despeH**a**do] clear
despertador m [despairtad**o**r] alarm clock
despertar to wake
despertarse [–t**a**rseh] to wake up
despierto [desp-y**ai**rto] awake
desprendimiento de terreno danger: landslides
despreocupado [despreh-okoop**a**do] thoughtless
después [despw**e**s] afterwards
después de [deh] after
destinatario m addressee
destino m destination
el avión con destino a ... the plane for ...
destornillador m [destornee-yad**o**r] screwdriver
destruir [destrw**ee**r] to destroy

desvestirse [desbest**ee**rseh] to undress
desviación f [desb-yas-y**o**n] diversion
desvío m [desb**ee**-o] detour, diversion
desvío provisional temporary diversion
detener [deten**air**] to arrest; to stop
detergente en polvo m [detairH**e**nteh] washing powder
detergente lavavajillas [lababaH**ee**-yas] washing-up liquid
detrás (de) [deh] behind
devolver [debolb**air**] to give back; to vomit
D.F. m [deh **e**feh] Mexico City
di I gave; tell me
día m [d**ee**-a] day
día de Año Nuevo [deh **a**n-yo nw**e**bo] New Year's Day
Día de los Muertos [deh los mw**ai**rtos] Day of the Dead, All Souls Day
día feriado [fer-y**a**do] public holiday
diamante m [d-yam**a**nteh] diamond
diapositiva f [d-yaposeet**ee**ba] slide
diario (m) [d-y**a**r-yo] diary; daily newspaper; daily
diarrea f [d-yarr**eh**-a] diarrhoea
días feriados public holidays
días laborables [labor**a**b-les] weekdays; working days
dibujar [deebooH**a**r] to draw
dibujos animados mpl [deeb**oo**Hos] cartoons
diccionario m [deeks-yon**a**r-yo] dictionary
dice [d**ee**seh] he/she says; you say
dicho [d**ee**cho] said
diciembre m [dees-y**e**mbreh] December
diecinueve [d-yeseenw**e**beh] nineteen
dieciocho [d-yesee-**o**cho] eighteen
dieciséis [d-yesees**ay**s] sixteen
diecisiete [d-yesees-y**e**teh] seventeen
diente m [d-y**e**nteh] tooth
dieron [d-y**ai**ron] they gave; you gave
diesel m [d**ee**sel] diesel
dieta f [d-y**e**ta] diet
a dieta on a diet
diez [d-yes] ten
difícil [deef**ee**seel] difficult
dificultad f [deefeekoolt**a**] difficulty
diga tell me
digo I say
dije [d**ee**Heh] I said
dijeron [deeH**ai**ron] they said; you said
dijiste [deeH**ee**steh] you said
dijo [d**ee**Ho] he/she said; you said
¿qué dijo? what did you say?; what did he/she say?
dilatar to delay; to be late
diminuto tiny

Dinamarca f Denmark
dinero m [deen**ai**ro] money
Dios m [d-yos] God
¡Dios mío! [m**ee**-o] my God!
dirección f [deereks-y**o**n] direction; address; steering; management
director m, **directora** f manager; director; headteacher
directorio m telephone directory
dirigir [deereeH**ee**r] to direct; to lead
disco m record
disconformidad f [deeskonformeed**a**] disagreement
discoteca f record shop; disco
disculparse [deeskoolp**a**rseh] to apologize
disculpe [deesk**oo**lpeh] excuse me
disculpen las molestias we apologize for any inconvenience
discurso m speech
discusión f [deeskoos-y**o**n] discussion; argument
discutir to argue
diseñador de modas m [deesen-yad**o**r deh] fashion designer
disimular [deeseemool**a**r] to pretend
disqueta f [deesk**e**ta] diskette
distancia f [deest**a**ns-ya] distance
distinto different
distraído [deestra-**ee**do] absent-minded; distracted
distribuidor m [deestreebweed**o**r] distributor
Distrito Federal m [fedair**a**l] Federal District, Mexico City
distrito postal m postcode, zip code
disuélvase en agua dissolve in water
divertido [deebairt**ee**do] entertaining; funny
divertirse [deebairt**ee**rseh] to have a good time
divisas fpl [deeb**ee**sas] foreign currency
divorciado [deebors-y**a**do] divorced
divorciarse [deebors-y**a**rseh] to divorce
divorcio m [deeb**o**rs-yo] divorce
divulgar [deeboolg**a**r] to publicize
doble [d**o**bleh] double
doble sentido two-way
doce [d**o**seh] twelve
docena (de) f [dos**e**na] dozen
dólar m dollar
doler [dol**ai**r] to hurt
dolor m pain
dolor de garganta [deh] sore throat
dolor de cabeza [kab**e**sa] headache
dolor de muelas [mw**e**las] toothache
dolor de oídos [o-**ee**dos] earache
doloroso painful
domicilio m [domees**ee**l-yo]

place of residence
domingo m Sunday
domingos y feriados Sundays and public holidays
donativa f donations
donde [d**o**ndeh] where
¿dónde? where?
dorado (m) gold, golden; type of fish
dormido asleep
dormir to sleep
dormitorio m [dormeet**o**r-yo] bedroom; dormitory
dos two
doscientos [dos-y**e**ntos] two hundred
doy I give
droga f drug
drogadicto m [drogad**ee**kto] drug addict
drogado in debt
drogarse [drog**a**rseh] to take drugs; to get into debt
droguería f [drogair**ee**-a] drugstore
ducha f shower
ducharse [dooch**a**rseh] to have a shower
dudar to doubt; to hesitate
duele [dw**e**leh] it hurts
dulce [d**oo**lseh] sweet; gentle
dulces mpl [d**oo**ls-es] sweets, candies
dunas fpl sand dunes
durante [door**a**nteh] during
Durex® m Sellotape®, Scotch tape®
duro hard

E

E parking
e [eh] and
echar to throw; to throw away
  echar a faltar to miss
  echo de menos a mi ... [deh] I miss my ...
echar al buzón [boos**o**n] to post, to mail
echar al correo [korr**eh**-o] to post, to mail
echar el cerrojo [sairr**o**Ho] to bolt
echar sangre [s**a**ngreh] to bleed
echarse la siesta [ech**a**rseh] to have a nap
ecológico [ekol**o**Heeko] ecological
ecologista m/f environmentalist, Green
economía f economy
económico cheap, inexpensive; economic; economical
ecuatoriano (m) [ekwator-y**a**no] Ecuadorean
edad f [ed**a**] age
  ¿qué edad tienes? [keh – t-y**e**n-es] how old are you?
edificio m [edeef**ee**s-yo] building
edredón m quilt, eiderdown; duvet
educado polite
EE.UU. (Estados Unidos) USA
efectivo: en efectivo [efekt**ee**bo] in cash
eje m [**e**Heh] axle
eje del cigüeñal [seegwen-y**a**l]

crankshaft
ejemplo m [eHemplo] example
por ejemplo for example
ejidatario m [eHeedatar-yo] member of an agricultural community
ejido m [eHeedo] communal land
el the
él he; him
elástico elastic
elecciones fpl [eleks-yon-es] elections
electricidad f [elektreeseeda] electricity
electricista m [elektreeseesta] electrician
eléctrico electric
electrodomésticos mpl electrical appliances
elegir [eleh-Heer] to choose
ella [eh-ya] she; her
ellas [eh-yas] they; them
ellos [eh-yos] they; them
embajada f [embaHada] embassy
embalse m [embalseh] reservoir
embarazada [embarasada] pregnant
embotellamiento m [emboteh-yam-yento] traffic jam
embrague m [embrageh] clutch
emergencia f [emairHens-ya] emergency
emisión f [emees-yon] programme; emission; distribution date; issue
emocionante [emos-yonanteh] exciting
empacar to pack
empalme m [empalmeh] junction
empaquetado m [empaketado] packing
empaste m [empasteh] filling
empeorar [empeh-orar] to get worse
empezar [empesar] to begin
empieza a las ocho [emp-yesa] it starts at eight
empinado steep
empleada f [empleh-ada], **empleado** m white collar worker, employee
empresa f firm, enterprise
empresario m businessman
empujar [empooHar] to push
en in; at; on; by
enamorados: día de los enamorados m [dee-a deh] St Valentine's day
encantado delighted
¡encantado! pleased to meet you!
encantador lovely
encantar to please
encendedor m [ensendedor] lighter
encerrar [ensairrar] to lock in; to lock up
enchufe m [enchoofeh] plug; socket
encima [enseema] above
encima de [deh] on top of
encontrar to find
encontrarse (con/a) [–trarseh] to meet
encuentra: se encuentra [seh

enkwentra] is located
encuentro (m) [enk**we**ntro] meeting, encounter; I find
endrogarse [–g**a**rseh] to get into debt
enemigo m enemy
enero m [en**ai**ro] January
enfermarse [–m**a**rseh] to become ill, to get sick
enfermedad f [enfairmed**a**] disease
enfermedad venérea [ben**ai**reh-a] VD
enfermera f [enfairm**ai**ra], **enfermero** m nurse
enfermo [enf**ai**rmo] ill, sick
enfrente de [enfr**e**nteh deh] opposite
enganche [eng**a**ncheh] deposit
engañar [engan-y**a**r] to cheat; to trick
enmicado m [enmeek**a**dó] plastic covering (for documents)
enojado [enoH**a**do] angry
enojarse [–H**a**rseh] to get angry
enorme [en**o**rmeh] enormous
enseñar [ensen-y**a**r] to teach
entender [entend**ai**r] to understand
no entiendo I don't understand
entero [ent**ai**ro] whole; in one piece
entiendo [ent-y**e**ndo] I understand
entierro m [ent-y**ai**rro] funeral
entonces [ent**o**ns-es] then; therefore
entrada f entrance, way in; ticket
entrada gratis admission free
entrada libre [l**ee**breh] admission free
entrar to go in, to enter
entre [**e**ntreh] among; between
entretanto meanwhile
entrevista f [entreb**ee**sta] interview
enviar [emb-y**a**r] to send
envolver [embolb**ai**r] to wrap up; to involve
equipaje m [ekeep**a**Heh] luggage, baggage
equipaje de mano [deh] hand luggage
equipajes mpl [ekeep**a**H-es] left-luggage office, (US) baggage check
equipo m [ek**ee**po] team; equipment, tools
equivocado [ekeebok**a**do] wrong
equivocarse [–**a**rseh] to make a mistake
equivocarse de número [deh n**oo**mairo] to dial the wrong number
era [air**a**] I/he/she/it was; you were
éramos [**ai**ramos] we were
eran [**ai**ran] they were; you were
eras [**ai**ras] you were
eres [**ai**r-es] you are
erupción f [airoops-y**o**n] rash; eruption
es he is; you are
esa that

ésa that (one)
esas those
ésas those (ones)
escala f intermediate stop; scale; ladder
escalera automática f escalator
escaleras fpl stairs
escarcha f frost
escayola f [eskī-y**o**la] plaster cast
escocés [eskos-**e**s] Scottish
Escocia f [esk**o**s-ya] Scotland
escoger [eskoH**air**] to choose
esconder [eskond**air**] to hide
escorpión m [eskorp-y**o**n] scorpion
escribir to write
escrito written
por escrito in writing
escritura f deed; document
escuchar to hear
escuela f [eskw**e**la] school
escuela de párvulos [deh p**a**rboolos] kindergarten
escuincle m/f [eskw**ee**nkleh] kid, nipper; runt
escurrir a mano to wring by hand
ese [**e**seh] that
ése that (one)
esencial [esens-y**a**l] essential
esfuerzo m [esfw**air**so] effort
esmalte de uñas m [esm**a**lteh deh **oo**n-yas] nail polish
esmeralda f emerald
eso that
eso es that's it, that's right
esos those
ésos those (ones)
espalda f back
espantoso dreadful; frightening
España f [esp**a**n-ya] Spain
español (m) [espan-y**o**l], **española** (f) Spanish; Spaniard
especialista m/f [espes-yal**ee**sta] specialist
especialmente [espes-yalm**e**nteh] especially
espectáculo m show, spectacle
espejo m [esp**e**Ho] mirror
esperar [espair**a**r] to wait; to hope
espere [esp**ai**reh] please wait
¡espéreme! [esp**ai**remeh] wait for me!
espero que sí I hope so
espeso thick
esponja f [esp**o**nHa] sponge
esposa f wife
esposo m husband
espuma de afeitar f [deh afayt**a**r] shaving foam
esquí acuático [esk**ee** akw**a**teeko] waterski; waterskiing
esquina f [esk**ee**na] corner
esta this
ésta this one
estación f [estas-y**o**n] station; season
estacionamiento m [estas-yonam-y**e**nto] car park, parking lot
estacionamiento limitado restricted parking
estacionamiento privado private parking
estacionamiento reservado this

parking place reserved
estacionamiento subterráneo underground parking
estacionamiento vigilado supervised parking
estacionarse [estas-yon**ar**seh] to park
estación de autobuses [deh owtob**oo**s-es] bus station
estación de ferrocarril train station
estación de servicio [sairb**ee**s-yo] service station
estadio de fútbol m [est**a**d-yo deh] football stadium
Estados Unidos mpl [oon**ee**dos] United States
estallar [esta-y**ar**] to explode
estampilla f [estamp**ee**-ya] stamp
estaño m [est**a**n-yo] tin; pewter
estar to be
estas these
éstas these ones
estatua f [est**a**twa] statue
este m [**e**steh] east
este this
éste this (one)
esterilizado [estaireeleees**a**do] sterilized
esto this
estómago m stomach
estornudar to sneeze
estos these
éstos these (ones)
estoy I am
estrecho narrow; tight
estrella f [estr**eh**-ya] star
estrellarse contra [estreh-y**a**rseh] to run into; to crash into
estreno m new film/movie release
estreñido [estren-y**ee**do] constipated
estreñimiento m [estren-yeem-y**e**nto] constipation
estropear [estropeh-**ar**] to damage
estudiante m/f [estood-y**a**nteh] student
estudiar [estood-y**ar**] to study
estupefaciente m [–fas-y**e**nteh] hallucinogenic drug
estupendo wonderful, great
estúpido stupid
etiqueta f [eteek**e**ta] label
... de etiqueta [deh] formal ...
europeo [eh-oorop**eh**-o] European
evidente [ebeed**e**nteh] obvious
exactamente [–m**e**nteh] exactly
¡exacto! exactly!
excelente [esel**e**nteh] excellent
excepto [es**e**pto] except
excepto domingos y feriados except Sundays and holidays
excepto sábados except Saturdays
exceso de equipaje m [es**e**so deh ekeep**a**Heh] excess baggage
exceso de velocidad [beloseed**a**] speeding
excursión f [eskoors-y**o**n] trip
excusados mpl [eskoos**a**dos] toilets, rest rooms

expedir [espedeer] to despatch
expendio m [ekspend-yo] stall; kiosk; shop, store
explicación f [espleekas-yon] explanation
explicar to explain
exportación f [esportas-yon] export
exposición f [esposees-yon] exhibition
exprés m [espres] fast train; special delivery
exterior (m) [estair-yor] exterior, outer; foreign; overseas
Secretaría de Asuntos Exteriores Ministry of Foreign Affairs
extintor (de incendios) m [deh eensend-yos] fire extinguisher
extra four-star petrol, (US) premium gas
extranjera (f) [estranHaira], **extranjero** (m) [estranHairo] foreign; foreigner
en el extranjero abroad, overseas
extrañar [estranyar] to miss
extraño [estran-yo] strange

F

fábrica f factory
fabricado por ... made by ...
fácil [faseel] easy
facilidad: con facilidades payment by instalments
factura f bill, (US) check; invoice
facturación f [faktooras-yon] check-in
facturar el equipaje [ekeepaHeh] to check in luggage/baggage
falda f skirt; hillside
fallar [fa-yar] to fail; to break down
falso false
falta f lack; mistake; defect; fault
no hace falta ... [aseh] it's not necessary to ...
faltaba más don't mention it
falta de visibilidad poor visibility
faltar to be missing; to be absent
faltan tres there are three missing
faltan seis kilómetros para llegar there are six kilometres to go before we get there
¿cuánto falta (para) ...? how much further is it (to) ...?
echar a faltar to miss
familia f [fameel-ya] family
famoso famous
farmacia f [farmas-ya] chemist's, pharmacy
farmacia de turno [deh toorno] emergency chemist's/pharmacy, duty chemist
faro m light; headlight; lighthouse
faro antiniebla [anteen-yebla] fog lamp

favor: a favor de [fab**o**r deh] in favour of
por favor please
si hace favor [**a**seh] if you don't mind
fayuca f [fī-y**oo**ka] contraband goods
fayuquero m [fī-yook**ai**ro] seller of contraband goods
febrero m [febr**ai**ro] February
fecha f date
fecha de caducación, fecha de caducidad expiry date
fecha de nacimiento [deh naseem-y**e**nto] date of birth
fecha límite de venta sell-by date
¡Felices Pascuas y Próspero Año Nuevo! [fel**ee**s-es p**a**skwas ee pr**o**spairo **a**n-yo nw**e**bo] Merry Christmas and a Happy New Year!
felicidad f [feleeseed**a**] happiness
¡felicidades! [feleeseed**a**d-es] happy birthday!; congratulations!
felicitar [feleeseet**a**r] to congratulate
feliz [fel**ee**s] happy
¡feliz cumpleaños! [koompleh-**a**n-yos] happy birthday!
feo [f**eh**-o] ugly
feria f [f**ai**r-ya] fair; loose change
feriado: días feriados [fair-y**a**dos] public holidays
ferretería f [fairretair**ee**-a] hardware store
ferrocarril m railway, railroad
festividad f [festeebeed**a**] celebration
festivos bank holidays, public holidays
fibras naturales natural fibres
fiebre f [f-y**e**breh] fever; high temperature
fiebre del heno [**e**no] hay fever
fierro m [f-y**ai**ro] iron
fiesta f public holiday; party
fiesta de ... [deh] feast of ...
fila f row
fila india single file
filmar [feelm**a**r] to film
filtro m filter
filtro solar sunblock
fin m [feen] end; purpose
por fin at last, finally
a fin de que [deh keh] so that
final m [feen**a**l] end
final de autopista end of motorway/highway
fin de semana [deh] weekend
fin de serie discontinued articles
fingir [feenH**ee**r] to pretend
fino fine; delicate
firma f signature; company
firmar to sign
flaco thin, skinny
flequillo m [flek**ee**-yo] fringe
flete m [fl**e**teh] carriage, transport cost
flojera: me da flojera [floH**ai**ra] I can't be bothered

flojo [fl**o**Ho] lazy
flor f flower
florería f [florair**ee**-a] florist
florero m [flor**air**o] vase
flotadores mpl lifebelts
flotar to float
FMT [efemet**eh**] tourist card
foco m light bulb
folleto m [fo-y**e**to] pamphlet
Folleto de Migración Turística [deh meegras-y**o**n] tourist card
fonda f simple restaurant; boarding house
fondo m bottom; background
al fondo (de) at the bottom (of)
fondos mpl funds, money
fontanero m [fontan**air**o] plumber
footing m jogging
forma f form
en forma fit
fósforo m match
foto f photograph
sacar fotos to take photographs
fotografía f photograph; photography
fotografiar [fotograf-y**a**r] to photograph
fotógrafo m photographer
fotómetro m light meter
fraccionamiento m [fraks-yonam-y**e**nto] housing estate
francamente [–m**e**nteh] frankly
francés [frans-**e**s] French
Francia f [fr**a**ns-ya] France
franqueado [frankeh-**a**do] franked
franqueo m [frank**eh**-o] postage
frazada f [fras**a**da] blanket, rug
frecuencia: con frecuencia [frekw**e**ns-ya] often
fregadero m [fregad**air**o] sink
fregar to keep on at; to annoy
fregarlo to screw up
fregar los platos to do the washing up
freír [freh-**ee**r] to fry
frenar to brake
freno m brake
freno de mano [deh] handbrake
frente f [fr**e**nteh] forehead
hacer frente a ... [as**air**] to face up to ...
fresco fresh
frigorífico m fridge
frío [fr**ee**-o] cold
hace frío [**a**seh] it's cold
frontera f [front**air**a] border
la Frontera the Mexican-US border
frutería f [frootair**ee**-a] fruit shop; greengrocer's
fue [fweh] he/she/it went; he/she/it was; you went; you were
fuego m [fw**e**go] fire
¿tiene fuego? have you got a light?
fuegos artificiales [arteefees-y**a**l-es] fireworks

fuente f [fw**e**nteh] fountain; source; font
fuera [fw**ai**ra] outside; he/she/it was; he/she/it went; you were; you went
fuera de [deh] apart from
fuera de horas pico off-peak hours
fuera de servicio [deh sairb**ee**s-yo] out of order
fuéramos [fw**ai**ramos] we were; we went
fueran [fw**ai**ran] they were; they went; you were; you went
fueron [fw**ai**ron] they were; they went; you were; you went
fuerte [fw**ai**rteh] strong; loud
fuerza f [fw**ai**rsa] force; strength
fui [fwee] I was; I went
fuimos [fw**ee**mos] we were; we went
fuiste [fw**ee**steh] you were; you went
fumadores [foomad**o**r-es] smoking
fumar to smoke
funcionar [foons-yon**a**r] to work
funcionario m [foons-yon**a**r-yo] civil servant
función de noche late showing
función de tarde early showing
funeraria f [foonair**a**r-ya] undertaker's
funicular m [fooneekool**a**r] cable car
furioso [foor-y**o**so] furious
furúnculo m abscess; boil
fusible m [foos**ee**bleh] fuse
fútbol m football
futuro (m) [foot**oo**ro] future

G

gachupín m [gachoop**ee**n] Spaniard
gafas fpl glasses, (US) eyeglasses
gafas de bucear [deh booseh-**a**r] goggles
gafas de sol sunglasses
galería f [galair**ee**-a] gallery; enclosed balcony
galería de arte [deh **a**rteh] art gallery
Gales m [g**a**l-es] Wales
galés [gal-**e**s] Welsh
gama: toda la gama the whole range
gamuza f [gam**oo**sa] suede
ganadería f [–dair**ee**-a] cattle farming
ganadero m [–d**ai**ro] (cattle) rancher
ganado m cattle
ganar to win; to earn
ganga f bargain
ganso m goose
garaje m [gar**a**Heh] garage
garantía f guarantee
garantizar [–tees**a**r] to guarantee
garganta f throat

gasolina f petrol, (US) gas
gasolina normal two-star petrol, (US) regular (gas)
gasolina super [s**oo**pair] four-star petrol, (US) premium (gas)
gasolinera f [gasoleen**ai**ra] petrol/gas station, filling station
gastar to spend
gato m cat; jack
gemelos mpl [Hem**e**los] twins; cufflinks
general: por lo general [Henair**a**l] usually
en general generally, in general
genio m [H**e**n-yo] genius
gente f [H**e**nteh] people
una gente a person
gerente m/f [Hair**e**nteh] manager; manageress
gestionar [Hest-yon**a**r] to negotiate
gimnasia f [Heemn**a**s-ya] gymnastics
gimnasio m gymnasium
ginecólogo m [Heenek**o**logo] gynaecologist
gira f [H**ee**ra] tour
girar [Heer**a**r] to turn
gire a la izquierda [H**ee**reh] turn left
giro [H**ee**ro] money order
gis m [Hees] chalk
gitano m [Heet**a**no] gypsy
globo m balloon
glorieta f [glor-y**e**ta] roundabout
gobierno m [gob-y**ai**rno] government
gol m goal
Golfo (de México) m Gulf of Mexico
golpe m [g**o**lpeh] blow
de golpe all of a sudden
golpear [golpeh-**a**r] to hit; to beat up
golpiza f [golp**ee**sa] beating
goma f glue
gomita f rubber band
gordo fat
gorra f cap
gorro m bonnet, cap
gorro de baño [deh b**a**n-yo] bathing cap
gorro de ducha shower cap
gota f drop
gotera f [got**ai**ra] leak
gozar [gos**a**r] to enjoy
grabadora f tape recorder
gracias [gr**a**s-yas] thank you
gracias a Usted [oost**eh**] thank you (more emphatic)
gracioso [gras-y**o**so] funny
grado m degree
grafitos mpl graffiti
gramática f grammar
gramo m gramme
Gran Bretaña f [bret**a**n-ya] Great Britain
grande [gr**a**ndeh] big, large; old
grandes almacenes mpl [gr**a**nd-es almas**e**n-es] large department store
granizo m [gran**ee**so] hail
granja f [gr**a**nHa] farm

granjero m [granHairo] farmer
grano m grain; spot
grapa f paper clip
grasa f fat
grasiento [gras-yento] greasy
grasoso greasy
gratis free
grave [grabeh] serious; very ill/sick
gravilla loose chippings
Grecia f [gres-ya] Greece
gremio m trade union
grifo m tap, (US) faucet
gripe f [greepeh] flu
gris grey
gritar to shout
Grito: el Grito the Declaration of Independence by Miguel Hidalgo on 16 Sept 1810, repeated by the President every Independence Day
grosería [grosairee-a] swearword, oath
  decir groserías [deseer] to swear
grosero [grosairo] rude
grúa f [groo-a] tow truck, breakdown lorry; crane
grueso [grweso] thick
grupo m group
grupo sanguíneo [sangeeneh-o] blood group
guacamayo m [gwakamī-yo] parrot
guajolote m [gwaHoloteh] turkey
guante m [gwanteh] glove
guapo [gwapo] handsome
guardacostas m/f [gwardakostas] coastguard
guardar [gwardar] to keep; to put away
guardarropa m [gwardarropa] cloakroom, (US) checkroom
guardería (infantil) f [gwar-dairee-a (infanteel)] crèche; nursery school
guárdese en lugar fresco keep in a cool place
guardia m/f [gward-ya] guard
guarura m/f [gwaroora] thug, hood
guata f [gwata] belly
guatemalteco (m) [gwatemalteko] Guatemalan
guayabera f [gwī-yabaira] embroidered shirt
guero [gwairo] blond, light skinned
guerra f [gairra] war
guerra civil civil war
guía m/f [gee-a] guide
guía telefónica f phone book, telephone directory
guía turístico m tourist guide
guisar [geesar] to cook
guitarra f [geetarra] guitar
gusano m worm
gustar to please
  me gusta ... [meh] I like ..
  (si) gusta pasar would you like to go in?
  me gustaría ... I'd like to ...
gusto: mucho gusto [moocho] pleased to meet you
  con mucho gusto certainly, with great pleasure

el gusto es mío how do you do; it is a pleasure
¡qué gusto de verte! [keh – deh b**ai**rteh] it's good to see you!

H

h is not pronounced in Spanish

ha he/she/it has; you have
hábil [**a**beel] skilful
días hábiles working days
habitante m/f [abeet**a**nteh] inhabitant
habitar to live
hablador talkative
hablar to speak
hable aquí speak here
habrá there will be; he/she/it will have; you will have
habrán they will have; you will have
habrás you will have
habré [abr**eh**] I will have
habremos we will have
habría [abr**ee**-a] I would have; he/she/it would have; you would have
habríamos [abr**ee**-amos] we would have
habrían [abr**ee**-an] they would have; you would have
habrías [abr**ee**-as] you would have
hacer [as**ai**r] to make; to do
hace tres días [**a**seh] three days ago
hace calor/sol it is hot/sunny
se me hace que ... [seh meh – keh] I believe that ...
no le hace [leh] don't worry about it
¿cuánto se hace de México a Veracruz? how long does it take from Mexico to Veracruz?
hacerse [as**ai**rseh] to become
hacia [**a**s-ya] towards
haga: ¡hágalo ahora! do it now!
hago I do; I make
hallar [a-y**a**r] to find
hamaca f [am**a**ka] hammock
hambre: tengo hambre [**a**mbreh] I'm hungry
han they have; you have
haré [ar**eh**] I will do
harto full, stuffed
estar harto (de) [deh] to be fed up (with)
es harto difícil [deef**ee**seel] it's very difficult
has you have
hasta even; until
hasta que [keh] until
hasta luego [lw**e**go] goodbye, cheerio, see you later
¡hasta mañana! [man-y**a**na] see you tomorrow!
¡hasta pronto! see you soon!
hay [ī] there is; there are
haz [as] do; make
¡hazlo tú! you do it!
he [eh] I have
hecho (m) made; done; fact
hecho a la medida made-to-measure

h is not pronounced in Spanish

helada f frost
heladería f [eladairee-a] ice-cream parlour
helado m ice cream
helar to freeze
hembra f female
hemos we have
henequén m [eneken] sisal-type fibre from the henequen plant, used for making rope and fabrics
herida f [aireeda] wound
herido injured
hermana f [airmana] sister
hermano m [airmano] brother
hermoso [airmoso] beautiful
herramientas fpl [airram-yentas] tools
hervir [airbeer] to boil
hice [eeseh] I made; I did
hidratante: crema hidratante f [eedratanteh] moisturizer
hielo m [yelo] ice
hierba f [yairba] grass
hierro m [yairro] iron
hija f [eeHa] daughter
hijo m [eeHo] son
¡hijo de la chingada! son of a bitch!
¡híjole! [eeHoleh] hell!, damn!
hilo m thread
hipermercado [eepairmairkado] hypermarket
hipo m hiccups
hipódromo m horse-racing track
historia f [eestor-ya] history; story
hizo [eeso] he/she made; he/she did; you made; you did
hogar m home; household goods
hoja f [oHa] leaf; sheet of paper
hoja de afeitar [deh afaytar] razor blade
hojalata f [oHalata] aluminium
¡hola! hello!, hi!
hombre m [ombreh] man
hombre de negocios [deh negos-yos] businessman
hombro m shoulder
hondo deep
hondureño (m) [ondooren-yo] Honduran
honrado honest
hora f hour
¿qué hora es/qué hora tiene/me da su hora? what time is it?
hora local local time
horario m [orar-yo] timetable, (US) schedule
horario de camiones [deh kam-yon-es] bus timetable/schedule
horario de invierno [eemb-yairno] winter timetable/schedule
horario de recogidas [rekoHeedas] collection times
horario de trenes [tren-es] train timetable/schedule
horario de verano [bairano] summer timetable/schedule

horas de consulta surgery hours, (US) office hours
horas de oficina [ofeese**e**na] opening hours
horas de visita [beese**e**ta] visiting hours
horas pico rush hour
hormiga f ant
horno m oven
horquilla m [ork**ee**-ya] hairslide, hairpin
hospedarse [osped**a**rseh] to stay
hotel-garaje m [–gar**a**Heh] hotel where rooms are rented by the hour
hoy [oy] today
hoyo m [**o**-yo] hole
huaraches mpl [war**a**ch-es] leather sandals
hube [**oo**beh] I had
hubieron [oob-y**ai**ron] they had; you had
hubimos [oob**ee**mos] we had
hubiste [oob**ee**steh] you had
hubo [**oo**bo] he/she/it had; you had; there was/were
húbole: ¿qué húbole? [keh **oo**boleh] how's it going?
huele: huele a ... [weleh] it smells of ...
huelga f [w**e**lga] strike
huella f [w**e**ya] print; trace
huellas digitales [deeHeet**a**l-es] fingerprints
hueso m [w**e**so] bone; stone (of fruit etc)
huésped m/f [w**e**sped] guest
huipil m [w**ee**pil] short, embroidered blouse
hule m [**oo**leh] rubber
humedad f [oomed**a**] humidity, dampness
húmedo damp
humo m smoke
humor m humour
hundirse [oond**ee**rseh] to sink
huracán m hurricane

I

idéntico (a/que) [keh] identical (to)
idioma m [eed-y**o**ma] language
idiota m/f [eed-y**o**ta] idiot
iglesia f [eegl**e**s-ya] church
ignorar: ignoro si ... I don't know whether ...
igual [eegw**a**l] equal; like
me da igual [meh] it's all the same to me
imbécil (m) [eemb**e**seel] idiot; stupid
impaciente [eempas-y**e**nteh] impatient
impactante [eempakt**a**nteh] striking; shocking
impermeable (m) [eempairmeh-**a**bleh] waterproof; raincoat
importación f [eemportas-y**o**n] import; importing
artículos de importación imported goods
importante [eemport**a**nteh] important
importar: no importa it doesn't matter
¿le importa si ...? [leh] do you

mind if ...?
importe m [eemp**o**rteh] amount, sum
importe total total due
imposible [eempose**e**bleh] impossible
impreso m [eempr**e**so] form
impuesto m [eempw**e**sto] tax
incendiar [eensend-y**a**r] to set fire to
incendio m [eens**e**nd-yo] fire (blaze)
incluido [eenkloo-**ee**do] included
incluso even
inconsciente [eenkons-y**e**nteh] unconscious; unaware
increíble [eenkreh-**ee**bleh] incredible
indemnizar [eendemnees**a**r] to compensate
independiente [eendepend-y**e**nteh] independent
indicaciones fpl [eendeekas-y**o**n-es] instructions
indicador m indicator
indicador de nivel [deh neeb**e**l] gauge
indicar to indicate
indígena (m/f) [eend**ee**Hena] Indian; native inhabitant
indignado indignant
indispuesto [eendeespw**e**sto] unwell
industria f industry; factory
infantil children's
infarto m heart attack
infección f [eenfeks-y**o**n] infection
infectarse [eenfekt**a**rseh] to become infected
inflamado swollen
inflamarse [eenflam**a**rseh] to swell
influenciar [eenflwens-y**a**r] to influence
información f [eenformas-y**o**n] information
información de vuelos flight information
información turística tourist information
información y turismo tourist information office
informar to inform
informarse (de/sobre) [–m**a**rseh (deh/s**o**breh)] to get information (on/about)
informe m [inf**o**rmeh] report
infracción f [eenfraks-y**o**n] offence
ingeniero m [eenHen-y**ai**ro] engineer
Inglaterra f [eenglat**ai**rra] England
inglés (m) [eeng-l**e**s] English; Englishman
inglesa f Englishwoman
ingresar to enter
ingreso m [eengr**e**so] income; entry
ingresos mpl income; deposits
iniciales fpl [eenees-y**a**l-es] initials
inmediatamente [eenmed-yatam**e**nteh] immediately
inocente [eenos**e**nteh] innocent
inscribirse [–b**ee**rseh] to

register, to enrol
insistir to insist
insolación f [eensolas-y**o**n] sunstroke
instrucciones fpl [eenstrooks-y**o**n-es] instructions
instrucciones de lavado washing instructions
íntegro [**ee**ntegro] complete; intact
inteligente [eenteleeH**e**nteh] intelligent
intentar to try
interés m [eentair-**e**s] interest
interesante [eentairesanteh] interesting
intereses mpl [eentair**e**s-es] interest
interino: en el interino [eentair**ee**no] meanwhile
interior (m) [eentairee-**o**r] interior, inner; domestic, home
intermedio (m) [eentairm**e**d-yo] intermission, interval; intermediate
intermitente m [eentairmeet**e**nteh] indicator
intérprete m/f [eent**ai**rpreteh] interpreter
interruptor m [eentairroopt**o**r] switch
interurbano long-distance
intoxicación alimenticia f [eentokseekas-y**o**n aleement**ee**s-ya] food poisoning
introduzca el dinero exacto insert exact amount
introduzca la tarjeta y marque insert card and dial
introduzca moneda insert coin
inundación f [eenoondas-y**o**n] flood
inundar to flood
inútil useless, pointless
inversión f [eenbairs-y**o**n] investment
invierno m [eemb-y**ai**rno] winter
invitada f [eembeet**a**da], **invitado** m guest
invitar [eenbeet**a**r] to invite
inyección f [een-yeks-y**o**n] injection
ir [eer] to go
ir de paseo [deh pas**eh**-o] to go for a walk
Irlanda f [eerl**a**nda] Ireland
Irlanda del Norte [n**o**rteh] Northern Ireland
irlandés (m) [eerland-**e**s] Irish; Irishman
irlandesa f Irishwoman
irse [**ee**rseh] to leave, to go away
isla f [**ee**sla] island
itinerario m [eeteenair**a**r-yo] itinerary
IVA (impuesto sobre el valor añadido) [**ee**ba] VAT
izq. (izquierda) left
izquierda f [eesk-y**ai**rda] left
a la izquierda (de) [deh] on the left (of)

J

jabón m [Habon] soap
jabón de afeitar [deh afaytar] shaving soap
jacal m [Hakal] straw hut; shack
jaiba f [Hība] crab
jalar [Halar] to pull
jaliscense [Haleesenseh] from/of Jalisco
jamás [Hamas] ever; never
jardín m [Hardeen] garden
jardín de niños [deh neen-yos] kindergarten
jardines públicos mpl [Hardeen-es] park, public gardens
jarocho [Harocho] from/of Veracruz
jarra f [Harra] jug
jarrón m [Harron] vase
jefe m [Hefeh] boss; chief
jefe de tren [deh] guard
jícara f [Heekara] gourd
joder [Hodair] to irritate, to annoy; to mess about; to screw up
¡lo jodiste! [Hodeesteh] you screwed up!
jodido [Hodeedo] annoying, a nuisance; knackered
jornada f [Hornada] working day
jorocho [Horocho] from/of Veracruz
jorongo m [Horongo] poncho
joropo m [Horopo] dance from Veracruz
joven (m/f) [Hoben] young; young man; young woman
joyas fpl [Hoyas] jewellery
joyería f [Hoyairee-a] jewellery; jeweller's
jubilación f [Hoobeelas-yon] pension
jubilada f [Hoobeelada], jubilado m retired person, pensioner
jubilarse [Hoobeelarseh] to retire
judío [Hoodee-o] Jewish
juego (m) [Hwego] game; I play
el juego gambling
jueves m [Hweb-es] Thursday
jugar [Hoogar] to play
jugos y licuados juices and milkshakes
juguete m [Hoogeteh] toy
juguetería f [Hoogetairee-a] toy shop
juicio m [Hwees-yo] judgement; opinion; trial
llevar una persona al juicio to take someone to court
julio m [Hool-yo] July
junio m [Hoon-yo] June
juntar [Hoontar] to collect, to gather
junto (a) [Hoonto] next (to)
juntos together
justo [Hoosto] just; exact, precise
juventud f [Hoobentoo] youth; the young
juzgar [Hoosgar] to judge

K

kínder m [k**ee**ndair] kindergarten
klaxon m [kl**a**kson] horn

L

la the; her; it
labios mpl [l**a**b-yos] lips
laborables weekdays, working days
laca f hair spray
LADA national telephone system
Ladatel long-distance phone
lado m side
al lado de [deh] beside, next to
ladrar to bark
ladridos mpl barking
ladrillo m [ladr**ee**-yo] tile
ladrón m thief
lagartija f [lagart**ee**Ha] lizard
lagarto m alligator
lago m lake
lágrimas fpl tears
lámpara f lamp
lana f wool; money
lana pura pure wool
lanzar [lans**a**r] to throw
lápiz m [l**a**pees] pencil
lápiz de ojos [deh **o**Hos] eyeliner
lapizlabios m [l**a**pees-l**a**b-yos] lipstick
larga distancia [deest**a**ns-ya] long-distance
largo (m) length; long
a lo largo de [deh] along
¡lárguese! [l**a**rgeseh] go away!
las the; them; you
las que ... the ones that ...
lata f tin; can
dar lata to be a nuisance
latinoamericana (f), **latinoamericano** (m) Latin American
latón m brass
lavabo m [lab**a**bo] washbasin
lavado m [lab**a**do] washing
lavado de carros [deh] carwash
lavadora f [labad**o**ra] washing machine
lavandería f [labandair**ee**-a] laundry
lavandería automática [owtom**a**teeka] launderette, laundromat
lavar [lab**a**r] to wash
lavar a mano wash by hand
lavar en seco dry clean
lavar la ropa to do the washing
lavarse [lab**a**rseh] to wash
lavarse la cara to wash one's face
lavar separado wash separately
lavavajillas m [lababaH**ee**-yas] dishwasher
laxante m [laks**a**nteh] laxative
le [leh] him; her; you
lección f [leks-y**o**n] lesson
leche limpiadora f [leemp-yad**o**ra] skin cleanser

lechería f [lechair**ee**-a] dairy; dairy shop
lectura f [lekt**oo**ra] reading
leer [leh-**air**] to read
lejano [leh-H**a**no] distant, faraway
lejía f [leH**ee**-a] bleach
lejos [**le**Hos] far away
lejos de [deh] far from
lengua f [l**e**ngwa] tongue; language
lenguaje m [lengw**a**Heh] language
lentes de contacto fpl [l**e**nt-es deh] contact lenses
lentillas fpl [lent**ee**-yas] contact lenses
lentillas blandas soft lenses
lentillas duras hard lenses
lentillas porosas gas permeable lenses
lento slow
les them; you
letra f letter; banker's draft
levantar [lebant**a**r] to raise, to lift
levantarse [lebant**a**rseh] to get up
ley f [lay] law
libra f pound
libre [**lee**breh] free; vacant
libre de impuestos [deh eempw**e**stos] duty-free
librería f [leebrair**ee**-a] bookshop, bookstore
librero m [leebr**ai**ro] bookshelves
libreta de ahorros f [deh a-**o**rros] savings account book
libreta de direcciones [deereks-y**o**n-es] address book
libro m book
libro de bolsillo [deh bols**ee**-yo] paperback
libro de frases [fr**a**s-es] phrasebook
licenciado m [leesens-y**a**do] graduate
líder m [l**ee**dair] leader
liga f elastic band; suspender
ligero [leeH**ai**ro] light
lima de uñas f [deh **oo**n-yas] nailfile
límite f [**lee**meeteh] limit
límite de altura maximum height
límite de peso weight limit
límite de velocidad [deh beloseed**a**d] speed limit
limpiaparabrisas m [–br**ee**sas] windscreen wiper
limpiar [leemp-y**a**r] to clean
limpieza f [leemp-y**e**sa] cleanliness; cleaning
limpieza en seco dry-cleaning
limpio [l**ee**mp-yo] clean
lindo [l**ee**ndo] beautiful, lovely
línea f [l**ee**neh-a] line
linterna f [leent**ai**rna] torch
lío m [l**ee**-o] mess
liquidación f [leekeedas-y**o**n] sale; redundancy pay
liquidación total clearance sale
liso flat; plain; straight
lista f list

lista de correos [deh korr**eh**-os] poste restante, (US) general delivery
lista de espera [esp**ai**ra] standby; waiting list
listo clever; ready
litera f [leet**ai**ra] couchette
litro m litre
llamada f [yam**a**da] call
llamada por cobrar reverse charge call
llamar [yam**ar**] to call; to name
llamar por teléfono to call, to phone
llamarse [yam**ar**seh] to be called
¿cómo te llamas? [teh y**a**mas] what's your name?
llame a la puerta please knock
llame al timbre please ring
llame antes de entrar knock before entering
llamo: me llamo ... [meh y**a**mo] my name is ...
llanos mpl [y**a**nos] plains
llanta f [y**a**nta] tyre, (US) tire
llantero m [yant**ai**ro] tyre repairs
llave f [y**a**beh] key; spanner, (US) wrench; tap, (US) faucet
llave inglesa [eengl**e**sa] spanner, (US) wrench
llegada f [yeg**a**da] arrival
llegadas internacionales [eentairnas-yon**a**l-es] international arrivals
llegadas nacionales [nas-yon**a**l-es] domestic arrivals
llegar [yeg**ar**] to arrive; to get to
llegué [yeg**eh**] I arrived
llenar [yen**ar**] to fill
llenar el depósito to fill up
lleno [y**e**no] full
llevar [yeb**ar**] to carry; to take; to bring
llevo dos años trabajando aquí I've been working here for two years
llevar a juicio [Hw**ee**s-yo] to take to court
llevarse [yeb**ar**seh] to take away; to remove
llorar [yor**ar**] to cry
llover [yob**air**] to rain
lloviendo: está lloviendo [yob-y**e**ndo] it's raining
llovizna f [yob**ee**sna] drizzle
llueve [yw**eh**-beh] it is raining
lluvia f [y**oo**b-ya] rain
lo it; the
localidad f [lokaleed**a**] place; seat
localidades fpl [lokaleed**a**d-es] ticket office
loción antimosquitos f [los-y**o**n anteemosk**ee**tos] insect repellent
loción bronceadora [bronseh-ad**o**ra] suntan lotion
loción para después del afeitado [despw**e**s del afayt**a**do] aftershave
loco (m) mad; madman
locomotora f engine

locutor m [lokoot**o**r], **locutora** f television presenter
lodo m mud
loma f hill
lonchería f lunch counter
Londres [l**o**nd-res] London
longitud f [lonHeet**oo**] length
los the
los que ... the ones that ...
loza f [l**o**sa] crockery
luces de cruce [l**oo**s-es deh kr**oo**seh] dipped headlights
luces de posición fpl [posees-y**o**n] sidelights
luces traseras [tras**ai**ras] rear lights
lucha f [l**oo**cha] fight, struggle
lucha libre [l**ee**breh] all-in wrestling
luchar to fight
luego [lw**e**go] then; afterwards; soon
luego luego right away, immediately
lugar m place
en lugar de [deh] instead of
lugar de veraneo [bairan**eh**-o] summer resort
lugares de interés [loog**a**r-es deh eentair-**e**s] places of interest
lujo m [l**oo**Ho] luxury
lujoso [looH**o**so] luxurious
luna f moon
lunes m [l**oo**n-es] Monday
luto m mourning
luz f [loos] light
luz de carretera full beam

M

machista m male chauvinist, sexist
macho m male; large banana
machete m [mach**e**teh] long, broad knife
madera f [mad**ai**ra] wood
madrazo m [madr**a**so] beating
madre f [m**a**dreh] mother
dar en la madre a uno to give someone a good beating
¡me vale madre! [meh b**a**leh] I don't give a shit!
madrina f [madr**ee**na] godmother
madrugada f small hours
las cuatro de la madrugada four o'clock in the morning
madrugador m someone who stays up very late/gets up very early, early riser
madrugar to stay up very late; to get up very early
madurar to mature, to ripen; to come to term
maduro ripe
maestra f [ma-**e**stra], **maestro** m teacher; primary school teacher
magna sin [seen] unleaded
maguey m [mag**ay**] agave cactus
maíz m [ma**ee**s] maize, (US) corn
mal (m) wrong; evil; bad; badly

maleducado rude
malentendido m misunderstanding
maleta f suitcase
hacer las maletas to pack
maletero m [maletairo] boot (of car), (US) trunk
mal genio m [Hen-yo] bad temper
mal humor m [oomor] bad mood; bad temper; anger
Malinche f [maleencheh] Cortés' interpreter who later became his lover
malinchismo m betrayal of one's country
malo bad; sick, ill, unwell
mamá f mum
mamón! idiot!
manantial m [manant-yal] spring
mancha f stain
manchar to stain, to dirty
mandar to send; to order
mandatario: el primer mandatario [mandator-yo] leader; President; Prime Minister
mandato m period in government
¿mande? [mandeh] sorry?, pardon (me)?
mandíbula f jaw
manejar [maneHar] to drive
maneje con cuidado drive with care
manejo [maneHo] I drive
manera: de esta manera [deh – manaira] in this way
de manera que so (that)
manga f sleeve
sin manga sleeveless
manglar m mangrove swamp
mango m handle; mango
manifestación f [maneefestas-yon] demonstration; manifestation
mano f hand; pal, mate, buddy
manoplas fpl mittens
manta f blanket, rug
mantel m tablecloth
mantelerías fpl [mantelairee-as] table linen
mantenga limpia la ciudad keep our city tidy
manténgase en lugar fresco store in a cool place
manténgase fuera del alcance de los niños keep out of the reach of children
mantenimiento m [manteneem-yento] maintenance
manzana f [mansana] apple; city block
mañana (f) [man-yana] morning; tomorrow
por la mañana/de mañana in the morning
¡hasta mañana! see you tomorrow!
pasado mañana the day after tomorrow
mañana por la mañana tomorrow morning
mañana por la tarde [tardeh] tomorrow afternoon; tomorrow evening

mañanitas: cantar las mañanitas [man-yan**ee**tas] to serenade someone for their birthday
mapa m map
mapa de carreteras [deh karret**ai**ras] road map
mapa de recorrido network map
maquiladora f [makeelad**o**ra] foreign-owned assembly plant located in Mexico
maquillaje m [makee-y**a**Heh] make-up
maquillarse [makee-y**a**rseh] to put one's make-up on
máquina de afeitar eléctrica f [m**a**keena deh afayt**a**r] electric shaver
máquina de escribir typewriter
máquina de fotos camera
maquinaria f [makeen**a**r-ya] machinery
máquina tragaperras slot machine
maquinilla de afeitar f [makeen**ee**-ya deh afayt**a**r] electric shaver
mar m sea
maravilloso [marabee-y**o**so] marvellous
marcar to dial; to mark
marca registrada f [reHeestr**a**da] registered trade mark
marcar el número dial the number
marcha f gear
marcha atrás reverse gear
marcharse [march**a**rseh] to go away
marea f [mar**eh**-a] tide
mareado [mareh-**a**do] dizzy; sick; drunk
mareo m [mar**e**h-o] sickness; faintness
marica m, maricón m queer
marido m husband
marina f navy
mariposa f butterfly; fairy, pansy
marisquería f [mareeskair**ee**-a] shellfish restaurant
marque ... dial ...
martes m [m**a**rt-es] Tuesday
martes de carnaval [deh karnab**a**l] Shrove Tuesday
martillo m [mart**ee**-yo] hammer
marzo m [m**a**rso] March
más more
más de/que [deh/keh] more than
más pequeño smaller
el más caro the most expensive
ya no más that's enough
más o menos more or less
matar to kill
matrícula f licence plate; registration; registration fees
máximo personas maximum number of people
maya (m/f) [mī-ya] Maya; Mayan
mayo m [m**ī**-yo] May
mayor [mī-y**o**r] adult; bigger; older; biggest; oldest

la mayor parte (de) [parteh (deh)] most (of)
mayor de edad of age (18), adult
mayoría: la mayoría [mī-yoree-a] most; the majority
me me; myself
me duele aquí [dweleh] I have a pain here
mecánico m mechanic
mecate m [mekateh] string; rope; cord
media docena (de) f [med-ya dosena (deh)] half a dozen
media hora f [ora] half an hour
mediano [med-yano] medium; average
medianoche f [med-yanocheh] midnight
media pensión f [pens-yon] half board
medias fpl [med-yas] stockings; tights, pantyhose
ir/pagar a medias to go Dutch, to share the costs
medicina f [medeeseena] medicine
médico m [medeeko] doctor
médico general [Henairal] GP
medida f size; measure
medida del cuello f [kweh-yo] collar size
medio m [med-yo] middle
por medio de [deh] by (means of)
de tamaño medio [taman-yo] medium-sized
medio boleto m half fare
mediodía m [med-yodee-a] midday
medio litro m half a litre
medir to measure
medusa f jellyfish
mejor [meHor] better; best
mejorar [meHorar] to improve
se está mejorando [seh] he's getting better
mencionar [mens-yonar] to mention
menor smaller; younger; smallest; youngest
menor de edad minor, under-age
menos less; least; fewer; fewest
a menos que [keh] unless
mensual [menswal] monthly
mentar: mentarle la madre a uno [mentarleh la madreh] to insult someone, to swear at someone
menú turístico m set menu
menudo tiny, minute
a menudo often
mercado m [mairkado] market
mercado cubierto [koob-yairto] indoor market
mercado de divisas [deh deebeesas] exchange rates
mercería f [mairsairee-a] haberdashery
merendar to have an afternoon snack
merendero m [mairendairo] open-air café
merienda f [mair-yenda] tea,

afternoon snack
mero [m**ai**ro] exact; almost, nearly
ya mero any minute now, right away
el mero mero the big cheese
está aquí mero it's just near here
mes m month
mesa f table
mesera f [mes**ai**ra] waitress; chambermaid
mesero m waiter
mesón m restaurant specializing in regional dishes
mestizo [mest**ee**so] mixed race, interracial
meta f goal
metate m [met**a**teh] mortar and pestle
metro m metre; underground, (US) subway
mexicana (f), [meHeek**a**na] mexicano (m) Mexican
México m [m**e**Heeko] Mexico; Mexico City
mezquita f [mesk**ee**ta] mosque
mi my
mí me
mía [m**ee**-a] mine
microondas: horno microondas [**o**rno meekro-**o**ndas] microwave oven
miedo m [m-y**e**do] fear
tengo miedo (de/a) [deh] I'm afraid (of)
miel f [m-yel] honey
mientras [m-y**e**ntras] while
mientras que [keh] whereas
mientras tanto meanwhile
miércoles m [m-y**ai**rkol-es] Wednesday
miércoles de ceniza [deh sen**ee**sa] Ash Wednesday
¡mierda! [m-y**ai**rda] shit!
mil [meel] thousand
militar m soldier, serviceman
millón m [mee-y**o**n] million
un millón de ... [deh] a million ...
milpa f maize field
mina f mine
minifalda f mini-skirt
minúsculo tiny
minusválido (m) [meenoosb**a**leedo] disabled; disabled person
minuto m minute
mío [m**ee**-o] mine
miope [m-y**o**peh] short-sighted
mirador m scenic view; vantage point
mirar to look (at); to see
mis my
misa f mass
mismo same
mitad f [meet**a**] half
mitad de precio [deh pr**e**s-yo] half price
mixteca (f) [meest**e**ka] from/of the Mixtec region; indigenous language of Southern Mexico
M.N. (moneda nacional) f national currency
mochila f rucksack
moda f fashion

de moda fashionable
moda juvenil [Hoobeneel] young fashions
modas caballeros fpl [kaba-yairos] men's fashions
modas niños/niñas [neen-yos] children's fashions
modas pre-mamá maternity fashions
modas señora [sen-yora] ladies' fashions
modelo m model; design; style
moderno [modairno] modern
modista f dressmaker; fashion designer
modisto m fashion designer
modo: de modo que [deh – keh] so (that)
ni modo that's how it is, what can you do?
modo de empleo instructions for use
mojado [moHado] wet
molcajete m [molkaHeteh] mortar and pestle
moldeado con secador de mano [moldeh-ado – deh] blow-dry
molestar to disturb; to bother
molesto annoying
monasterio m [monastair-yo] monastery
moneda nacional f [nas-yonal] national currency
monedas fpl coins
monedero m [monedairo] purse
montacargas m service lift, service elevator
montaje m [montaHeh] assembly
montaña f [montan-ya] mountain
montaña rusa f big dipper, roller coaster
montañismo m [montan-yeesmo] climbing
montar to get in; to ride; to assemble
montar a caballo [kaba-yo] to go horse-riding
montar en bicicleta [beeseekleta] to cycle
morado purple
morbo m morbid interest
mordedura f bite
morder [mordair] to bite
mordida f bribe
moreno dark-haired; dark-skinned
moretón m bruise
morir to die
mosca f fly
mostrador m counter
mostrar to show
motel-garaje m [garaHeh] hotel where rooms are rented by the hour
moto f motorbike
motora f motorboat
mover [mobair] to move
mucha [moocha] much; a lot; a lot of
muchacha f girl
muchacho m boy
muchas a lot; a lot of; many
muchas gracias [gras-yas] thank

you very much
muchísimas gracias thank you very much indeed
muchísimo enormously, a great deal
mucho [m**oo**chos] much; a lot; a lot of
mucho más a lot more
mucho menos a lot less
mucho gusto a pleasure to meet you
muchos a lot; a lot of; many
muebles mpl [mw**e**bl-es] furniture
muela f [mw**e**la] tooth
sacarse una muela [sak**a**rseh] to have a tooth taken out
muela del juicio [Hw**ee**s-yo] wisdom tooth
muelle m [mw**eh**-yeh] spring; quay
muerte f [mw**air**teh] death
muerto (m) [mw**air**to] dead; dead person
mugriento [moogr-y**e**nto] filthy
mujer f [mooH**air**] woman; wife
muletas fpl crutches
multa f fine; parking ticket
multa por uso indebido penalty for misuse
mundo m world
muñeca f [moon-y**e**ka] wrist; doll
muro m wall
músculo m muscle
museo m [moos**eh**-o] museum
museo de arte [deh **a**rteh] art gallery
música f music
muslo m thigh
musulmán Muslim
muy [mwee] very
muy bien [b-yen] very well

N

N$ m new peso
nácar m mother of pearl
nacer [nas**air**] to be born
nacido [nas**ee**do] born
nacimiento m [naseem-y**e**nto] birth; Nativity
nacional [nas-yon**a**l] domestic
el turismo nacional Mexican tourism, local tourism
nacionalidad f [nas-yonaleed**a**] nationality
nacionalismo m [nas-yonal**ee**smo] nationalism
nacionalización f [nas-yonaleesas-y**o**n] nationalization
nada nothing
de nada [deh] you're welcome, don't mention it
antes que nada [**a**nt-es keh] first of all
nada que declarar nothing to declare
nadar to swim
nadie [n**a**d-yeh] nobody
náhuatl (m) [n**a**watl] Aztec; language of the Aztecs
narcotraficante m/f [–k**a**nteh] drug trafficker
narcotráfico m drug trade, drug traffic

nariz f [nar**ee**s] nose
natación f [natas-y**o**n] swimming
natural [natoor**a**l] natural
al natural at room temperature
naturaleza f [natooral**e**sa] nature
naturalmente [–m**e**nteh] naturally; of course
náusea: siento náuseas [s-y**e**nto n**ow**seh-as] I feel sick
navaja f [nab**a**Ha] penknife; flick knife
Navidad f [nabeed**a**] Christmas
¡feliz Navidad! [fel**ee**s] merry Christmas!
nayarita [nī-yar**ee**ta] from/of Nayarit
neblina f mist
necesario [neses**a**r-yo] necessary
necesitar [neseseet**a**r] to need
negar to deny
negativa f [negat**ee**ba] denial; refusal
negativo m negative
negocio m [neg**o**s-yo] business
negro (m) black; furious; black man
nena f baby girl; little girl
nene m [n**e**neh] baby boy; little boy
nervioso [nairb-y**o**so] nervous
me pone nervioso [meh p**o**neh] it makes me nervous
neurótico [neh-oor**o**teeko] neurotic
nevar [neb**a**r] to snow
nevería f [neber**ee**-a] ice cream parlour
ni neither; nor
¡ni modo! what can you do!
ni ... ni ... neither ... nor ...
nica m/f Nigaraguan
nicaraguense (m/f) [neekaragw**e**nseh] Nicaraguan
niebla f [n-y**e**bla] fog
nieta f [n-y**e**ta] granddaughter
nieto m [n-y**e**to] grandson
nieva [n-y**e**ba] it is snowing
nieve f [n-y**e**beh] snow; ice cream; sorbet
ningún none; not one; no ...
en ningún sitio [s**ee**t-yo] nowhere
ninguno nobody; none; not one
niña f [n**ee**n-ya] child
niñera f [neen-y**ai**ra] nanny
niño m [n**ee**n-yo] child
nivel del aceite m [neeb**e**l del as**ay**teh] oil level
no no; not
noche f [n**o**cheh] night
de noche at night
buenas noches [bw**e**nas n**o**ch-es] good night
esta noche tonight
por la noche at night
pasar la noche to spend the night
Nochebuena f [nocheh-bw**e**na] Christmas Eve
Nochevieja f [n**o**cheh-b-y**e**Ha]

New Year's Eve
no contiene alcohol does not contain alcohol
nocturno [noktoorno] night
no estacionarse no parking
no estacionarse, se usa grúa illegally parked vehicles will be towed away
no exceda la dosis indicada do not exceed the stated dose
no fumadores [foomador-es] no smoking
no fumar no smoking
no funciona [foons-yona] out of order
no hay de qué [ī deh keh] you are welcome
no hay localidades sold out
no le hace [leh aseh] don't worry about it
nomás just, only
díselo nomás [deeselo] just tell him/her
nombre m [nombreh] name
nombre de pila [deh] first name
nombre de soltera [soltaira] maiden name
no molestar do not disturb
nopal m cactus leaf
no para en ... does not stop in ...
no pisar el pasto keep off the grass
nordeste m [nordesteh] north-east
no rebasar no overtaking, no passing
no recomendada para menores de 18 años not recommended for those under 18 years of age
normal (m) [nor-mal] normal; lower grade petrol, (US) regular (gas)
normalmente [–menteh] usually
noroeste m [noro-esteh] north-west
norte m [norteh] north
al norte de la ciudad [deh la s-yooda] north of the city
norteamericana (f) [norteh-amaireekana], norteamericano (m) North American
norteño [norten-yo] from the north of Mexico
Noruega f [norwega] Norway
nos us; ourselves
no se admiten devoluciones no refunds given
no se admiten perros no dogs allowed
no ... sino ... not ... but ...
nosotras, nosotros we; us
nota f note
nota de consumo [deh] receipt
noticias fpl [notees-yas] news
noticiero m [notees-yairo] news bulletin
no tocar please do not touch
no utilizar lejía do not bleach
nova f [noba] two-star petrol, (US) regular gas
nova plus four-star petrol, (US) premium gas

novecientos [nobes-**y**entos] nine hundred
novecito [nobes**ee**to] very new
novela f [nob**e**la] novel
noveno [nob**e**no] ninth
noventa [nob**e**nta] ninety
novia f [n**o**b-ya] girlfriend; fiancée; bride
noviembre m [nob-**y**embreh] November
novillada f [nobee-y**a**da] bullfight featuring young bulls
novio m [n**o**b-yo] boyfriend; fiancé; groom
Nte. north
nube f [n**oo**beh] cloud
nublado cloudy
nuboso cloudy
nuera f [nw**ai**ra] daughter-in-law
nuestra [nw**e**stra], **nuestras, nuestro, nuestros** our
Nueva York [nw**e**ba] New York
nueve [nw**e**beh] nine
nuevo [nw**e**bo] new
nuevoleonés [nweboleh-on-**e**s] from/of Nuevo Leon
nuevo peso m new peso
número m [n**oo**mairo] number; size
número de calzado [deh kals**a**do] shoe size
número de teléfono phone number
nunca never
nutritivo [nootreet**ee**bo] nutritious

O

o or
o ... o ... either ... or ...
oaxaqueño [waHak**e**n-yo] from/of Oaxaca
obispo m [ob**ee**spo] bishop
objeción f [obHes-y**o**n] objection
objetar [obHet**a**r] to object
objetivo m [obHet**ee**bo] lens; objective
objetos de escritorio [obH**e**tos deh eskreet**o**r-yo] office supplies
objetos perdidos lost property, lost and found
obra f work; play
obras fpl roadworks
obrero m [obr**ai**ro] worker
obsequio m [obs**e**k-yo] gift
obstruido [obstroo-**ee**do] blocked
obturador m shutter
ocasión f [okas-y**o**n] occasion; opportunity; bargain
de ocasión [deh] second hand
occidental [okseedent**a**l] Western
occidente m [okseed**e**nteh] West
Océano Pacífico m [os**eh**-ano] Pacific Ocean
ochenta eighty
ocho eight
ochocientos [ochos-**ye**ntos] eight hundred
ocho días mpl [d**ee**-as] week

ocote m [ok**o**teh] resinous pine used for burning
octavo [okt**a**bo] eighth
octubre m [okt**oo**breh] October
oculista m/f optician
ocultar to hide
oculto hidden
ocupado engaged; occupied; busy
ocupar to occupy
ocurrir [okoor**ee**r] to occur, happen
ocurre que [ok**oo**rreh keh] it so happens that
odiar [od-y**a**r] to hate
odio (m) [**o**d-yo] hate, hatred; I hate
odioso odious, revolting; horrible
oeste m [o-**e**steh] west
al oeste de la ciudad [deh la s-yood**a**] west of the city
ofender [ofend**air**] to offend
oferta f [of**air**ta] special offer
oficial (m/f) [ofees-y**a**l] officer; official
oficina f [ofees**ee**na] office
oficina de correos [deh korr**eh**-os] post office
oficina de correos y telégrafos post office and telegrams
oficina de información y turismo [eenformas-y**o**n] tourist information office
oficina de objetos perdidos [obH**e**tos] lost property office, lost and found
oficina de reclamaciones [reklamas-y**o**n-es] complaints department
oficina de registros [reH**ee**stros] registrar's office
oficina de turismo tourist information office
oficinista m/f [ofeeseen**ee**sta] office worker
oficio m [of**ee**s-yo] job; trade
ofrecer [ofres**air**] to offer
oído (m) [o-**ee**do] ear; hearing; heard
¡oiga! [**oy**ga] listen here!; excuse me!
oigo I am listening
oír [o-**ee**r] to listen
ojo m [**o**Ho] eye
¡ojo! watch out!
ola f wave
ola de calor [deh] heatwave
oler [ol**air**] to smell
olfato m sense of smell
olmeca from/of ancient Olmec culture
olor m smell
olvidar [olbeed**a**r] to forget
once [**o**nseh] eleven
ONU f [o **e**neh oo] UN
operación f [opairas-y**o**n] operation
operadora f operator
operarse [opair**a**rseh] to have an operation
oportunidad f [oportoonid**a**] chance, opportunity
oposición f [oposees-y**o**n] opposition
óptica f optician's
óptico m optician
optimista optimistic

¡órale! [**o**raleh] go on then!, get on with it!
orden f order, instruction
a sus órdenes at your service
orden m order
en orden in order
organización f [organeesas-y**o**n] organization
organizar [organeesa**r**] to organize
orgulloso [orgoo-y**o**so] proud
oriental east, eastern
orientar to direct, to guide
oriente m [or-y**e**nteh] east
orilla f [or**ee**-ya] shore; side
oro m gold
orquesta f [ork**e**sta] orchestra
oscuro dark
Ote. east
otoño m [ot**o**n-yo] autumn, (US) fall
otorrinolaringólogo m ear, nose and throat specialist
otra vez [bes] again
otro another (one); other
oveja f [ob**e**Ha] sheep
overol m [obair**o**l] overall
oye [**o**-yeh] he/she listens; you listen; he/she hears; you hear

P

pabellón m [pabeh-y**o**n] (hospital) ward
pachanga f party; partying
paciente m/f [pas-y**e**nteh] patient
padecer [pades**air**] to suffer
padecer del corazón [koras**o**n] to have a heart condition
padre m [p**a**dreh] father
¡está padre! it's great!
padres mpl [p**a**d-res] parents
padrino m [padr**ee**no] godfather
pagadero [pagad**ai**ro] payable
pagar to pay
página f [p**a**Heena] page
páginas amarillas [amar**ee**-yas] yellow pages
pago m payment
país m [pa-**ee**s] country
paisaje m [pīs**a**Heh] landscape; scenery
pájaro m [p**a**Haro] bird
pala f spade
palabra f word
palacio m [pal**a**s-yo] palace
Palacio de Justicia [deh Hoost**ee**s-ya] Law Courts
palanca de velocidades f [beloseed**a**d-es] gear lever
palco m box (at theatre)
paleta f ice lolly
paliacate m [pal-yak**a**teh] headscarf
palmera f [palm**ai**ra] palm tree
palo m stick; tree
palomitas fpl popcorn
palos de golf mpl [deh] golf clubs
paludismo m [palood**ee**smo] malaria
PAN (Partido de Acción Nacional) m National Action Party (centre-right party)

panadería f [panadair**ee**-a] baker's
panal m honeycomb
panameño (m) [panam**e**n-yo] Panamanian
pantalla f [pant**a**-ya] screen
pantalón corto m shorts
pantalones mpl [pantal**o**n-es] trousers, (US) pants
panteón m [panteh-**o**n] cemetery
pantimedias fpl tights, pantyhose
panza f [p**a**nsa] belly
pañal m [pan-y**a**l] nappy, diaper
pañuelo m [panw**e**lo] handkerchief; scarf
papa f [p**a**pa] potato
papá m dad
papalote m [–l**o**teh] kite
papel m [pap**e**l] paper; rôle
papel de envolver [deh embolb**air**] wrapping paper
papel de escribir writing paper
papel de plata silver foil
papelera f [papel**ai**ra] litter; litter bin
papelería f [papelair**ee**-a] stationery, stationer's
papel sanitario [saneet**a**r-yo] toilet paper
papel tapiz [tap**ee**s] wallpaper
paquete m [pak**e**teh] packet; package holiday
paquetería f [paketair**ee**-a] left luggage office, baggage check
par m pair
para for; in order to
cuarto para las tres quarter to three
parabrisas m windscreen
paracaidismo m [parakīd**ee**smo] parachuting; squatting
paracaidista m/f squatter; parachutist
parachoques m [parach**o**k-es] bumper, (US) fender
parada f stop
parada de camión [deh] bus stop
paradero f [parad**ai**ro] stop
paraguas m [par**a**gwas] umbrella
para que [keh] in order that
parar to stop
pararse to stand (up)
para uso del personal staff only
para uso externo not to be taken internally
parcela f [pars**e**la] plot (of land)
parecer [pares**air**] to seem; to resemble
parece que sí/no it seems so/not
me parece (que) ... I think (that) ...
parecido [pares**ee**do] similar
pared f [par**eh**] wall
pareja f [par**e**Ha] pair; couple; partner
parezco [par**e**sko] I am like
pariente m/f [par-**ye**nteh]

relative
parir to give birth
parque m [p**a**rkeh] park
parque de atracciones [deh atraks-y**o**n-es] amusement park
parque de bomberos [bomb**ai**ros] fire station
parque de recreo [rekr**eh**-o] amusement park
parque infantil [eenfant**ee**l] children's park
parrilla f [parr**ee**-ya] grill
párroco m parish priest
parte m [p**a**rteh] report
parte f [p**a**rteh] part
en todas partes [p**a**rt-es] everywhere
en otra parte elsewhere
en alguna parte somewhere
¿de parte de quién? [deh – k-yen] who's calling?
participar [parteeseep**a**r] to take part; to inform
particular [parteekool**a**r] private
un particular a private individual
partida f game
partido m match, game, bout; (political) party
partir to cut (into pieces); to leave, to go
a partir de mañana from tomorrow onwards
parto m birth
parvulario m [parbool**a**ree-o] nursery school
pasado last
la semana pasada last week
pasado mañana [man-y**a**na] the day after tomorrow
pasado de moda [deh] out of fashion
pasaje m [pas**a**Heh] ticket; fare
pasajero m [pasaH**ai**ro] passenger
pasajeros de tránsito transit passengers
pasaporte m [pasap**o**rteh] passport
pasaportes passport control
pasar to pass; to overtake; to happen
pasar la aduana [adw**a**na] to go through Customs
pasarlo bien [b-yen] to enjoy oneself
pasatiempo m [pasat-y**e**mpo] hobby
Pascua [p**a**skwa] Easter
pase [p**a**seh] come in
pasear [paseh-**a**r] to go for a walk; to take for a walk
paseo m [pas**eh**-o] walk; drive; ride
paseo de ... ... avenue
pasillo m [pas**ee**-yo] corridor
paso m passage; pass; step
estar de paso [deh] to be passing through
pasó: ¿qué pasó? how's it going?, what's happening?
paso a desnivel underpass
paso a nivel level crossing, (US) grade crossing
paso de contador [deh] (metered) unit

paso de peatones [peh-at**o**n-es] pedestrian crossing
paso prohibido no admittance, no entry
paso subterráneo pedestrian underpass
pasta de dientes f [deh d-y**e**nt-es] toothpaste
pastelería f [pastelair**ee**-a] cake shop
pastilla f [past**ee**-ya] pill, tablet
pastillas para la garganta throat pastilles
patatas fritas crisps, (US) potato chips
patinaje m [pateen**a**Heh] skating
patinar to skid; to skate
patria f [p**a**tree-a] motherland, home country
las fiestas patrias celebration of national independence
paz f [pas] peace
PB ground floor, (US) first floor
peatón m [peh-at**o**n] pedestrian
peatonal pedestrian
peatón, circula por tu izquierda pedestrians keep to the left
peatones [peh-at**o**n-es] pedestrians
pecado m sin
pecho m chest; breast
pedazo m [ped**a**so] piece
pediatra m/f [pedee-**a**tra] pediatrician
pedir to order; to ask for
pedir hora [**o**ra] to ask the time
pedir disculpas to apologize
pegar to hit; to stick
no me pega la gana I don't feel like it
peinar [payn**a**r] to comb
peinarse [payn**a**rseh] to comb one's hair
peine m [p**ay**neh] comb
pelado cropped; bare, barren; skint, penniless
pelea f [pel**eh**-a] fight
peletería f [peletair**ee**-a] furs, furrier
película f film, movie
película de color [deh] colour film
película en versión original [bairs-y**o**n oreeHeen**a**l] film/movie in the original language
peligro m danger
peligro de incendio danger: fire hazard
peligro deslizamientos slippery road surface
peligroso dangerous
es peligroso bañarse danger: no swimming
es peligroso asomarse do not lean out
pelirrojo [peleerr**o**Ho] redheaded
pelo m hair
pelón bald
pelota f ball
peluca f wig

peluquera f [pelook**ai**ra], **peluquero** m hairdresser
peluquería f [pelookair**ee**-a] hairdresser's
peluquería de caballeros [deh kaba-y**ai**ros] gents' hairdresser's
peluquería de señoras [sen-y**o**ras] ladies' salon
Pemex State-owned oil company
pena f sadness, sorrow
¡qué pena! [keh] what a pity!
me da mucha pena [meh] I'm very sorry
tener pena [ten**air**] to be shy, embarrassed
penca f cactus leaf
pendejada f [pendeH**a**da] (piece of) stupidity
pendejo m [pend**e**Ho] bloody idiot, (US) jerk
pendiente m [pend-y**e**nteh] slope
estar pendiente de [deh] to be waiting for
estar al pendiente de to watch out for
pene m [p**e**neh] penis
penetrar [penetr**a**r] to enter
penicilina f [peneeseel**ee**na] penicillin
pensamiento m [pensam-y**e**nto] thought
pensar to think
pensión f [pens-y**o**n] guesthouse, boarding house; pension
pensión completa [kompl**e**ta] full board
pensionista m [pens-yon**ee**sta] old-age pensioner
peña f [p**e**n-ya] rock, boulder; singing club
peón m [peh-**o**n] labourer; pawn
peor [peh-**o**r] worse; worst
pepenar to scavenge, to scour rubbish tips
pequeño (m) [pek**e**n-yo] small; child
perder [paird**air**] to lose
echar a perder to miss
perderse [paird**air**seh] to get lost
pérdida f [p**ai**rdeeda] loss
perdón [paird**o**n] sorry, excuse me; pardon, pardon me
perfecto [pairf**e**kto] perfect
perfumería f [pairfoomair**ee**-a] perfume shop
periódico m [pair-y**o**deeko] newspaper
periodista m/f [pair-yod**ee**sta] journalist
período m [pair**ee**-odo] period
perla f [p**ai**rla] pearl
permiso m [pairm**ee**so] licence; permit
con permiso excuse me, may I pass
permitir [pairmeet**ee**r] to allow
pero [p**ai**ro] but
perro m [p**ai**rro] dog
perro caliente m [kal-y**e**nteh] hot dog

persona f [pairs**o**na] person
persona mayor [mī-y**o**r] elderly person, senior citizen
pesadilla f [pesad**ee**-ya] nightmare
pesado heavy; boring, tedious
pésame: **dar el pésame** [p**e**sameh] to offer one's condolences
pesar: **a pesar de que** [deh keh] despite the fact that
a pesar de in spite of
pesca f fishing
ir a pescar to go fishing
pescadería f [peskadair**ee**-a] fishmonger's
pescar to fish; to catch out
pesero m [pes**ai**ro] collective taxi
peso m weight; Mexican national currency
peso máximo maximum weight
peso neto net weight
pestañas fpl [pest**a**n-yas] eyelashes
petate m [pet**a**teh] straw mat
petróleo para lámparas m [petr**o**leh-o] paraffin oil, kerosene oil
pez m [pes] fish
picadura f bite
picante [peek**a**nteh] hot, spicy
picar to sting; to itch
pico: **horas pico** fpl rush hour
picor m itch
picoso [peek**o**so] hot

pidió [peed-y**o**] he/she asked for; you asked for
pie m [p-yeh] foot
a pie on foot
piedra f [p-y**e**dra] stone
piedra preciosa [pres-y**o**sa] precious stone
piel f [p-yel] skin
pienso [p-y**e**nso] I think
pierna f [p-y**ai**rna] leg
pijama m [peeH**a**ma] pyjamas
pila f battery
píldora f pill
piloto m pilot
pilotos mpl rear lights
pincel m [peens**e**l] paint brush
pinchazo m [peench**a**so] puncture
pinche [p**ee**ncheh] bloody, lousy
pintada f graffiti
pintar to paint
pintura f painting; paint
pinzas fpl [p**ee**nsas] tweezers
piña f [p**ee**n-ya] pineapple
pipa f pipe
piragua f [peer**a**gwa] canoe
piragüismo m [peeragw**ee**smo] canoeing
pirámide f [peer**a**meedeh] pyramid
piscina f [pees**ee**na] swimming pool
piscina cubierta [koob-y**ai**rta] indoor swimming pool
piso m floor
pista f track; clue
pista de baile [deh b**ī**leh] dance floor

pista de tenis tennis court
pistola f gun
placa f [pl**a**ka] number plate, licence plate
plancha f iron
planchar to iron
planear [planeh-**a**r], **planificar** [planeefeek**a**r] to plan
plano (m) flat; map
planta f plant; floor
planta baja [b**a**Ha] ground floor, (US) first floor
plástico (m) plastic
plata f silver; money, (US) dough
plateado [plateh-**a**do] silver
plática [pl**a**teeka] conversation; talk
platicar [plateek**a**r] to talk, to converse
platillo m [plat**ee**-yo] saucer
plato m plate; dish, course
playa f [pl**ī**-ya] beach
playera f [plī-y**ai**ra] T-shirt
playeras fpl [plī-y**ai**ras] trainers
plaza f [pl**a**sa] square; seat
plaza de toros [deh] bullring
plazas libres [l**ee**b-res] seats available
plomero m [plom**ai**ro] plumber
pluma f pen; feather
plumón m [ploom**o**n] felt tip pen
población f [poblas-y**o**n] village; town; population
poblano from/of Puebla
pobre [p**o**breh] poor
pobreza f [pobr**e**sa] poverty
pocho americanized (used to refer to americanized Mexican)
poco little; rarely
poco profundo shallow
pocos few
  unos pocos a few
poder (m) [pod**ai**r] to be able to; power
podrido rotten
policía f [polees**ee**-a] police
policía m/f policeman; policewoman
política f politics
político (m) politician; political
póliza de seguros f [p**o**leesa deh] insurance policy
polvo m [p**o**lbo] powder; dust
pólvora f [p**o**lbora] gunpowder
pomada f ointment
pon put
poner [pon**ai**r] to put
ponerse de pie [pon**ai**rseh deh p-yeh] to stand up
ponerse en marcha to set off
pongo I put
poniente m [pon-y**e**nteh] west
popote m [pop**o**teh] (drinking) straw
poquito: un poquito [pok**ee**to] a little bit
por by; through; for
  por allí [a-y**ee**] over there
  por fin [feen] at last
  por lo menos at least
  por qué [keh] why
  por semana per week
por avión [ab-y**o**n] airmail
porcentaje m [porsent**a**Heh] percentage

por ciento [s-y**e**nto] per cent
por correo terrestre [korr**eh**-o tairr**e**streh]
por favor [fab**o**r] please
porfiriato m [porfeer-y**a**to] period under rule of Porfirio Diaz 1876-1911
por qué [keh] why
porque [p**o**rkeh] because
portada f cover
portaequipajes m [porta-ekeep**a**H-es] luggage rack
portátil [port**a**teel] portable
portero m [port**ai**ro] porter; doorman; goalkeeper
portugués [portoog-**e**s] Portuguese
posada f hotel
posible [pos**ee**bleh] possible
postal f [pos-t**a**l] postcard
potosino from/of San Luis Potosí
PRD (Partido Revolucionario Democrático) m Democratic Revolutionary Party (left-wing party)
precaución f [prekows-y**o**n] caution
precio m [pr**e**s-yo] price
precios fijos [f**ee**Hos] fixed prices
precioso [pres-y**o**so] beautiful; precious
precio unidad [ooneed**a**] price per unit, price per item
preferencia f [prefair**e**ns-ya] right of way; preference
preferir [prefair**ee**r] to prefer
prefijo m [pref**ee**Ho] dialling code, area code
pregunta f question
preguntar to ask
premio m [pr**e**m-yo] prize
prenda las luces switch on your lights
prendas fpl clothing
prender [prend**ai**r] to light; to switch on
prender luces de cruce switch headlights on
prensa f press; newspapers
preocupado [preh-okoop**a**do] worried
preocuparse [preh-okoop**a**rseh] to worry (about)
¡no te preocupes! [teh preh-ok**oo**p-es] don't worry!
preparar to prepare
prepararse [prepar**a**rseh] to get ready
prepa(ratoria) f pre-university level school
prepotente [prepot**e**nteh] arrogant
presentar to introduce
preservativo m [presairbat**ee**bo] condom
presidencia f [preseed**e**ns-ya] Presidency
presión f [pres-y**o**n] pressure
presión de las llantas [deh las y**a**ntas] tyre pressure
prestado: pedir prestado to borrow
prestar to lend
PRI (Partido Revolucionario Institucional) m Institutional

Revolutionary Party (party of government since 1920)
prieto [pree-y**e**to] dark-skinned; black
prima f cousin
primavera f [preemab**ai**ra] spring
primera (clase) f [kl**a**seh] first class
primera especial [espes-y**a**l] deluxe first-class
primero first
primeros auxilios [owk-s**ee**l-yos] first-aid post
primer piso first floor, (US) second floor
primer plato m first course
primo m cousin
principal [preenseep**a**l] main
principiante m/f [preenseep-y**a**nteh] beginner
principio m [preens**ee**p-yo] beginning
prioridad a la derecha give way/ yield to vehicles coming from the right
prisa: tener prisa to be in a hurry
privado (m) [preeb**a**do] private; cul-de-sac
privatización f [preebateesas-y**o**n] privatization
probablemente [probableh-m**e**nteh] probably
probador m fitting room
probarse [prob**a**rseh] to try on
problema m problem
producto preparado con ingredientes naturales product prepared using natural ingredients
productos alimenticios [prod**oo**ktos aleement**ee**s-yos] foodstuffs
productos de belleza [deh beh-y**e**sa] beauty products
profesor m, **profesora** f teacher; lecturer
profundidad f [profoondeed**a**] depth
profundo deep
prohibida la entrada no entry, no admission
prohibida la entrada a menores de ... no admission for those under ... years of age
prohibida la vuelta en U no U-turns
prohibida su reproducción copyright reserved
prohibida su venta not for sale
prohibido [pro-eeb**ee**do] prohibited, forbidden; no
prohibido asomarse do not lean out of the window
prohibido bañarse no swimming
prohibido cantar no singing
prohibido echar basura no litter
prohibido el paso no entry; no trespassing
prohibido escupir no spitting
prohibido estacionarse no parking
prohibido estacionarse excepto carga y descarga no parking except for loading and unloading

prohibido fijar carteles stick no bills
prohibido fumar no smoking
prohibido girar a la izquierda no left turn
prohibido hablar con el chofer do not speak to the driver
prohibido hacer auto-stop no hitch-hiking
prohibido pescar no fishing
prohibido pisar el pasto keep off the grass
prohibido prender fuego no campfires
prohibido sacar fotografías no photographs
prohibido tocar el claxon do not sound your horn
prometer [promet**air**] to promise
prometida f fiancée
prometido (m) engaged; fiancé
pronóstico del tiempo m [t-y**e**mpo] weather forecast
pronto early; soon
de pronto suddenly
¡hasta pronto! [**a**sta] see you soon!
llegar pronto [yeg**a**r] to be early
pronunciar [pronoons-y**a**r] to pronounce
propaganda f advertising; publicity; propaganda
propiedad privada [prop-yed**a** preeb**a**da] private property
propietario m [prop-yet**a**r-yo] owner
propina f tip
propósito: a propósito deliberately
proteger [proteH**air**] to protect
provecho: ¡buen provecho! [bwen prob**e**cho] enjoy your meal!
provincia f [prob**ee**ns-ya] province
en provincia in the country, in the provinces
provocar [probok**a**r] to cause
¿te provoca un café? [teh] do you feel like a coffee
próximo next
la semana próxima next week
prudente [prood**e**nteh] careful
prueba de alcoholemia f [prw**e**ba deh alko-ol**e**m-ya] breath test
prueba de embarazo [embar**a**so] pregnancy test
Pte. west
público (m) public; audience
pueblo m [pw**e**blo] village; people; nation; ordinary people
puede [pw**e**deh] he/she can; you can
puede ser [sair] maybe
puedo [pw**e**do] I can
puente m [pw**e**nteh] bridge
puente aéreo [a-**ai**reh-o] shuttle flight
puente colgante [kolg**a**nteh] rope bridge
puente de cuota [kw**o**ta] toll bridge

puerta f [pw**ai**rta] door; gate
por la otra puerta use other door
puerta de embarque [emb**a**rkeh] gate
puerta nº. gate no.
puerto m [pw**ai**rto] harbour, port
puerto de montaña [deh mont**a**n-ya] mountain pass
puerto deportivo marina
pues [pwes] since; so
puesta de sol f [pw**e**sta deh] sunset
puesto de periódicos m [pair-y**o**deekos] newspaper kiosk
puesto de socorro first-aid post
puesto que [keh] since
pulga f flea
pullman m luxury bus
pulmones mpl [poolm**o**n-es] lungs
pulmonía f [poolmon**ee**-a] pneumonia
pulque m [p**oo**lkeh] drink made from fermented agave cactus sap
pulquería f [poolkair**ee**-a] bar specializing in pulque
pulsera f [pools**ai**ra] bracelet
pulso m pulse
punto m dot; spot; point
hacer punto [as**ai**r] to knit
punto de vista [deh b**ee**sta] point of view
puntual: llegar puntual [yeg**a**r poontw**a**l] to arrive on time
pura lana virgen pure new wool
puro (m) [p**oo**ro] cigar; pure
es la pura verdad [vaird**a**] it's the absolute truth
puse [p**oo**seh] I put

Q

que [keh] who; that; which; than
¿qué? what?; which?
quedar [ked**a**r] to stay; to remain
quédate con él [k**e**dateh] keep it
no me queda otra [meh k**e**da] I've no choice
¿dónde queda? [d**o**ndeh] where is it?
queda muy cerca it's very near
quedarse [ked**a**rseh] to stay
quedarse con to keep
quedarse sin gasolina to run out of petrol/gas
¿qué hubo? [**oo**bo] what's happening?; how's things?
quejarse [keh-H**a**rseh] to complain
quemadura f [kemad**oo**ra] burn
quemadura de sol [deh] sunburn
quemar [kem**a**r] to burn
quemarse [kem**a**rseh] to burn oneself
querer [ker**ai**r] to love; to want
querido [kair**ee**do] dear

queso m [k**e**so] cheese
qué tal? how do you do?
¡qué va! [ba] no way!
¿quién? [k-yen] who?
quiero [k-y**ai**ro] I want; I love
no quiero I don't want to
¿quihubo? [k-y**oo**bo] how's it going?
quince [k**ee**nseh] fifteen
quince días [d**ee**-as] fortnight
quinientos [keen-y**e**ntos] five hundred
quinto [k**ee**nto] fifth
quiosco m [k-y**o**sko] kiosk
quisiera [kees-y**ai**ra] I would like; he/she would like; you would like
quiso [k**ee**so] he/she wanted; you wanted
quitaesmalte m [keeta-esm**a**lteh] nail polish remover
quitar [keet**a**r] to remove
quizá(s) [kees**a**(s)] maybe

R

rabia f [r**a**b-ya] rage; rabies
me da rabia it makes me mad
rabioso [rab-y**o**so] furious
ración f [ras-y**o**n] portion
radiador m [rad-yad**o**r] radiator
radio m [r**a**d-yo] spoke
radio f radio
radiografía f [rad-yograf**ee**-a] X-ray
rajarse [raH**a**rseh] to back down, to run away
ranchero m [ranch**ai**ro] small farmer
rancho m small farm, smallholding
rápidamente [–m**e**nteh] quickly
rápido fast
raro rare; strange
rascar to scratch
rasgar to tear
rasgo m feature
rasuradora f shaver
rasurarse [rasoor**a**rseh] to shave
rata f rat
rato: espera un rato wait a minute, wait a bit
pasar buen/mal rato to have a good/bad time
cada rato every now and then
ratón m mouse
rayas: de rayas [deh r**ī**-yas] striped
razón f [ras**o**n] reason; rate
tiene razón [t-y**e**neh] you're right
con razón ... so that's why ...
razonable [rason**a**bleh] reasonable
realizar [reh-alees**a**r] to carry out
realmente [reh-alm**e**nteh] really; in fact
rebajado [rebaH**a**do] reduced
rebajas fpl [reb**a**Has] reductions, sale
rebajas de verano [deh bair**a**no]

summer sale
rebasar to overtake, to pass
rebozo m [reb**o**so] shawl
recado m message
¿quiere dejar recado? would you like to leave a message?
recámara f bedroom
recepción f [reseps-y**o**n] reception
recepcionista m/f [reseps-yon**ee**sta] receptionist
receta f [res**e**ta] recipe; prescription
con receta médica only available on prescription
recetar [reset**a**r] to prescribe
recibir [reseeb**ee**r] to receive
recibo m [res**ee**bo] receipt
recién [res-y**e**n] recently
recién salía de casa cuando ... I'd just left home when ...
recién pintado wet paint
reclamación de equipajes f [reklamas-y**o**n deh ekeep**a**H-es] baggage claim
reclamaciones fpl [reklamas-y**o**n-es] complaints
recoger [rekoH**air**] to collect; to pick up
recogida de equipajes f [rekoH**ee**da deh ekeep**a**H-es] baggage claim
recoja su boleto take your ticket
recomendar to recommend
reconocer [rekonos**air**] to recognize; to examine
reconocimiento m [rekonoseem-y**e**nto] examination
reconocimiento médico medical examination
recordar to remember
recorrer [rekor**air**] to travel; to travel through; to move along
recorrido m journey
recreo m [recr**eh**-o] playtime, break
recto straight
todo recto straight ahead
recuerdo (m) [rekw**air**do] memory; souvenir; I remember
red f [reh] network; net
redondo round
reduzca la velocidad reduce speed now
reembolsar [reh-embols**a**r] to refund
reembolsos refunds
reestreno m [reh-estr**e**no] re-release (of a classic movie)
refacciones fpl [refaks-y**o**n-es] spare parts, spares
regadera f [regad**air**a] shower
regalo m present
regalón spoiled
regatear [regateh-**a**r] to haggle
regenta f [reH**e**nta], **regente** m [reH**e**nteh] mayor
régimen m [**re**Heemen] diet; regime
regiomontano [reH-yomont**a**no] from/of Monterrey
registrar [reHeestr**a**r] to search; to register, to certify

registro de equipajes m [reHeestro deh ekeepaH-es] check in
regla f rule; period
reglamento m rule
regresar to return
regresar a casa to go home
regreso m return
reina f [rayna] queen
Reino Unido m United Kingdom
reír [ray-eer] to laugh
relajarse [relaHarseh] to relax
relajo m [relaHo] disorder; noise, hubbub
rellenar [reh-yenar] to fill in; to fill
reloj m [reloH] watch; clock
reloj de pulsera [deh poolsaira] watch, wristwatch
relojería f [reloHairee-a] watches and clocks; watchmaker's shop
remar to row
remate m [remateh] sale, auction sale; the final detail
remitente m/f [remeetenteh] sender
remo m oar
remolque m [remolkeh] trailer
renta f rent; rental
rentado rented
rentar to rent; to hire
se renta to rent, for hire
renunciar [renoons-yar] to resign
reparación f [reparas-yon] repair(s)
reparación de calzado [deh kalsado] shoe repairs
reparaciones [reparas-yon-es] faults service
reparar to repair
repelente de mosquitos m [repelenteh deh] mosquito repellent
repente: de repente [deh repenteh] suddenly
repetir to repeat; to have a second helping
reponerse [reponairseh] to recover
representante m/f [representanteh] representative, agent
repuestos mpl [repwestos] spare parts
repugnante [repoognanteh] disgusting
requisito m [rekeeseeto] requirement, condition
res m cow, bull
resbaladizo [resbaladeeso] slippery
resbalar to slip
rescatar to rescue
reserva f [resairba] reservation
reserva de asientos [deh as-yentos] seat reservation
reservado [resairbado] reserved
reservado el derecho de admisión the management reserve the right to refuse admission
reservar [resairbar] to reserve;

to book
reservas fpl reservations
resfriado m [resfree-**a**do] cold
respeto m respect
respirar to breathe
responder [respond**air**] to answer, to reply
responsable (m/f) [respons**a**bleh] the person in charge; responsible
respuesta f [respw**e**sta] answer
restaurante m [restowr**a**nteh] restaurant
resto m rest
retar to challenge
rete: está rete lindo [r**e**teh] it's really beautiful
reumatismo m [reh-oomat**ee**smo] rheumatism
reunión f [reh-oon-y**o**n] meeting
revelado m [rebel**a**do] film processing
revelar [rebel**a**r] to develop; to reveal
revisar [rebees**a**r] to check
revisor m [rebees**o**r] conductor; guard
revista m [reb**ee**sta] magazine
revolución f [reboloos-y**o**n] revolution
la Revolución Mexicana the Mexican Revolution 1910-17
rey m [ray] king
Reyes: día de los Reyes m [d**ee**-a deh los r**ay**-es] 6th of January, Epiphany
rico rich
ridículo ridiculous
riego: tierras de riego fpl irrigated land
rímel m mascara
rincón m corner
riñón m [reen-y**o**n] kidney
río m [r**ee**-o] river
risa f laughter
me da risa [meh] it makes me laugh
rizado [rees**a**do] curly
robar to steal
robo m theft
roca f rock
rodilla f [rod**ee**-ya] knee
rogar to beg
rojo [r**o**Ho] red
rómpase en caso de emergencia break in case of emergency
romper to break
ropa f clothes
ropa de caballeros [deh kaba-y**ai**ros] men's clothes
ropa de cama bed linen
ropa de señoras [sen-y**o**ras] ladies' clothes
ropa infantil [eenfant**ee**l] children's clothes
ropa interior [eentair-y**o**r] underwear
ropa sucia [s**oo**s-ya] laundry
rosa (f) pink; rose
roto broken
rubeola f [roob**eh**-ola] German measles
rubí m [roob**ee**] ruby
rubio [r**oo**b-yo] blond
rueda f [rw**e**da] wheel

rueda de repuesto f [deh repw**e**sto] spare wheel
ruega: se ruega ... [seh rw**e**ga] please ...
ruego I request
ruido m [rw**ee**do] noise
ruidoso [rweed**o**so] noisy
ruinas fpl [rw**ee**nas] ruins
rural [roor**a**l] rural, country
ruta f route

S

S.A. (Sociedad Anónima) PLC, Inc
sábado m Saturday
sábana f sheet
saber [sab**air**] to know
saber a to taste of
sabor m taste
sabroso tasty, delicious
sacacorchos m corkscrew
sacar to take out; to get out
sacar una foto to take a photo
sacar un boleto to buy a ticket
saco m jacket
sal (f) salt; leave
sala f room; lounge; hall
sala climatizada [kleematis**a**da] air-conditioned
sala de belleza [beh-y**e**sa] beauty salon
sala de cine [deh s**ee**neh] cinema, movie theater
sala de conciertos [kons-y**ai**rtos] concert hall
sala de embarque [emb**a**rkeh] departure lounge
sala de espera [esp**ai**ra] waiting room
sala de exposiciones [esposees-y**o**n-es] exhibition hall
sala de tránsito transit lounge
salado salty
sala X X-rated cinema, adult movie theater
saldar to sell at a reduced price
saldo m clearance; balance
sales de baño fpl [s**a**l-es deh b**a**n-yo] bath salts
salgo I'm leaving, I'm going out
salida f exit; departure
salida ciudad take this direction to leave the city
salida de ambulancias ambulance exit
salida de autopista end of motorway/highway; motorway/highway exit
salida de camiones heavy goods vehicle exit, works exit
salida de emergencia [deh emairHens-ya] emergency exit
salida de incendios [eens**e**nd-yos] fire exit
salida de socorro f emergency exit
salidas fpl departures
salidas internacionales [eentairnas-yon**a**l-es] international departures

salidas nacionales [nas-yon**al**-es] domestic departures
salir to go out; to leave
salón de baile m [deh bīleh] dance hall
salón de belleza [beh-y**e**sa] beauty salon
salón de demostraciones [demostras-y**o**n-es] exhibition hall
salón de peluquería [pelookair**ee**-a] hairdressing salon
salpicadera f [salpeekad**ai**ra] mudguard
saltar to jump
Salubridad f Ministry of Health
salud f [sal**oo**] health
saludar to greet
saludos best wishes
salvadoreño (m) [salbador**e**n-yo] Salvadorean
salvo que [keh] except that
sangrar to bleed
sangre f [s**a**ngreh] blood
sanitarios mpl [saneet**a**r-yos] toilets, rest rooms
sano healthy
sarampión m [saramp-y**o**n] measles
sarape m [sar**a**peh] woven blanket
sartén f frying pan
sastre m [s**a**streh] tailor
scotch m Sellotape®, Scotch tape®
se [seh] himself; herself; itself; yourself; themselves; yourselves; oneself
sé I know
no sé I don't know
se aceptan tarjetas de crédito we accept credit cards
secador de pelo m [deh] hair dryer
secar to dry
secarse el pelo [sek**a**rseh] to dry one's hair, to have a blow-dry
sección f [seks-y**o**n] department
seco dry
secretaria f, **secretario** m secretary
secretaría f Ministry
Secretaría de Turismo Ministry of Tourism
secreto secret
Sectur tourist office
sed: tengo sed [seh] I'm thirsty
seda f silk
seda natural pure silk
sede f [s**e**deh] head office, headquarters
seguida: en seguida [seg**ee**da] immediately, right away
seguido [seg**ee**do] often
seguir [seg**ee**r] to follow
según according to
segunda (clase) f [kl**a**seh] second class
segundo (m) second
de segunda mano second-hand
segundo piso m second floor,

(US) third floor
seguridad f [segooreed**a**] safety; security
seguro (m) safe; sure; insurance; safety pin
seguro de viaje m [deh b-y**a**Heh] travel insurance
se habla inglés English spoken
se hacen fotocopias photocopying service
seis [says] six
seiscientos [says-y**e**ntos] six hundred
selva f [s**e**lba] jungle; rain forest
semáforo m traffic lights
semana f week
semanal weekly
Semana Santa Holy Week
senador m Senator
sencillo [sens**ee**-yo] simple
se necesita ... ... needed, required
sensible [sens**ee**bleh] sensitive
sentar: sentar bien (a) [b-yen] to suit
sentarse [sent**a**rseh] to sit down
sentido m direction; sense; meaning
sentir to feel; to hear
señas fpl [s**e**n-yas] address
señor [sen-y**o**r] gentleman, man; sir
el señor López Mr López
señora f [sen-y**o**ra] lady, woman; madam
la señora López Mrs López
señoras fpl ladies; ladies' toilet, ladies' room; ladies' department
señores mpl [sen-y**o**r-es] men; gents' toilet, men's room
señorita f [sen-yor**ee**ta] young lady, young woman; miss
la señorita López Miss López
separado separate; separated
por separado separately
se precisa ... ... needed
se prohibe ... ... forbidden
se prohibe echar basura no litter
se prohibe fumar no smoking
se prohibe hablar con el chofer do not speak to the driver
se prohibe la entrada no entry, no admittance
se prohibe la entrada a mujeres, uniformados e integrantes de la fuerzas armadas no admittance to women, members of the armed forces and anyone in uniform
septiembre m [set-y**e**mbreh] September
séptimo [s**e**pteemo] seventh
sequía f [sek**ee**-a] drought
ser [sair] to be
a no ser que [keh] unless
se renta for hire, to rent
se renta departamento flat to let, apartment for rent
se rentan cuartos rooms to rent
serio [s**ai**r-yo] serious
en serio seriously
serpiente f [sairp-y**e**nteh] snake

serranía f mountains
se ruega please ...
se ruega desalojen su cuarto antes de las doce please vacate your room by twelve noon
se ruega no ... please do not ...
se ruega no estacionarse no parking please
se ruega no molestar please do not disturb
se ruega pagar en caja please pay at the desk
se vende for sale
servicio a través de operadora operator-connected calls
servicio automático direct dialling
servicio de cuarto [sairb**ee**s-yo deh kw**a**rto] room service
servicio de fotocopias photocopying service
servicio estrella [estr**eh**-ya] first class (coach) service
servicios mpl [sairb**ee**s-yos] toilets, rest rooms
servicios de rescate [deh resk**a**teh] mountain rescue
servicios de socorro emergency services
servilleta f [sairbee-y**e**ta] serviette, napkin
servir [sairb**ee**r] to serve
sesenta [ses**e**nta] sixty
sesión continua continuous showing
setecientos [setes-y**e**ntos] seven hundred
setenta seventy
sexenio m six year Presidential term
sexo m sex
sexto [s**e**sto] sixth
si [see] if
sí yes; oneself; herself; itself; yourself; themselves; yourselves; each other
SIDA m [s**ee**da] AIDS
sido been
siempre [s-y**e**mpreh] always
siempre que [keh] whenever; as long as
siento [s-y**e**nto] I sit down; I feel; I regret
sierra f [s-y**ai**rra] mountain range
siesta f siesta, nap
siete [s-y**e**teh] seven
siga recto straight ahead
siglo m century
significado m meaning
significar to mean
siguiente [seeg-y**e**nteh] next
al día siguiente [d**ee**-a] the day after
silencio m [seel**e**ns-yo] silence
silla f [s**ee**-ya] chair
silla de ruedas [deh rw**e**das] wheelchair
sillita de ruedas [see-y**ee**ta] pushchair, buggy
sillón m [see-y**o**n] armchair
simpático nice
sin [seen] without
sinagoga f synagogue
sincero [seens**ai**ro] sincere

sindicalista m/f trade unionist
sindicato m trade union, labor union
sin duda undoubtedly
sin embargo however, neverthless
sino: no ... sino ... not ... but ...
si no otherwise
sino que [keh] but
sin plomo unleaded
siquiera [seek-y**ai**ra] even if; at least
sírvase [s**ee**rbaseh] please
sírvase frío serve cold
sírvase Usted mismo help yourself
sitio m [s**ee**t-yo] place
en ningún sitio [neen-g**oo**n] nowhere
smoking m [sm**o**keen] dinner jacket
sobrar to be left over; to be too many
sobre (m) [s**o**breh] envelope; on; above
sobrecarga [sobrek**a**rga] excess weight; extra charge
sobrevivir [sobrebeeb**ee**r] to survive
sobrina f niece
sobrino m nephew
sobrio [s**o**br-yo] sober
sociedad f [sos-yed**a**] society; company
socio m [s**o**s-yo] associate; member
socorrer [sokor**ai**r] to help
socorrista m/f lifeguard
¡socorro! help!
sois [soys] you are
sol m sun
al sol in the sun
solamente [solam**e**nteh] only
soleado [soleh-**a**do] sunny
solo lonely
sólo only
no sólo ... sino también ... [tamb-y**e**n] not only ... but also ...
sólo camiones buses only
sólo carga y descarga loading and unloading only
sólo laborables weekdays only
sólo motos motorcycles only
sólo para residentes (del hotel) hotel patrons only
soltera (f) [solt**ai**ra] single; single woman
soltero (m) [solt**ai**ro] single; bachelor
solterón m [soltair**o**n] bachelor
solterona f [soltair**o**na] spinster
sombra f shade; shadow
sombra de ojos [deh **o**Hos] eyeshadow
sombrero m [sombr**ai**ro] hat
sombrilla f [sombr**ee**-ya] parasol
somnífero m [somn**ee**fairo] sleeping pill
somos we are
son they are; you are
sonreír [sonreh-**ee**r] to smile
sonrisa f smile
sordo deaf

sorprendente [sorprend**e**nteh] surprising
sorpresa f surprise
sótano m lower floor; basement
soy I am
sport: de sport [deh] casual
Sr (Señor) Mr
Sra (Señora) Mrs
Sres (Señores) Messrs
Srta (Señorita) Miss
su [soo] his; her; its; their; your
suave [sw**a**beh] soft; quiet
subir to go up; to get on; to get in; to take up
subtitulado sub-titled
subtítulos mpl subtitles
suburbios mpl [soob**oo**rb-yos] suburbs; poor quarters
suceder [soosed**air**] to happen
sucio [s**oo**s-yo] dirty
sucursal f branch
sudamericana (f) [soodamaireek**a**na], **sudamericano** (m) South American
sudar to sweat
Suecia f [sw**e**s-ya] Sweden
sueco [sw**e**ko] Swedish
suegra f [sw**e**gra] mother-in-law
suegro m [sw**e**gro] father-in-law
suela f [sw**e**la] sole
suelo (m) floor; I am used to
suelto [sw**e**lto] small change
sueño (m) [sw**e**n-yo] dream; I dream
tener sueño [ten**air**] to be tired/sleepy
suerte f [sw**air**teh] luck
por suerte luckily, fortunately
¡buena suerte! [bw**e**na] good luck!
suéter m [sw**e**tair] sweater
suficiente: es suficiente [soofees-y**e**nteh] that's enough
sufragio efectivo, no reelección effective suffrage, no re-election (slogan on many official documents)
suicidarse [sweeseed**a**rseh] to commit suicide
Suiza f [sw**ee**sa] Switzerland
sumar to add; to add up to
supe [s**oo**peh] I knew
súper [s**oo**pair] four-star petrol, (US) premium (gas); supermarket
supermercado m [soopairmairk**a**do] supermarket
supuesto: por supuesto [soopw**e**sto] of course
sur m south
al sur de [deh] south of
sureste m [soor**e**steh] south-east
suroeste m [sooro-**e**steh] south-west
surtido m assortment
sus [soos] his; her; its; their; your
susto m shock
susurrar to whisper
sutil subtle

suya [s**oo**-ya], **suyas, suyo, suyos** his; hers; its; theirs; yours

T

tabaco m tobacco; cigarettes
tabasqueño [tabask**e**n-yo] from/of Tabasco
tabique m [tab**ee**keh] brick
tabla de surf f [deh soorf] surfboard
tabla de windsurf f sailboard
tablero de instrumentos m [tabl**ai**ro deh eenstroom**e**ntos] dashboard
tablón de anuncios m [an**oo**ns-yos] notice board, bulletin board
tablón de información [deh eenformas-y**o**n] indicator board
tacón m heel
tacones altos [tak**o**n-es] high heels
tacones planos flat heels
tal such
con tal (de) que provided that
talco m talcum powder
talla f [t**a**-ya] size
¿qué número talla? what size are you?
tallas grandes [gr**a**nd-es] large sizes
tallas sueltas [sw**e**ltas] odd sizes
taller mecánico m [ta-y**air** mek**a**neeko] garage
talón m heel
talonario (de cheques) m [talon**a**r-yo (deh ch**e**k-es)] cheque book, checkbook
talón de equipajes [ekeep**a**H-es] baggage slip
tal vez [bes] maybe
tamaño m [tam**a**n-yo] size
tamaulipeco [tamowleep**e**ko] from/of Tamaulipas
también [tamb-y**e**n] also
yo también me too
tampoco neither, nor
yo tampoco me neither, nor me
tan: tan bonito so beautiful
tan pronto como as soon as
tanque m [t**a**nkeh] tank
tantito: espere tantito wait a moment
tanto (m) so much; point
tanto ... como ... both ... and ...
tantos so many
tapa f lid
tapar to cover
tapas fpl savoury snacks, tapas
tapatío from/of Guadalajara
tapete m [tap**e**teh] rug, carpet
tapón m plug
taquería f [takair**ee**-a] taco restaurant, taco stall
taquilla f [tak**ee**-ya] ticket office
tarahumara m/f [tara-oom**ara**] indigenous person from northern Mexico
tarasco (m) indigenous

person from Michoacan; from/of Tarascan culture
tardar: **¿cuánto tarda?** [kw**a**nto] how long does it take?
no tarda he/she won't be long
no tardes [t**a**rd-es] don't be long
tarde (f) [t**a**rdeh] afternoon; evening; late
a las tres de la tarde [deh] at 3 p.m.
esta tarde this afternoon, this evening
por la tarde in the evening
llegar tarde [yeg**a**r] to be late
tarifa f charge, charges
tarifa especial estudiante [espes-y**a**l estood-y**a**nteh] student reduced rate
tarifa normal standard rate
tarifa reducida [redoos**ee**da] reduced rate
tarjeta f [tarH**e**ta] card
tarjeta verde Green Card (tourist permit in Mexico)
tarjeta bancaria [bank**a**r-ya] cheque card
tarjeta de crédito [deh kr**e**deeto] credit card
tarjeta de embarque [emb**a**rkeh] boarding pass
tarjeta postal postcard
tarjeta telefónica phonecard
tauromaquia f [towrom**a**k-ya] bullfighting
taxista m/f taxi driver
taza f [t**a**sa] cup
te [teh] you; yourself
té m tea
teatro m [teh-**a**tro] theatre
techo m ceiling
teclado m keyboard
técnica f technique; technology
técnico technical
tecnología f [teknoloH**ee**-a] technology
tecolote m [–l**o**teh] owl
tejado m [teH**a**do] roof
tejanos mpl [teH**a**nos] jeans
tejidos mpl [teH**ee**dos] materials, fabrics
tela f material
teleférico m cable car
teléfono m telephone
teléfono interurbano long-distance phone
teléfonos de emergencia emergency telephone numbers
telesilla m [teles**ee**-ya] chairlift
Televisa largest Mexican television corporation
televisión f [t**e**lebees-y**o**n] television
televisor m television (set)
temblor m earthquake
temer [tem**air**] to fear
temor m fear
tempestad f [tempest**a**] storm
templo m temple; church
temporada f season
ten hold
tenedor m fork
tener [ten**air**] to have
tener derecho to have the right

tener prisa to be in a hurry
tener prioridad [pree-oreeda] to have right of way
tener que [keh] to have to
¡tenga cuidado! [kweedado] be careful!
tengo I have
tengo que I have to, I must
tensión f [tens-yon] blood pressure
teñirse el pelo [ten-yeerseh to dye one's hair, to have one's hair dyed
tepetate m [tepetateh] type of soft stone used for building
tercera edad f [eda] old age
tercero third
tercer piso m [tairsair] third floor, (US) fourth floor
tercio m [tairs-yo] third
terciopelo m [tairs-yopelo] velvet
terco [tairko] stubborn
terminal f [tairmeenal] terminus; terminal
terminar to finish
termo m thermos flask
termómetro m thermometer
terrateniente m/f [tairra-ten-yenteh] large landowner
terreno m [tairreno] piece/plot of land
testigo m witness
testimonio m [testeemon-yo] evidence; statement
tetera f [tetaira] teapot
tezontle m [tesontleh] volcanic marble-like rock
ti [tee] you
tía f [tee-a] aunt
tianguis m [t-yangees] market
tibio [teeb-yo] lukewarm
tiburón m shark
tiempo m [t-yempo] time; weather
a tiempo on time
al tiempo at room temperature
tiempo de recreo [deh rekreh-o] leisure
tiempo libre [leebreh] free time
tienda f [t-yenda] shop, store; tent
esta tienda se traslada a ... this business is transferred to ...
tienda de abarrotes f [deh abarrot-es] grocer's, dry goods store
tienda de artículos de piel [p-yel] leather goods shop
tienda de campaña tent
tienda de comestibles [komesteebl-es] grocer's
tienda de deportes [deport-es] sports shop
tienda de electrodomésticos electrical goods shop
tienda de muebles [mwebl-es] furniture shop
tienda de regalos gift shop
tienda de ultramarinos grocer's
tienda de vinos y licores [beenos ee leekor-es] off-licence, liquor store

tienda libre de impuestos [l**ee**breh deh eempw**e**stos] duty-free shop
tiene: ¿tiene ...? [t-y**e**neh] have you got ...?, do you have ...?; do you sell ...?
tiene que [keh] he/she must; you must
tierra f [t-y**ai**rra] earth; land
tifo m typhus
tijeras fpl [teeH**ai**ras] scissors
tiliches mpl [teel**ee**ch-es] bits and pieces
timbre m [t**ee**mbreh] bell; stamp
timbre de alarma [deh] alarm bell
tímido shy
tina f bath(tub)
tintorería f [teentorair**ee**-a] dry-cleaner's
tío m [t**ee**-o] uncle
tipo de cambio m [deh k**a**mb-yo] exchange rate
tirita f Elastoplast®, Bandaid®
tiro m shot
tlapalería f [tlapalair**ee**-a] hardware store
toalla f [to-**a**-ya] towel
toalla de baño [deh b**a**n-yo] bath towel
tobillo m [tob**ee**-yo] ankle
tocadiscos m record player
tocar to touch; to play
tocayo m [tok**ī**-yo] namesake
todavía [todab**ee**-a] still; yet
todavía no not yet
todo all, every; everything
todos los días every day
todo derecho straight on
todo recto straight ahead
todos everyone
tolteca from/of Toltec culture
tomado drunk
tomar to take; to drink
tomar el sol to sunbathe
tomavistas m cine-camera
tómese antes de las comidas to be taken before meals
tómese después de las comidas to be taken after meals
tómese ... veces al día to be taken ... times per day
tome Usted [t**o**meh oost**eh**] take
tonelada f tonne
tono m dialling tone; shade
tonto silly
topes mpl 'sleeping policemen', speed bumps
torcer [tors**air**] to twist; to sprain; to turn
torcerse el tobillo [tob**ee**-yo] to twist one's ankle
torero m [tor**ai**ro] bullfighter
tormenta f storm
tormentoso stormy
tornillo m [torn**ee**-yo] screw
toro m bull
toros mpl bullfighting
torpe [t**o**rpeh] clumsy
torre f [t**o**rreh] tower
tos f cough
toser [tos**air**] to cough
tosferina f [tosfair**ee**na] whooping cough

total: **en total** [tot-**a**l] altogether
totalmente [tot-alm**e**nteh] absolutely
tóxico [t**o**kseeko] poisonous
toxicómano m [tokseek**o**mano] drug addict
trabajador (m) [trabaHad**o**r], **trabajadora** (f) worker; industrious
trabajar [trabaj**a**r] to work
trabajo m [trab**a**Ho] work; job
traducir [tradoos**ee**r] to translate
traer [tra-**air**] to bring
tráfico: **tráfico de drogas** drug traffic; drug-trafficking
tragar to swallow
traigo [trīgo] I bring
tráiler m [trīlair] large truck; caravan, (US) trailer
tráiners mpl [trīnairs] trainers
traje (m) [tr**a**Heh] I brought; suit; clothes
traje de baño [deh b**a**n-yo] swimming costume
traje de noche [n**o**cheh] evening dress
traje de señora [sen-y**o**ra] lady's suit
traje típico traditional regional costume
trámites mpl [tr**a**-meet-es] bureaucracy, paperwork
tranquilizante [trankeeleees**a**nteh] tranquillizer
tranquilizarse [trankeelees**a**rseh] to calm down
tranquilo [trank**ee**lo] quiet
transar to sell out, to compromise
tránsito m traffic
tras after
trasbordo m transfer; change
hacer trasbordo en ... change at ...
trasero (m) [tras**air**o] bottom; back; rear
trasladar to move
se traslada under new management
trasnochar to spend the night
tratamiento m [–m-y**e**nto] treatment
tratar to treat; to try
trato m way of treating people
través: **a través de** [trav-**e**s deh] across, through
travieso [trab-y**e**so] mischievous
trece [tr**e**seh] thirteen
treinta [tr**ay**nta] thirty
tren m train
tren de carga [deh] goods train
tren de lavado automático [lab**a**do owtom**a**teeko] carwash
tren de pasajeros [pasaH**air**os] passenger train
tren directo through train
tren tranvía [tranb**ee**-a] stopping train
tres three
trescientos [tres-y**e**ntos] three hundred
tres cuartos de hora mpl [kw**a**rtos deh **o**ra] three

quarters of an hour
tribunal m [treeboon**a**l] court; tribunal
tripulación f [treepoolas-y**o**n] crew
triste [tr**ee**steh] sad
tristeza f [treest**e**sa] sadness
tronco m body; buddy
tropezar [tropes**a**r] to trip
trueno m [trw**e**no] thunder
tu [too] your
tú you
tubo de escape m [deh esk**a**peh] exhaust
tubo de respirar snorkel
tuerce a la izquierda turn left
tuerza [tw**ai**rsa] turn
tú mismo yourself
túnel m [t**oo**-nel] tunnel
turismo m tourism; luxury bus; tourist office
turista m/f tourist
turístico [toor**ee**steeko] tourist
turno m [t**oo**rno] turn; round; shift
  es mi turno it's my turn/round
tus [toos] your
tuya [t**oo**-ya], **tuyas, tuyo, tuyos** yours

U

u [oo] or
ubicarse [oobeek**a**rseh] to be located
  ¿lo ubicas? do you know the one I mean?
Ud (Usted) [oost**eh**] you
Uds (Ustedes) [oost**e**des] you
úlcera (de estómago) f [**oo**lsaira] (stomach) ulcer
últimamente [oolteemam**e**nteh] recently, lately
último last; latest
  últimos días [d**ee**-as] last days; last few days
ultramarinos m grocer's
un [oon] a
una [**oo**na] a
unas some
universidad f [ooneebairseed**a**] university
uno one; someone
unos some; a few
uña f [**oo**n-ya] fingernail
urbanización f [oorbaneesas-y**o**n] housing estate
urbano urban, city
urgencias [oorH**e**ns-yas] casualty (department); emergencies
uruguayo [ooroogw**ī**-yo] Uruguayan
usado used; secondhand
usar to use
  no se usa [seh] it isn't done
uso use
  el uso del tabaco es perjudicial para su salud smoking can damage your health
uso externo not to be taken internally
uso obligatorio cinturón de seguridad seatbelts must be worn

Usted [oost**eh**] you
Ustedes [oost**e**d-es] you
útil useful

V

> **v** is pronounced more like a **b** than an English **v**

va he/she/it goes; you go
vaca f cow
vacaciones fpl [bakas-y**o**n-es] holiday, vacation
vacilar [baseel**a**r] to party, to have a good time
vacilón [baseel**o**n] fun-loving
vacío [bas**ee**-o] empty
vacuna f vaccination
vacunarse [bakoon**a**rseh] to be vaccinated
vagón m carriage, coach
vagón de literas [deh leet**ai**ras] sleeping car
vagón restaurante [restowr**a**nteh] restaurant car
vajilla f [baH**ee**-ya] dinner service, set of crockery
vale: ¿cuánto vale? [kw**a**nto b**a**leh] how much is it?
me vale (madre) [m**a**dreh] I don't give a shit
valer [bal**air**] to be worth
valiente [bal-y**e**nteh] brave
valla f [b**a**-ya] fence
valle m [b**a**-yeh] valley
valores mpl [bal**o**r-es] securities
válvula f valve
vamos we go
van they go; you go
vapor m steam
vaquero m [bak**ai**ro] cowboy
vaqueros mpl jeans
variar [bar-y**a**r] to vary
para variar for a change
varicela f [barees**e**la] chickenpox
varios [b**a**r-yos] several; different
varón m male
varonil manly
vas you go
vasco Basque
vaso m glass
vatio m [b**a**t-yo] watt
vaya [bī-ya] go; I/he/she/you should go; I/he/she/you might go
Vd (Usted) you
Vds (Ustedes) you
ve [beh] go; he/she sees; you see
veces: a veces [b**e**s-es] sometimes
vecindad f [beseend**a**] inner city slum
vecino m [bes**ee**no] neighbour
vehículos pesados heavy vehicles
veinte [b**ay**nteh] twenty
vejez f [beH-**e**s] old age
vela f candle; sail
velero m [bel**ai**ro] sailing boat
velocidad f [beloseed**a**] speed
velocidad controlada por radar

radar speed checks
velocidades fpl [beloseed**a**d-es] gears
velocidad limitada speed limits apply
velocímetro m [belos**ee**metro] speedometer
ven [ben] come; they see; you see
vena f vein
venda f bandage
vendar to dress (wound)
vendemos a ... selling rate
vender [bend**air**] to sell
veneno m poison
venezolano [benesol**a**no] Venezuelan
vengo I come
venir to come
venta f sale
de venta aquí on sale here
venta de estampillas stamps sold here
venta de localidades tickets (on sale)
ventana f window
ventanilla f [bentan**ee**-ya] window; ticket office
ventas a crédito credit terms available
ventas al contado cash sales
ventas a plazos hire purchase, installment plan
ventilador m fan
ver [bair] to see; to watch
veraneante m/f [bairaneh-**a**nteh] holiday-maker, vacationer
veranear [bairaneh-**a**r] to holiday, to take a vacation
veraneo: centro de veraneo [s**e**ntro deh bair**a**neh-o] holiday resort
verano m [bair**a**no] summer
veras: de veras [deh b**ai**ras] really, honestly
verdad f [baird**a**] truth
¿verdad? don't you?; do you?; isn't it?; isn't he?; is he? etc
verdadero [bairdad**ai**ro] true
verde (m) [b**ai**rdeh] green
verguenza f [bairgw**e**nsa] shame
versión f [bairs-y**o**n] version
en versión original [oreegeen**a**l] in the original language
vestido m dress
vestir to dress
vestirse [best**ee**rseh] to get dressed; to dress
vestuarios mpl [bestw**a**r-yos] fitting rooms; changing rooms
vez f [bes] time
una vez once
en vez de [deh] instead of
vi [bee] I saw
vía f [b**ee**-a] platform, (US) track
vía aérea: por vía aérea [a-**air**-eh-a] by air mail
viajar [b-yaH**a**r] to travel
viaje m [b-y**a**Heh] journey
¡buen viaje! [bwen] have a good trip!

> **v** is pronounced more like a **b** than an English **v**

viaje de negocios [deh neg**o**s-yos] business trip
viaje de novios [n**o**b-yos] honeymoon
viaje organizado [organeesa**d**o] package tour
viajero m [b-yaHairo] traveller
vía oral orally
vía rectal per rectum
víbora f [b**ee**bora] snake
vida f life
vidrio m [b**ee**dr-yo] glass; window
viejo (m) [b-y**e**Ho] old; mate, buddy
mi viejo my old man, my father
mis viejos my parents
viene: la semana que viene [keh b-y**e**neh] next week
viento m [b-y**e**nto] wind
vientre m [b-y**e**ntreh] stomach
viernes m [b-y**ai**rn-es] Friday
Viernes Santo Good Friday
vine [b**ee**neh] I came
vinos y licores wines and spirits
viñedo [been-y**e**do] vineyard
violación f [b-yolas-y**o**n] rape
violar [b-yol**a**r] to rape
violencia f [b-yol**e**nsee-a] violence
violento [b-yol**e**nto] violent
visita f visit
visita con guía [g**ee**-a] guided tour
visitante m/f [beeseet**a**nteh] visitor
visitar to visit
visor m viewfinder
víspera f [b**ee**spaira] the day before
vista f view
visto seen
viuda f [b-y**oo**da] widow
viudo m widower
vivir to live
vivo alive; I live
VO (versión original) original language
voceador m [bosead**o**r] newspaper seller
vocero m [bos**ai**ro] spokesman
volante m [bol**a**nteh] steering wheel
volar to fly
volcán m [bolk**a**n] volcano
volibol m [boleeb**o**l] volleyball
voltaje m [bolt**a**Heh] voltage
voltear [bolteh-**a**r] to turn over; to knock over
volver [bolb**ai**r] to come back
volver a hacer algo to do something again
vomitar to vomit
v.o. subtitulada version in the original language with subtitles
voy I go
voz f [bos] voice
vuelo m [bw**e**lo] flight
vuelo nacional [nas-yon**a**l] domestic flight

vuelo regular scheduled flight
vuelta f [bw**e**lta] tour, trip
a la vuelta around the corner
dar una vuelta to go for a walk
vuelto m [bw**e**lto] change
vuelvo [bw**e**lbo] I return
vulcanizadora f [boolkaneesad**o**ra] vulcanizer, tyre repairs

Y

y [ee] and
ya already; now
ya está there you are
ya mero [m**ai**ro] right here, right now
yace [y**a**-seh] lies
yanqui m/f [y**a**nkee] Yankee, North American
ya que [keh] since
yerba f [y**ai**rba] herb
yerno m [y**ai**rno] son-in-law
yo I; me
yo mismo myself
yucateco [yookat**e**ko] from/of Yucatán

Z

zacateco [sakat**e**ko] from/of Zacatecas
zafarse [saf**a**rseh] to get away, to escape
zancudo m [sank**oo**do] mosquito
zapatería f [sapatair**ee**-a] shoe shop/store
zapatero m [sapat**ai**ro] cobbler; shoe repairer
zapatismo m [sapat**ee**smo] peasant movement led by Emiliano Zapata (1911-19); peasant movement in Chiapas 1994-
zapatista m/f follower of the above
zapatos mpl [sap**a**tos] shoes
zapoteco [sapot**e**ko] from/of Zapotec culture
zenzontle m [sens**o**ntleh] mockingbird
zócalo m [sok**a**lo] central square
zona f [s**o**na] area
zona arqueológica [arkeh-ol**o**geeka] archaeological site
zona de servicios [deh sairb**ee**s-yos] service area
zona industrial [eendoostree-**a**l] industrial estate
zona monumental historic monuments
zona postal [pos-t**a**l] postcode, zip code
zona (reservada) para peatones pedestrian precinct
zopilote m [sopeel**o**teh] vulture
zurdo [s**oo**rdo] left-handed

Menu Reader:

Food

ESSENTIAL TERMS

bread el pan
butter la mantequilla [mantekee-ya]
cup la taza [tasa]
dessert el postre [postreh]
fish el pescado
fork el tenedor
glass (tumbler) el vaso [baso]
(wine glass) la copa
knife el cuchillo [koochee-yo]
main course el plato principal
meat la carne [karneh]
menu la carta
pepper (spice) la pimienta [peem-yenta]
plate el plato
salad la ensalada
salt la sal
set menu el menú, la comida corrida
soup la sopa
spoon la cuchara
starter la entrada
table la mesa

another ..., please otro/otra ..., por favor [fabor]
waiter! ¡señor! [sen-yor]
waitress! ¡señorita! [sen-yoreeta]
could I have the bill, please? me pasa la cuenta, por favor [meh pasa la kwenta]

aceite [as**ay**teh] oil
aceite de oliva [deh ol**ee**ba] olive oil
aceitunas [asayt**oo**nas] olives
aceitunas aliñadas [aleen-y**a**das] olives with salad dressing
aceitunas negras [n**eh**-gras] black olives
aceitunas rellenas [reh-y**e**nas] stuffed olives
achicoria [acheek**o**r-ya] chicory, endive
achiote [achee-**o**teh] spicy seasoning from Yucatán
acocil [akos**ee**l] freshwater shrimp
adobado tossed in adobo seasoning
adobo red chilli paste used for cooking, in marinades etc
aguacate [agwak**a**teh] avocado
ahumado [a-oom**a**do] smoked
ajo [**a**Ho] garlic
a la brasa barbecued
a la crema creamed
a la criolla [kree-**o**-ya] in hot, spicy sauce
a la marinera [mareen**ai**ra] in white wine sauce with garlic
a la mexicana [meHeek**a**na] with chilli peppers, onions and garlic
a la parrilla [parr**ee**-ya] grilled
a la plancha grilled
a la romana fried in batter
a la Tampiqueña [tampeek**e**n-ya] with chilli sauce and black refried beans
a la Veracruzana [bairakroos**a**na] in a tomato-based sauce with olives, capers and chillies
al carbón grilled
al mojo de ajo [m**o**Ho deh **a**Ho] in a garlic sauce
al natural [natoor**a**l] plain
albahaca [alba-**a**ka] basil
albóndigas meatballs
albóndigas de lomo [deh] pork meatballs
alcachofas artichokes
alcachofas a la romana artichokes in batter
alcaparras capers
al horno [**o**rno] baked
aliñado [aleen-y**a**do] with salad dressing
ali oli garlic mayonnaise
almejas [alm**eh**-Has] clams
almejas a la marinera [mareen**ai**ra] clams stewed in white wine
almejas al natural [natoor**a**l] live clams
almendras almonds
almuerzo [almw**ai**rso] set menu; lunch
anchoas [anch**o**-as] anchovies
anchoas a la barquera [bark**ai**ra] marinated anchovies with capers
anguila [ang**ee**la] eel
antojitos [antoH**ee**tos] snacks
apio [**a**p-yo] celery
arroz [arr**o**s] rice
arroz a la cubana boiled rice with fried eggs and either bananas or chillies

arroz a la mexicana [meHeek**a**na] rice with garlic, tomato and coriander
arroz blanco boiled white rice
arroz con leche [l**e**cheh] rice pudding
arroz con mariscos rice with seafood
arroz verde [b**ai**rdeh] rice with olives and green peppers
asado roast; roast meat
ate [**a**teh] quince jelly
atún tuna
avellanas [abeh-y**a**nas] hazelnuts
aves [**a**b-es] poultry
azafrán [asafr**a**n] saffron
azúcar [as**oo**kar] sugar

bacalao a la vizcaína [bakal**ow** – beeska-**ee**na] cod served with ham, peppers and onions
bacalao al pil pil [peel] cod cooked in olive oil
baleada [baleh-**a**da] corn meal pancake filled with beans, cheese and eggs
barbacoa barbecued meat
berenjena [bairenH**e**na] aubergine, eggplant
besugo bream
besugo al horno [**o**rno] baked sea bream
besugo asado baked sea bream
besugo mechado sea bream stuffed with ham and bacon
betabel beetroot
bien hecho [b-yen **e**cho] well-done
bife [b**ee**feh] steak
birria [b**ee**r-ya] mutton stew
bistec steak
bistec de ternera [deh tairn**ai**ra] veal steak
bizcocho [beesk**o**cho] sponge finger
blanquillo [blank**ee**-yo] egg
bolillo [bol**ee**-yo] bread roll
bollo [b**o**-yo] roll
bomba helada [el**a**da] baked Alaska
bonito tuna
bonito al horno [**o**rno] baked tuna
bonito con jitomate [Hitom**a**teh] tuna with tomato
boquerones fritos [bokair**o**n-es] fried fresh anchovies
borracho cake soaked in rum
botanas snacks
brazo de gitano [br**a**so deh Heet**a**no] swiss roll
brochetas kebabs
budín bread pudding
buey [boo-**eh**] beef
buñuelos [boon-yw**e**los] light fried pastries; doughnuts
burritos stuffed tortilla parcels

cabeza [kab**e**sa] pig's head (brains, cheeks etc)
cabrilla [kabr**ee**-ya] sea bass
cabrito kid
cabrito al pastor grilled kid
cabrito asado roast kid
cacahuates [kakaw**a**t-es] peanuts

caguama [kagw**a**ma] turtle
cajeta [kaH**e**ta] fudge
calabacines [kalabas**ee**n-es] courgettes, zucchini; marrow, squash
calabacitas courgettes, zucchini
calabaza [kalab**a**sa] pumpkin, (US) squash
calamares a la romana [kalam**a**r-es] squid rings fried in batter
calamares en su tinta squid cooked in their ink
calamares fritos fried squid
caldeirada [kaldair**a**da] fish soup
caldillo [kald**ee**-yo] stew
caldo de ... [deh] ... soup
caldo de perdiz [paird**ee**s] partridge soup
caldo de pescado clear fish soup
caldo de pollo [p**o**-yo] chicken soup
caldo gallego [ga-y**e**go] clear soup with green vegetables, beans
caldo tlalpeño [tlalp**e**n-yo] chicken broth with vegetables, chicken strips and coriander
caldo Xóchitl [s**o**cheetl] chicken broth with pumpkin blossoms
callos [k**a**-yos] tripe
camarones [kamar**o**n-es] prawns
camarones al mojo de ajo [m**o**Ho deh **a**Ho] garlic prawns
camote [kam**o**teh] sweet potato
campechana de camarón [deh] spicy prawn cocktail
canela cinnamon
canelones [kanel**o**n-es] canneloni
capirotada bread pudding
caracoles [karak**o**l-es] sea snails
carne [k**a**rneh] meat
carne de chancho [deh] pork
carne de puerco [pw**ai**rko] pork
carne de res beef
carne picada minced meat
carnero [karn**ai**ro] mutton
carnes [k**a**rn-es] meat; meat dishes
carnitas barbecued pork
carta menu
casero [kas**ai**ro] home-made
castañas [kast**a**n-yas] chestnuts
caza [k**a**sa] game
cazuela [kasw**e**la] casserole, stew
cazuela de hígado [deh **ee**gado] liver casserole
cazuela de mariscos seafood stew
cebolla [seb**o**-ya] onion
cebollitas [sebo-y**ee**tas] spring onions
cecina [ses**ee**na] sun-dried pork
cena [s**e**na] dinner, evening meal
cerdo [s**ai**rdo] pork, pig
cereza [sair**e**sa] cherry
ceviche [seb**ee**cheh] marinated raw seafood cocktail
chabacano apricot
chalupa fried tortilla with

filling
champiñones [champeen-y**o**n-es] mushrooms
chancho pork, pig
chayote [chī-y**o**teh] vegetable similar to marrow or squash
chicharrón pork crackling
chícharros peas
chilaquiles [cheelak**ee**l-es] fried tortillas in hot chilli sauce
chile [ch**ee**leh] chilli pepper
chile de árbol [deh] dried reddish chilli pepper
chile guero [g**ai**ro] very hot, white chilli pepper
chile habanero [aban**ai**ro] very hot red or green chilli
chile jalapeño [Halap**e**n-yo] green chilli pepper, usually in vinegar with onions and carrots
chile Pekin small, green, very hot chilli pepper
chile poblano large green bell pepper, usually stuffed
chile rubio very hot, white chilli pepper
chiles en nogada [ch**ee**l-es] stuffed peppers with a sauce made from walnuts and pomegranate seeds
chile serrano [sairr**a**no] very hot, thin green chilli pepper
chiles rellenos [reh-y**e**nos] stuffed green peppers
chimichanga stuffed, fried tortilla
chipirones [cheepeer**o**n-es] baby squid
chipotle [cheep**o**tleh] dark chilli sauce
chirimoya soursop – tart-flavoured fruit
cholgas mussels
chongos zamoranos [samor**a**nos] curds in syrup
chorizo [chor**ee**so] spicy red sausage
chuleta chop, cutlet
chuleta de cerdo [deh s**ai**rdo] pork chop
chuleta de cerdo empanizada [empanees**a**da] breaded pork chop
chuleta de chancho pork chop
chuleta de cordero [kord**ai**ro] lamb chop
chuleta de lomo ahumado [a-oom**a**do] smoked pork chop
chuleta de ternera [tairn**ai**ra] veal chop
chuleta de ternera empanizada [empanees**a**da] breaded veal chop
chuleta de venado [ben**a**do] venison chop
churrasco roast or grilled meat
churros [ch**oo**rros] long fritters
cigalas [seeg**a**las] crayfish
cigalas a la parrilla [parr**ee**-ya] grilled crayfish
cilantro [seel**a**ntro] coriander
ciruela [seerw**e**la] plum, greengage
ciruela pasa prune
cochinillo asado [kocheen**ee**-yo] roast sucking pig

cochinita pibil [p**ee**beel] barbecued pork
cocido [kos**ee**do] stew made from meat, chickpeas and vegetables
coco coconut
coctel de gambas [deh] prawn cocktail
coctel de langostinos king prawn cocktail
coctel de mariscos seafood cocktail
codornices [kodorn**ee**s-es] quails
codornices estofadas braised quails
coles de Bruselas [k**o**l-es deh] Brussels sprouts
corvina bass
coliflor cauliflower
coliflor con bechamel [besham**e**l] cauliflower in white sauce
comal griddle
comida set menu; meal; food
comida corrida set menu
comidas para llevar [yeb**a**r] take-away meals
comino cumin
conejo [kon**e**Ho] rabbit
congrio [k**o**n-gryo] conger eel
conservas [kons**ai**rbas] jams, preserves
consomé de pollo [deh p**o**-yo] chicken consommé
cordero [kord**ai**ro] lamb
cordero asado roast lamb
costillas [kost**ee**-yas] ribs
costillas de cerdo [deh s**ai**rdo] pork rib
coyotas biscuits, cookies
crema cream
crema de espárragos [deh] cream of asparagus soup
crema de espinacas cream of spinach soup
cremada dessert made from egg, sugar and milk
crepa sweet pancake
crep(e) pancake
crepes imperiales [kr**e**p-es eempair-y**a**l-es] crêpes suzette
criadillas [kree-ad**ee**-yas] bull's testicles
criadillas de ternera [deh tairn**ai**ra] calves' testicles
crocante [krok**a**nteh] ice cream with chopped nuts
croquetas [krok**e**tas] croquettes
croquetas de pescado [deh] fish croquettes
crudo raw
cubierto menu
cuerno [kw**ai**rno] croissant
cuitlacoche [kweetlak**o**cheh] type of edible mushroom which grows on the maize/corn plant

damasco apricot
dátiles [d**a**teel-es] dates
de fabricación casera [deh fabreekas-y**o**n kas**ai**ra] home-made
desayuno [desī-y**oo**no] breakfast
dorado type of fish
dulce de membrillo [d**oo**lseh deh membr**ee**-yo] quince jelly
dulces [d**oo**ls-es] sweets,

candies
durazno [doo**ra**sno] peach

ejotes [eH**o**t-es] green beans, runner beans
elote [el**o**teh] maize, corn on the cob, corncob
embutidos cured pork sausages
empanada pasty filled with meat or fish
empanizado [empaneess**a**do] in breadcrumbs
en escabeche [eskab**e**cheh] pickled
enchilada fried corn meal pancake filled with meat, vegetables and cheese
enchiladas rojas [r**o**Has] stuffed tortillas in red chilli sauce
enchilada suiza [sw**ee**sa] stuffed tortilla with soured cream
enchiladas verdes [b**ai**rd-es] stuffed tortillas in green chilli sauce
endivias [end**ee**b-yas] endive, chicory
ensalada salad
ensalada de frutas [deh] fruit salad
ensalada de pollo [p**o**-yo] chicken salad
ensalada mixta [m**ee**sta] mixed salad
ensalada verde [b**ai**rdeh] green salad
ensaladilla [ensalad**ee**-ya] vegetables and chicken in mayonnaise
ensaladilla rusa Russian salad
entrecot de ternera [deh tairn**ai**ra] veal entrecôte
entremeses [entrem**e**s-es] hors d'œuvres
entremeses variados [bar-y**a**dos] assorted hors d'œuvres
epazote [epas**o**teh] commonly used Mexican herb
escabeche de ... [eskab**e**cheh deh] pickled ...
escamoles [eskam**o**l-es] ants eggs
escarola curly endive
espada ahumado [a-oom**a**do] smoked swordfish
espaguetis [espag**e**tees] spaghetti
espárragos asparagus
espárragos con mayonesa [mī-yon**e**sa] asparagus with mayonnaise
espárragos dos salsas asparagus with mayonnaise and vinaigrette dressing
espárragos en vinagreta [beenagr**e**ta] asparagus in vinaigrette dressing
especia [esp**e**s-ya] spice
especialidad [espes-yaleed**a**] speciality
espinacas spinach
espinacas a la crema creamed spinach
estragón tarragon

fabada (asturiana) [astoor-y**a**na] bean stew with red sausage

fajitas [fa**H**ee**tas] soft wheat tortillas stuffed with chicken or beef, peppers and onion
faisán [fis**a**n] pheasant
faisán con castañas [kast**a**n-yas] pheasant with chestnuts
faisán estofado stewed pheasant
faisán trufado pheasant with truffles
fiambres [f-y**a**mb-res] cold meats, cold cuts
fideos [feed**eh**-os] thin pasta; noodles; vermicelli
filete [feel**e**teh] meat or fish steak
filete a la parrilla [parr**ee**-ya] grilled beef steak
filete a la plancha grilled beef steak
filete de puerco [deh pw**ai**rko] pork fillet
filete de res beef steak
filete de ternera [tairn**ai**ra] veal steak
flan crème caramel
flan con nata crème caramel with whipped cream
flan de café [deh kaf**eh**] coffee-flavoured crème caramel
flan de caramelo crème caramel
flan (quemado) al ron [kem**a**do] crème caramel with rum
flautas [fl**ow**tas] fried tacos
flor de calabaza [deh kalab**a**sa] pumpkin flower
frambuesas [frambw**e**sas] raspberries
fresas strawberries
fresas con nata strawberries and cream/whipped cream
frijol [freeH**o**l] bean
frijoles [freeH**o**l-es] kidney beans
frijoles blancos white beans
frijoles borrachos beans cooked with beer
frijoles de olla [deh **o**-ya] boiled beans in gravy-type sauce
frijoles negros [n**eh**-gros] black beans
frijoles refritos refried beans
fruta fruit
fruta variada [bar-y**a**da] selection of fresh fruit
frutas en almíbar fruit in syrup
frutillas [froot**ee**-yas] strawberries

galleta [ga-y**e**ta] biscuit, cookie
gallina [ga-y**ee**na] chicken
gamba large prawn
garbanzos [garb**a**nsos] chickpeas
garnachas tortillas with garlic sauce, typical of Veracruz
garobo iguana
gazpacho andaluz [gasp**a**cho andal**oo**s] cold soup made from tomatoes, onions, garlic, peppers and cucumber
gelatina [Helat**ee**na] gelatine; jelly, (US) jello
gorditas stuffed tortillas
granada pomegranate
gratinado au gratin – baked in

a cream and cheese sauce
grenadilla [grenad**ee**-ya] passion fruit
grosellas [gros**eh**-yas] redcurrants
guacamole [gwakam**o**leh] avocado dip
guanábana [gwan**a**bana] custard apple
guayaba [gwī-y**a**ba] guava
guinda [g**ee**nda] black cherry; alcoholic drink made from black cherries
guineo [geen**eh**-o] small banana
guisado [gwees**a**do] stew
gusanos de maguey [deh m**a**gay] maguey worms

hamburguesa [amboorg**e**sa] hamburger
harina [ar**ee**na] flour
harina de maíz [ma-**ee**s] cornflour
helado [el**a**do] ice cream
helado de chocolate [deh chokol**a**teh] chocolate ice cream
helado de fresa strawberry ice cream
helado de nata dairy ice cream
helado de vainilla [bīn**ee**-ya] vanilla ice cream
hierbas [y**ai**rbas] herbs
hígado [**ee**gado] liver
hígado con cebolla [seb**o**-ya] liver cooked with onion
hígado de ternera estofado [deh tairn**ai**ra] braised calves' liver
hígado encebollado [ensebo-y**a**do] liver in an onion sauce
hígado estofado braised liver
higos [**ee**gos] figs
higos con miel y nueces [m-yel ee nw**e**s-es] figs with honey and nuts
higos secos dried figs
hongos [**o**ngos] mushrooms
huachinango [wacheen**a**ngo] red snapper
huachinango al ajo [**a**Ho] red snapper with garlic butter
huevo [w**e**bo] egg
huevo duro [d**oo**ro] hard-boiled egg
huevo pasado por agua [**a**g-wa] boiled egg
huevos a la mexicana [meHeek**a**na] scrambled eggs with peppers, onions and garlic
huevos a la oaxaqueña [waHak**e**n-ya] eggs in chilli and tomato sauce
huevos cocidos [kos**ee**dos] hard-boiled eggs
huevos con jamón [Ham**o**n] ham and eggs
huevos con papas fritas fried eggs and chips/French fries
huevos con tocino [tos**ee**no] eggs and bacon
huevos escalfados poached eggs
huevos estrellados [estreh-y**a**dos] fried eggs
huevos fritos fried eggs
huevos fritos con chorizo

[chor**ee**so] fried eggs with Spanish sausage
huevos motuleños [motool**e**n-yos] eggs cooked in chillis and tomatoes, served on a fried tortilla and garnished with cheese, ham and chillis
huevos rancheros [ranch**ai**ros] fried eggs with hot tomato sauce and tortilla
huevos rellenos [reh-y**e**nos] stuffed eggs
huevos revueltos [rebw**e**ltos] scrambled eggs
huevo tibio [t**ee**b-yo] soft-boiled egg
humitas [oom**ee**tas] sweetcorn tamales

incluye pan, postre y vino includes bread, dessert and wine

jaiba [H**ī**ba] crab
jalapeños [Halap**e**n-yos] hot green chilli peppers
jalea [Hal**eh**-a] gelatine; jelly, (US) jello
jamón [Ham**o**n] ham
jamón serrano [sairr**a**no] cured ham, similar to Parma ham
jamón York boiled ham
jarabe [Har**a**beh] syrup
jícama [H**ee**kama] sweet turnip-like fruit eaten with lemon juice or chilli
jitomate [Heetom**a**teh] tomato

langosta lobster
langosta a la americana [amaireek**a**na] lobster with brandy and garlic
langosta fría con mayonesa [fr**ee**-a kon mī-yon**e**sa] cold lobster with mayonnaise
langosta gratinada lobster au gratin
langostinos a la plancha grilled king prawns
langostinos con mayonesa [mī-yon**e**sa] king prawns with mayonnaise
langostinos dos salsas king prawns cooked in two sauces
laurel [lowr**e**l] bay leaves
lechuga [lech**oo**ga] lettuce
lengua [l**e**ngwa] tongue
lengua de cordero estofada [deh kord**ai**ro] stewed lambs' tongue
lengua de res ox tongue
lenguado a la plancha [lengw**a**do] grilled sole
lentejas [lent**e**Has] lentils
lima [l**ee**ma] lime
limón lemon
lobina sea bass
lomo pork fillet, pork loin, tenderloin
longaniza [longan**ee**sa] cooked spicy sausage

macarrones [makarr**o**n-es] macaroni
macarrones gratinados macaroni cheese
machaca shredded meat
macho large green banana

maduro ripe
magdalena sponge cake, (US) muffin
maíz [ma-**ee**s] sweetcorn, maize, (US) corn
mamey [mam**ay**] round, apple-sized tropical fruit
mandarina tangerine
manitas de cerdo [deh s**ai**rdo] pig's trotters
manitas de cordero [kord**ai**ro] leg of lamb
mantequilla [mantek**ee**-ya] butter
manzana [mans**a**na] apple
manzanas asadas baked apples
maracuyá [marakoo-y**a**] passion fruit
mariscada cold mixed shellfish
mariscos shellfish
mariscos de temporada seasonal shellfish
masa dough
mayonesa [mī-yon**e**sa] mayonnaise
mazapán [masap**a**n] marzipan
mazorca f [mas**o**rka] corn on the cob, (US) corncob
medallones de anguila [meda-y**o**n-es deh ang**ee**la] eel steaks
medallones de merluza [mairl**oo**sa] hake steaks
mejillones [meHee-y**o**n-es] mussels
mejillones a la marinera [mareen**ai**ra] mussels in wine sauce with garlic
mejillones con salsa mussels with tomato and herb sauce
melón melon
membrillo [membr**ee**-yo] quince; quince jelly
menestra de verduras [deh baird**oo**ras] vegetable stew
menú [men**oo**] set menu
menú de la casa [deh] fixed-price menu
menú del día today's set menu
menudo tripe; sweetbreads
menú turístico set menu
merluza a la parrilla [mairl**oo**sa a la parr**ee**-ya] grilled hake
merluza a la riojana [r-yoH**a**na] hake with chillies
merluza a la romana hake steaks in batter
merluza frita fried hake
mermelada [mairmel**a**da] jam; marmalade
mermelada de ciruelas [deh seersw**e**las] plum jam
mermelada de damasco apricot jam
mermelada de durazno [door**a**sno] peach jam
mermelada de fresas strawberry jam
mermelada de limón lemon marmalade
mermelada de naranja [nar**a**nHa] orange marmalade
miel [m-yel] honey
milanesa breaded chop or escalope
milanesa de ternera [deh tairn**ai**ra] breaded veal escalope
mojarro [moH**a**rro] type of fish

mole [m**o**leh] sauce made with chilli peppers, chocolate and spices
mole de olla [deh **o**-ya] spicy meat stew
mole oaxaqueño [waHak**e**n-yo] type of black or green mole sauce
mole poblano rich mole sauce made from nuts, prunes and bananas, a Puebla speciality
mollejas de ternera [mo-y**e**Has deh tairn**ai**ra] calves' sweetbreads
molletes [mo-y**e**-tes] toasted roll with refried beans and cheese
mondongo tripe
morcilla [mors**ee**-ya] black pudding, blood sausage
morcilla de ternera [deh tairn**ai**ra] black pudding made from calves' blood
mortadela salami-type sausage
mostaza [most**a**sa] mustard
mousse de limón [deh] lemon mousse

nabo turnip
nacatamales [nakatam**a**l-es] corn meal dough filled with meat in sauce and steamed in banana leaves
nachos tortilla chips with cheese
naranja [nar**a**nHa] orange
nata cream
natilla [nat**ee**-ya] custard
natillas [nat**ee**-yas] cold custard with cinnamon
natillas de chocolate [deh chokol**a**teh] cold custard with chocolate
nieve [n-y**e**veh] sorbet; ice cream
níscalos wild mushrooms
nixtamal [neestam**a**l] maize dough, (US) corn dough
nopalitos chopped cactus-leaf salad
nueces [nw**e**s-es] walnuts
nuez [nwes] nut

ostión [ost-y**o**n] oyster

paella [pa-**eh**-ya] fried rice with seafood and chicken
paella valenciana [balens-y**a**na] paella with assorted shellfish
paleta ice lolly
palmito palm heart
palomitas popcorn
pan bread
pan blanco white bread
pan de cazón [kas**o**n] layered dish of tortillas, beans and dogfish with a hot sauce
pan de centeno [sent**e**no] brown bread
pan de higos [deh **ee**gos] dried fig cake with cinnamon
pan dulce [d**oo**lseh] buns and cakes, sweet pastries
pan integral [eentegr**a**l] wholemeal bread
pancita [pans**ee**ta] tripe
papa potato
papadzules [papads**u**l-es]

tortillas stuffed with hard-boiled eggs from Yucatán
papas a la criolla [cree-**o**-ya] potatoes in hot, spicy sauce
papas asadas baked potatoes
papas bravas potatoes in cayenne pepper
papas fritas chips, French fries
papaya papaya, pawpaw
parrillada de caza [parree-y**a**da deh k**a**sa] mixed grilled game
parrillada de mariscos mixed grilled shellfish
pasas raisins
pasta biscuit, cookie; pastry; pasta
pastel cake; pie
pastel de carne [k**a**rneh] brawn, jellied meat
pata foot, trotter
patatas (fritas) crisps, (US) potato chips
pato duck
pato a la naranja [nar**a**nHa] duck à l'orange
pato asado roast duck
pavo [p**a**bo] turkey
pavo relleno [reh-y**e**no] stuffed turkey
pay [pī] pie with a sweet filling
pay de queso [deh k**e**so] cheesecake
pechuga de pollo [deh p**o**-yo] breast of chicken
pepinillos [pepeen**ee**-yos] gherkins
pepinillos en vinagreta [beenagr**e**ta] gherkins in vinaigrette dressing
pepino cucumber
pera [p**ai**ra] pear
perdices [paird**ee**s-es] partridges
perdices a la campesina partridges with vegetables
perdices asadas roast partridges
perdices con chocolate [chokol**a**teh] partridges with chocolate
perdices encebolladas [ensebo-y**a**das] partridge with onion
perejil [paireh-H**ee**l] parsley
perro caliente [p**ai**rro kal-y**e**nteh] hot dog
pescaditos fritos fried sprats
pescado fish
pescado a la veracruzana [bairakroos**a**na] seasoned sea bass or red snapper fillets fried and served with tomato sauce on top
pez espada ahumado [a-oom**a**do] smoked swordfish
píbil cooked in a pit
picadillo [peekad**ee**-yo] minced meat
picadillo de pollo [deh p**o**-yo] minced chicken
picadillo de ternera [tairn**ai**ra] minced veal
picante hot, spicy
pichón pigeon
pichones estofados [peech**o**n-es] stewed pigeon
picoso hot, spicy
pierna [p-y**ai**rna] leg

piloncillo [peelons**ee**-yo] unrefined brown sugar
pimentón paprika
pimienta [peem-**y**enta] black pepper
pimienta blanca white pepper
pimienta de cayena [deh kī-**y**ena] cayenne pepper
pimiento rojo [r**o**Ho] red pepper
pimiento verde [b**ai**rdeh] green pepper
pinchitos snacks/appetizers served in bars; kebabs
pincho kebab
piña [p**ee**n-ya] pineapple
piña fresca fresh pineapple
piña gratinada pineapple au gratin
piñones [peen-y**o**n-es] pine nuts
pipián [peep-y**a**n] sauce of ground nuts, seeds and spices
pitahaya [peetah**ī**-ya] red fruit of a cactus plant with soft, sweet flesh
plátano banana
plátanos flameados [flameh-**a**dos] flambéed bananas
platos combinados meat and vegetables, hamburgers and eggs etc
poco hecho [**e**cho] rare
pollo [p**o**-yo] chicken
pollo al ajillo [aH**ee**-yo] fried chicken with garlic
pollo a la parrilla [parr**ee**-ya] grilled chicken
pollo al vino blanco [b**ee**no] chicken in white wine
pollo asado roast chicken
pollo con verduras [baird**oo**ras] chicken and vegetables
polvorones [polbor**o**n-es] sugar-based dessert (eaten at Christmas)
poro leek
postre [p**o**streh] dessert
pozole [pos**o**leh] thick broth of vegetables meat and corn
primer plato [pr**ee**mair] starter, appetizer
puerco [pw**ai**rko] pork
pulpitos con cebolla [seb**o**-ya] baby octopuses with onions
pulpo octopus
pupusa dumpling usually filled with cheese or meat
puré de papas [poor**eh** deh] mashed potatoes, potato purée

queque [k**e**keh] cake
quesadilla [kesad**ee**-ya] fried corn meal pancake usually filled with cheese
queso [k**e**so] cheese
queso con membrillo [mem-br**ee**-yo] cheese with quince jelly
queso fresco soft white cheese
queso fundido melted cheese
queso manchego hard, strong cheese
queso Oaxaca [waH**a**ka] soft white cheese used for cooking

rábanos radishes
ración [ras-y**o**n] portion

ración pequeña para niños [pek**e**n-ya p**a**ra n**ee**n-yos] children's portion
rajas [r**a**Has] strips of pickled green chillies; sliced green peppers in cream
ravioles [rab-y**o**l-es] ravioli
raya [rī-ya] skate
raya con manteca negra [n**eh**-gra] skate in butter and vinegar sauce
rebanada slice
refritos refried beans
relleno [reh-y**e**no] stuffed; stuffing
remolacha beetroot
repollo [rep**o**-yo] cabbage
res beef
riñones [reen-y**o**n-es] kidneys
riñones a la plancha grilled kidneys
riñones al jerez [Hair-**e**s] kidneys in a sherry sauce
róbalo bass
romero [rom**ai**ro] rosemary
ron rum
ropa vieja [b-y**eh**-Ha] shredded meat
rosca round sponge made at Christmas
roscas sweet pastries
rosquillas [rosk**ee**-yas] small sweet pastries

sal salt
salbute type of filled tortilla typical of Yucatán
salchicha sausage
salchichas de Frankfurt [deh] frankfurters
salchichón salami-type sausage
salmón [sal-m**o**n] salmon
salmón a la parrilla [par**ee**-ya] grilled salmon
salmón ahumado [a-oom**a**do] smoked salmon
salmón frío [fr**ee**-o] cold salmon
salmonetes [sal-mon**e**t-es] red mullet
salmonetes a la parrilla [par**ee**-ya] grilled red mullet
salmonetes en papillote [papee-y**o**teh] red mullet cooked in foil
salpicón de mariscos [deh] shellfish with vinaigrette dressing
salsa sauce
salsa allioli/ali oli [a-yee-**o**lee/ **a**lee **o**lee] garlic mayonnaise
salsa bechamel [besham**e**l] béchamel sauce, white sauce
salsa de jitomate [deh Heetom**a**teh] tomato sauce
salsa holandesa [oland**e**sa] hollandaise sauce
salsa mexicana/pico de gallo [meHeek**a**na/p**ee**ko deh g**a**-yo] hot sauce made with chillies, onions and red tomatoes
salsa romesco sauce made from peppers, tomatoes and garlic

salsa tártara tartare sauce
salsa verde [b**ai**rdeh] green sauce made from tomatillo and chillies
salsa vinagreta [beenagr**e**ta] vinaigrette dressing
salteado [salteh-**a**do] sautéed
sancocho vegetable soup with meat or fish
sandía [sand**ee**-a] water melon
sandwich sandwich
sandwich mixto [m**ee**sto] cheese and ham sandwich
sardina sardine
sardinas a la brasa barbecued sardines
sardinas a la parrilla [parr**ee**-ya] grilled sardines
sardinas fritas fried sardines
segundo plato main course
servicio incluido service charge included
servicio no incluido service charge not included
sesos a la romana brains in batter
sesos rebozados [rebos**a**dos] brains in batter
solomillo [solom**ee**-yo] fillet steak
solomillo con papas fritas fillet steak with chips/French fries
solomillo de cerdo [deh s**ai**rdo] fillet of pork
solomillo de ternera [tairn**ai**ra] fillet of veal
solomillo de vaca [b**a**ka] fillet of beef
solomillo frío [fr**ee**-o] cold roast beef
sopa soup
sopa de aguacate fría [deh agwak**a**teh] cold avocado soup
sopa de ajo [**a**Ho] garlic soup
sopa de arroz rice soup
sopa de fideos [feed**eh**-os] noodle soup
sopa de frijoles negros [freeH**o**l-es n**eh**-gros] black bean soup
sopa de gallina [ga-y**ee**na] chicken soup
sopa del día soup of the day
sopa de lentejas [lent**ee**Has] lentil soup
sopa de mariscos fish and shellfish soup
sopa de pescado fish soup
sopa de tortilla [tort**ee**-ya] soup with corn meal pancakes
sopa de tortuga turtle soup
sopa de verduras [baird**oo**ras] vegetable soup
sopa inglesa trifle
sopaipillas [sopīp**ee**-yas] sweet fritters
sopa seca rice or pasta dish served with a sauce on top
sopa tarasca creamy bean and tomato soup
sopes [s**o**p-es] garnished tortillas
sorbete [sorb**e**teh] sorbet
soufflé soufflé

soufflé de fresas [deh] strawberry soufflé
soufflé de naranja [nar**a**nHa] orange soufflé
soufflé de queso [k**e**so] cheese soufflé

taco stuffed maize/corn pancake
tacos al pastor tacos with grilled meat
tacos de pollo [deh p**o**-yo] tacos stuffed with chicken
tajadas [taH**a**das] fried banana strips
tallarines [ta-yar**ee**n-es] noodles
tallarines a la italiana [eetal-y**a**na] tagliatelle with tomato sauce
tamal filled maize/corn dough cooked in banana leaf, tamale
tamarindo tamarind
tapa de ternera rellena [deh tairn**ai**ra reh-y**e**na] stuffed veal hock
tapado stew
tapas appetizers
tarta cake
tarta Alaska baked Alaska
tarta de almendra [deh] almond tart or gâteau
tarta de arroz [arr**o**s] cake or tart containing rice
tarta de chocolate [chokol**a**teh] chocolate gâteau
tarta de fresas strawberry tart or gâteau
tarta de la casa tart or gâteau baked on the premises
tarta de manzana [mans**a**na] apple tart
tarta helada [el**a**da] ice cream gâteau
tarta mocha/moka [m**o**ka] mocha tart
tártar crudo raw minced steak, steak tartare
tejos de queso [t**e**Hos deh k**e**so] cheese pastries
tencas tench
tencas con jamón [Ham**o**n] tench with ham
ternera [tairn**ai**ra] veal
ternera asada roast veal
tocino [tos**ee**no] bacon
todo incluido all inclusive
tomate [tom**a**teh] green tomato
tomates rellenos [tom**a**t-es reh-y**e**nos] stuffed tomatoes
tomatillo [tomat**ee**-yo] green tomato used for sauces
tomillo [tom**ee**-yo] thyme
tordo thrush
tordos braseados [braseh-**a**dos] grilled thrushes
tordos estofados braised thrushes
toronja [tor**o**nHa] grapefruit
torrejas [torr**e**Has] French toast
torrijas [torr**ee**Has] sweet pastries
torta filled bread roll with salad, cream and tomato garnish
tortilla [tort**ee**-ya] maize

pancake, (US) corn pancake
tortilla de harina [deh ar**ee**na] wheat pancake
tortilla de huevo [w**e**bo] omelette
tortilla española [espan-y**o**la] Spanish omelette with potato, onion and garlic
tostada fried corn pancake topped with meat, vegetables and salsa; toast
totopo thin, fried tortilla
trucha [tr**oo**cha] trout
trucha ahumada [a-oom**a**da] smoked trout
trucha a la marinera [mareen**ai**ra] trout in white wine sauce
trucha con jamón [Ham**o**n] trout with ham
trucha escabechada marinated trout
tuétano [tw**e**tano] marrow, squash
tuna [t**oo**na] prickly pear
turrón nougat
turrón de coco [deh] coconut nougat
turrón de Jijona [HeeH**o**na] hard nougat
turrón de yema [y**e**ma] nougat with egg yolk

uchepos small sweet tamales
uvas [**oo**bas] grapes

vainilla [bīn**ee**-ya] vanilla
venado [ben**a**do] venison
verduras [baird**oo**ras] vegetables
verduras capeadas [kapeh-**a**das] courgettes and cauliflower in batter served with hot tomato sauce and cream
vinagre [been**a**greh] vinegar
vuelvealavida [bw**e**lbeh-a-lab**ee**da] marinated seafood cocktail with chilli

yema yolk
yerba [y**ai**rba] herb
yogur [yo-g**oo**r] yoghurt
yuca sweet potato

zanahoria [sana-**o**ree-a] carrot
zanahorias a la crema carrots à la crème
zapallo [sap**a**-yo] marrow, squash
zapote [sap**o**teh] sweet pumpkin
zarzamoras [sarsam**o**ras] blackberries
zarzuela de mariscos [sarsw**e**la deh] shellfish stew

Menu Reader:

Drink

ESSENTIAL TERMS

beer la cerveza [sairb**e**sa]
bottle la botella [bot**eh**-ya], el fr**a**sco
brandy el coñac [kon-y**a**k]
black coffee el café americano [kaf**eh** amaireek**a**no]
(strong) el café s**o**lo
coffee el café [kaf**eh**]
cup la taza [t**a**sa]
a cup of ... **u**na taza de ... [deh]
fruit juice el jugo de fr**u**tas [H**oo**go deh]
gin la ginebra [Heen**e**bra]
a gin and tonic un gintónic [jeent**o**neek]
glass (tumbler) el vaso [b**a**so]
(wine glass) la c**o**pa
a glass of ... un vaso de ... [deh], **una copa de ...**
milk la leche [l**e**cheh]
milkshake el licuado [leekw**a**do]
mineral water el agua mineral [**a**gwa meenair**a**l]
red wine el vino tinto [b**ee**no t**ee**nto]
soda (water) la s**o**da
soft drink el refr**e**sco
sugar el azúcar [as**oo**kar]
tea el té [teh]
tonic (water) la t**ó**nica
vodka el vodka [b**o**dka]
water el agua [**a**gwa]
whisky el wh**i**sky
white wine el vino bl**a**nco [b**ee**no]
wine el vino
wine list la lista de vinos [l**ee**sta deh b**ee**nos]

another ... **o**tro/**o**tra ...

agua [**a**gwa] water
agua de fruta fruit drink made from fruit and water
agua de granada [deh] grenadine juice
agua de jamaica [Ham**ī**ka] hibiscus blossom drink
agua de melón melon juice
agua de panela drink made from water and sugar
agua mineral [meenair**a**l] mineral water
agua mineral con gas fizzy mineral water
agua mineral sin gas [seen] still mineral water
aguardiente [agward-y**e**nteh] a clear spirit similar to brandy or white rum
al tiempo [t-y**e**mpo] at room temperature
añejo [an-y**eh**-Ho] vintage; mellow; mature
anís aniseed-flavoured spirit
aperitivo [apaireet**ee**bo] aperitif
api thick custard-like drink made from maize and cinnamon
aromáticas herb teas
atole [at**o**leh] thick drink made from maize/corn
azúcar [as**oo**kar] sugar

bebida drink
bebidas alcohólicas alcoholic drinks
Bohemia® brand of lager

cacao [kak**ow**] cocoa
café [kaf**eh**] coffee
café americano black coffee
café capuchino cappuccino
café con leche [l**e**cheh] coffee with milk (large cup)
café cortado coffee with a dash of milk (small cup)
café de olla [deh **o**-ya] coffee made with cinammon and raw sugar
café descafeinado [deskafay-een**a**do] decaffeinated coffee
café escocés [eskos-**e**s] black coffee, whisky/scotch and vanilla ice cream
café exprés [espr**e**s] strong black coffee
café instantáneo [eenstant**a**neh-o] instant coffee
café irlandés [eerland-**e**s] black coffee, whisky, vanilla ice cream and whipped cream
café negro [n**eh**-gro] black coffee, usually strong and often sweet
café perfumado coffee with a dash of brandy or other spirit
café solo black coffee, usually strong and often sweet
carta de vinos [deh b**ee**nos] wine list
Cava [k**a**ba] champagne
cebada [seb**a**da] drink made from fermented barley
cerveza [sairb**e**sa] beer, lager
cerveza clara light, lager-style beer
cerveza de barril draught beer
cerveza negra dark beer

cerveza oscura dark beer
champán [champan] champagne
chocolate caliente [chokolateh kal-yenteh] hot chocolate drink, sometimes sweetened with honey and flavoured with vanilla and spices
coctel cocktail
con azúcar [asookar] with sugar
con gas fizzy, sparkling
coñac [kon-yak] brandy
cosecha vintage
cubalibre [koobaleebreh] rum and cola
cubito de hielo [deh yelo] ice cube
cucaracha tequila and strong, alcoholic, coffee-flavoured drink

destornillador [destornee-yador] vodka and orange juice
Domecq [domek] Mexican wine producer
Dos Equis® [ekees] light Mexican beer

embotellado en ... bottled in ...
espumoso sparkling

gaseosa [gaseh-osa] lemonade
ginebra [Heenebra] gin
gintónic [jeentoneek] gin and tonic
granizada/granizado [graneesada] crushed ice drink
guinda [geenda] alcoholic drink made from black cherries; black cherry
guindada [geendada], guindilla [guindee-ya] cherry brandy

Hidalgo Mexican wine producer
hielo [yelo] ice
horchata [orchata] cold drink made from rice and water
horchata de chufas [deh] cold almond-flavoured milky drink

infusión [eenfoos-yon] herb tea

jarra de cerveza/vino [Harra deh sairbesa/beeno] jug of beer/ wine
jerez [Hair-es] sherry
jerez fino light, dry sherry
jerez oloroso sweet sherry
jugo [Hoogo] juice
jugo de damasco apricot juice
jugo de durazno [doorasno] peach juice
jugo de jitomate [Heetomateh] tomato juice
jugo de lima lime juice
jugo de limón lemon juice
jugo de naranja [naranHa] orange juice
jugo de piña [peen-ya] pineapple juice

leche [lecheh] milk
leche de soja [deh soHa] soya milk
leche desnatada skimmed milk
licor liqueur; spirit
licor de avellana [deh abeh-yana] hazelnut-flavoured liqueur

licor de manzana [mans**a**na] apple-flavoured liqueur
licor de durazno [door**a**sno] peach-flavoured liqueur
licor de melón melon-flavoured liqueur
licor de naranja [nar**a**nHa] orange-flavoured liqueur
licores [leek**o**r-es] spirits, liqueurs
licuado [leekw**a**do] milkshake
licuado de fresa [deh] strawberry milkshake
licuado de plátano banana milkshake
limonada fresh lemonade
lista de precios [pr**e**s-yos] price list

Málaga sweet wine
malta dark beer
malteada [malteh-**a**da] milkshake
manzanilla [mansan**ee**-ya] dry sherry-type wine; camomile tea
margarita cocktail of tequila, lime juice and either grenadine, Curaçao or triple sec
mate [m**a**teh] bitter tea made from the dried leaves of the yerba mate bush
media de agua [m**e**d-ya deh **a**g-wa] half bottle of mineral water
mediana bottle of beer
mezcal [mesk**a**l] spirit distilled from the maguey cactus

Negra Modelo® dark Mexican beer
Nescafe® [neskaf**eh**] instant coffee
Nochebuena® [nocheb**we**na] dark Mexican beer

Oporto port

Pacífico® brand of lager
piña colada [p**ee**n-ya] rum and pineapple cocktail
posh sugar cane liquor
pozol de cacao [pos**o**l deh kak**a**-o] cool drink made from ground maize/corn and chocolate
pulque [p**oo**lkeh] thick alcoholic drink distilled from the pulp of the maguey cactus
puro de caña [deh k**a**n-ya] sugar cane liquor

refresco soft drink, fizzy drink
rompope [romp**o**peh] egg nog, egg flip
ron rum
ron oro matured rum

sangría [sangr**ee**-a] mixture of red wine, lemon juice, spirits, sugar and fruit
sangrita orange juice, grenadine and chilli, drunk with tequila
San Miguel® [mig**e**l] type of lager
Sauza® [s**ow**sa] brand of tequila
semidulce [semeed**oo**lseh]

medium-sweet
sidra cider
sin azúcar [seen as**oo**kar] without sugar
sin gas still
Sol® brand of lager
Superior® [soopair-y**o**r] brand of lager

taxallate [taHa-y**a**teh] drink from Chiapas made from maize/corn and cocoa
té [teh] tea
Tecate® [tek**a**teh] light Mexican beer, usually served with lime and salt
té de hierbas [teh deh y**ai**rbas] herbal tea
Tehuacán® [teh-wak**a**n] mineral water
tequila [tek**ee**la] spirit distilled from the pulp of the agave cactus
tónica tonic
Tres Equis® [**e**kees] brand of lager

vino [b**ee**no] wine
vino blanco white wine
vino de casa [deh] house wine
vino de mesa table wine
vino del país [pa-**ee**s] local wine
vino rosado rosé wine
vino tinto red wine

yerbabuena [yairbabw**e**na] mint tea
yerba mate [y**ai**rba m**a**teh] bitter tea made from the dried leaves of the yerba mate bush